CARMARTHENSHIRE

THE HISTORIES OF WALES
SERIES EDITOR: CATRIN STEVENS

CARMARTHENSHIRE

THE CONCISE HISTORY

DYLAN REES

University of Wales Press
Cardiff
2006

British Library Cataloguing-in-Publication Data
A catalogue record for this book is available from the British Library.

ISBN 0-7083-1947-5

Printed in Malta by Gutenberg Press, Tarxien

i'm rhieni
Glan a Glenys
Y Felin, Llandybïe

Contents

List of Tables

Series Editor's Preface

The sense of belonging to *y filltir sgwâr* (the square mile), to its people and its values, has always had a special resonance for the people of Carmarthenshire. It found profound expression in the writings of author D. J. Williams, particularly in his autobiography, *Hen Dŷ Ffarm* (1953; translated into English as *The Old Farmhouse*, 1961), and whose love of Wales was merely an extension of his love for his native Rhydcymerau and thus for Sir Gâr itself. Sir Gaerfyrddin has inspired other poets and writers through the centuries both in Welsh, in the poetry of Gwenallt and J. Eirian Davies, and in English in the works of John Dyer and Lewis Morris. It has also focused the minds of historians, the greatest of whom, J. E. Lloyd, edited the two monumental volumes of *The History of Carmarthenshire* in 1935, and whose legacy can be traced through into the twenty-first century in the highly-acclaimed contributions of the Carmarthenshire Antiquarian Society, which celebrated its centenary in 2005 and whose erudite journal is ably edited by Muriel Bowen Evans.

Dylan Rees, the author of this volume, also belongs to his *milltir sgwâr,* as a native of Llandybïe in Sir Gâr. He was the obvious choice to respond to the challenge of further enhancing the county's already formidable historical reputation on the one hand, and presenting this scholarly discussion in an illuminating and readable style to fellow-historians and students of local history as well as to the general interested public, on the other. In his writing he has drawn heavily upon the research and expertise of both amateur and professional historians but he has sought to synthesise this scholarship into a new history which will serve to enrich our appreciation and understanding of this large, diverse and fascinating county. He has traced Carmarthenshire's history from prehistoric times to the present, pausing *en route* to marvel at Roman Moridunum, to pay homage to the medieval princes and lords of Deheubarth, to celebrate educationalists and hymn-writers and to join the ranks of the Rebecca Rioters, thus reflecting upon some of the myriad facets which form part of Sir Gâr's historical tapestry. I suspect it was a daunting task, but one which he undertook with resourcefulness and pride and I am greatly indebted to him for his perseverance, scholarship and dedication.

This concise history of Carmarthenshire is the second volume in The Histories of Wales Series, following the publication of David A. Pretty's *Anglesey* in the summer of 2005. It is sincerely hoped that when the series is complete, when all the counties, regions and cities have been duly chronicled in all their distinctiveness and complexity, each volume will contribute in its own unique way to the composite and intricate jigsaw which constitutes the history of Wales.

Catrin Stevens
Series Editor, The Histories of Wales

Acknowledgements

It was only when gathering resources, visiting sites and examining records that I became fully aware of the enormity of the task which I had so willingly agreed to undertake. My family ties are deeply rooted in the culture, land and history of Carmarthenshire and although nowadays an emigré – living in Swansea, I consider it a very great privilege to have been asked to write this book. Over half a century has lapsed since the last serious history of the county appeared in print. Much has changed in the intervening period. Now is perhaps an appropriate moment to reflect on these developments as we stand at the beginning of a new century and millennium. While it was beyond the scope of this volume to cover every conceivable trend or event in the county's past, I would hope that the content will provide an effective overview, stimulus and the wherewithal to enable those who wish to pursue their interests further.

My odyssey into Carmarthenshire's past has been as illuminating as it has been informative. In researching and writing this book I have incurred many debts for the inordinate number of favours I have requested. It is a pleasure to record my thanks here. No task has been too great or small for the staff at the County Records Office in Carmarthen and I am extremely grateful for the help I have received from Terry Wells. The staff at Swansea Central Library, Carmarthen County Library, Carmarthen County Museum, Carmarthenshire County Council, Llanelli Town Library, Dyfed Powys Health Authority and the South Wales Miners Library have all been courteous, helpful and professional, whenever approached.

Carmarthenshire Antiquarian Society generously provided me with a research grant to help support this project. I am extremely grateful for their help, and hope that this work in some small way returns the complement they have paid me. In addition the following officers and council members of the society – Dominic Conway, Edna Dale Jones, Tom Lloyd and Arfon Rees have all supported me in one way or another. I reserve a particular thanks to Muriel Bowen Evans who kindly read through early drafts of some of my chapters and suggested a number of useful amendments and additional lines of enquiry.

Among the many individuals who granted me interviews or assisted me with information on particular topics, I would like to thank the following: Harry Hancocks, Professor David Howells, Richard Millward, Ann Dorset, Rt. Hon Denzil Davies MP, Gareth Davies, Ray Gravell, Gwynfor and Dafydd Evans, David Cook, Pat Ward, Huw Thomas (WDA), Peter Davies (FUW), Keith Cobain, Tom Nash, Dilys Jenkins and David Lewis. A particular thanks to the artists Aneurin Jones RCA and Gordon Stuart RCA for providing two original works for inclusion in this volume. Catrin Stevens, my editor, has been a great help, and has freely made available her own extensive knowledge of Sir Gâr. Any errors or inaccuracies which remain are entirely my own responsibility.

My final and greatest debt is to my family Claire, Carys and Morgan. They have endured with tolerance, good grace and understanding the many hours required to research and refine this book.

Dylan Rees
Sgeti, Abertawe

I

Stone, Bronze and Iron:
Prehistory–AD 42

The Stone Age

Recorded history in Carmarthenshire as in Britain as a whole covers barely the last two millennia. Remains of *Homo sapiens* in the British Isles however date back to at least 500,000 years. The absence of written records, while clearly presenting problems for the historian, does not imply an absence of knowledge regarding these early societies. Their relationship with their environment has left evidence in various forms of their activities, habitations, material culture and rituals, much of it the detritus of their daily lives. That this evidence has survived at all is frequently due to chance. It has succeeded in avoiding the ravages of time, climate and modern intensive farming methods. Prehistory is very much the domain of archaeologists and we are dependent upon their field work for the collection, classification and interpretation of this primary evidence.

The Carmarthenshire of prehistory was for most of the time very different from contemporary Carmarthenshire. These differences were due to the interaction of climatic and physical factors. Climatic changes affected the physical features of the county which in turn had an impact upon human habitation. The main climatic force was the Ice Age of which there were several. The first human inhabitants for which there is evidence (from Pontnewydd in the Elwy valley, north Wales) arrived in Wales 250,000 years ago during the Pleistocene Ice Age (1,000,000–10,000 years ago). This generic term covers periods of glaciation interspersed by warm interludes. The consequence of this ebbing and flowing of the ice sheet and alternating warmer and colder periods was to sculpt and change the physical environment, and dramatically modify the native flora and fauna. Much evidence of human occupation may well have been destroyed in the process. Animals and plants that favoured a colder climate retreated north as the temperature rose. It has been estimated that the temperature in northern Europe was 2.5°c warmer than it is today.

Perhaps the most dramatic impact of the Ice Age was on the coastline.

The sea-level for most of the period of the Ice Age was much lower than it is today. Carmarthenshire would not have been a coastal county. Carmarthen Bay would have formed a low-lying plain, part of the much wider plain now occupied by the Severn estuary. The final retreat of the ice began around 10,000 BC. With the retreat of the glaciers the Severn estuary, Carmarthen Bay and the Irish Sea were born. F. J. North has estimated that some time during the Mesolithic period the Welsh coastline would have approximated the present 20 fathom submarine contour. The rising sea-levels probably account for the legend of Cantre'r Gwaelod. Exceptionally low tides have exposed traces of the remains of submerged forests. In 1971 at Amroth the stumps of a prehistoric forest were clearly visible, while A. L. Leach recorded in 1913 evidence of flint working at an exposed site near the village.

The system that is now used to classify the stages in man's development was developed by Christian Jurgensen Thomsen in Denmark in the early nineteenth century. He devised a three-age system based on the ages of stone, bronze and iron. Each was a technologically defined age, self-contained but more refined than the one preceding it. This classification has in turn been modified. Thomsen's Stone Age now has a tripartite division of Palaeolithic *c.*1,000,000 BC–*c.*8,000 BC (in turn divided into lower, middle and upper), Mesolithic *c.*8,000 BC–*c.*3,500 BC (subdivided into early and late) and Neolithic *c.*4,000 BC–*c.*2,200 BC (early, middle and late); the Bronze Age *c.*2,200 BC–*c.*800 BC and the Iron Age *c.*800 BC–*c.*AD 43 have also been divided up into early, middle and late. The examination of prehistoric Carmarthenshire will follow this classification. No evidence has been uncovered to date that Carmarthenshire was occupied during the lower Palaeolithic period – before 100,000 BC.

The Middle and Upper Palaeolithic Period *c.*100,000 BC–*c.*8,500 BC

The prehistoric inhabitants of Carmarthenshire were hunter-gatherers. Their basic lifestyle required a high degree of mobility searching for the animals upon which their lives depended for the provision of food (meat) and 'clothing' (hides and skins). As a consequence of this nomadic lifestyle very little archaeological evidence has survived. While there is no recorded evidence of the temporary structures which early man constructed within the county, there is evidence from a small number of caves which were occupied as shelters. Whether these were of a temporary or permanent nature is unclear, as is the duration of their occupation. The caves were natural features in the limestone outcrops which occur in the southern part of the county. Unfortunately some of the most important of these sites have in recent times been destroyed through quarrying.

The main source of evidence for human occupation during the Palaeolithic period in Carmarthenshire comes from Coygan cave near Laugharne. The cave was located in a steep carboniferous limestone promontory (rising to over 84m.) near East and West Marsh, between Pendine and Laugharne. This promontory was part of an old sea-cliff, backing on to a flat sandy area barely a few meters above sea level. As a result of modern quarrying the site has been destroyed but not before it was extensively surveyed and recorded by archaeologists. Significant quantities of finds were recovered and many of these are on display in the National Museum of Wales in Cardiff, and the county museum in Abergwili.

When Coygan was first recorded in 1867, it had a single narrow entrance from which a passage led into the rock for a distance of about 12m., increasing in size until it reached a main chamber. Two branches extended from the main chamber in the form of narrow passageways. The importance of the site lay in the rich layers of deposits which covered the cave floor. These contained primarily animal bones and also a small number of implements. The cave was excavated on five occasions between 1866 and the spring of 1963, when it became clear that the activities of Coygan Quarries were likely to destroy the site. The last excavation was undertaken at the behest of the then Welsh office of the Ministry of Works.

Given what has turned out to be the enormous importance of the site, it has unfortunately been rather ill served by some of those who conducted the earliest examinations. Much valuable information was destroyed, when techniques of rather dubious archaeological merit were employed. While considerable quantities of material were recovered from the cave, records of the location of the finds in relation to the layers were not made. The site was also entered and damaged by careless visitors and trophy hunters. F. C. Wardle who wrote up an account of the Eccles excavation of 1913 records his first glimpse of the cave:

> Mr Eccles put me in charge of the actual work. What did I find on my first introduction? After crawling on hands and knees through the then only known entrance, a scene of vandalism was witnessed. The stalagmite floor and the stalagtites were smashed and thrown in huge heaps, reaching in some places to the roof of the cave. The cave earth had been dug up and thrown over all in high mounds; and the result of these earlier and so called excavations were just a few bones and teeth, some of which, it

was to be feared were not even correctly named. The whole of this debris, about 120 tons had to be removed and sifted before anything else could be attempted in the way of fresh discoveries.[1]

In 1933 W. F. Grimes and L. F. Cowley excavated and catalogued the various layers and finds in the cave. They distinguished five layers which contained a large quantity of animal bones. These remains offer an indication of the fauna roaming the area and the climate and environment they lived in during the various ice ages. The species identified were: Woolly Rhinoceros (*Rhinoceros tichorhinus*); Horse (*Equus caballus*); Cave Hyaena (*Hyaena crocuta*, var. *spelae*); Mammoth (*Mammuthus primigenius*); Giant Ox (*Bos primigenius*); Irish Elk (*Cervus giganteus*); Cave Bear (*Ursus spelaeus*); Reindeer (*Rangifer tarandus*); Fox (*Vulpes vulpes*); Bison (*Bison bonasus*).

From an historical perspective the most important finds were the small number of human artifacts, which provided evidence of early man's existence in Carmarthenshire. The Eccles excavations recovered the first firm evidence of human occupation of the site. As Wardle recorded: 'On the 4th October (1913) six feet from the entrance and eighteen inches beneath the stalagmite Mr Eccles discovered the first indisputable work of Palaeolithic man and in close proximity to the first mammoth tooth to be found in situ.'

The artifacts discovered by Eccles in 1913 consisted of (i) a small scraper made from half a pebble; (ii) a scraper made from a ridge-backed twisted flake and (iii) two fragments forming part of a point of black chert. A second and more significant group was recovered during the Grimes and Wardle excavation (1933) and consisted of three specimens: (i) a flake of coarse grey-white chert with crude but clearly discernible secondary working; (ii) a small cordiform or heart-shaped point found close to the cave entrance and (iii) a thin flake of chert showing coarse primary flaking. They concluded that the artifacts provided satisfactory evidence that the cave was occupied during the Mousterian phase, and possibly also at a later date in the upper Palaeolithic period. The Mousterian phase is generally associated with Neanderthal communities. During this phase the implements which were made were flake tools and hand-axes. An estimate of when these items were produced would give a date of around 45,000 years before the present. These are the earliest tangible evidence to date of Carmarthenshire's first human inhabitants.

During the final excavation of the site in 1963, Clegg recovered, in addition to considerable quantities of bones, two hand-axes. The axes according to Clegg were of a type and shape linked to the late Acheulian tradition of the last glacial period. He noted that both displayed a similar pattern of workmanship and a common ovate shape. As they were discovered close together he concluded that they were not separated by a considerable period of time in their manufacture.

What sort of insight is provided for us by the evidence about Palaeolithic Carmarthenshire? Coygan cave was the only source of this evidence before its destruction. The large quantity of animal bones of various species provides excellent insight into the prevailing climatic conditions. A preponderance among the animal bones of species that inhabited cold climates similar to that now found near the Arctic Circle, suggests a tundra or northern steppe landscape – an area where grazing supported herds of Reindeer, Elk, Bison, Deer and Mammoth. These herds would have roamed the low plains, now submerged beneath Carmarthen Bay and the Bristol Channel, which the cave overlooked. While the evidence of human occupation is slight, it is nevertheless clear and suggests Neanderthal communities. For how long and by how many the cave was occupied is unknown. That these people were nomadic and possibly in contact with other groups is suggested by Grimes and Wardle who noted the similarity between one of the hand-axes they discovered, and finds from a cave near Torquay. The recovery of large quantities of Hyaena remains and gnawed bones would suggest that for most of the Palaeolithic period the cave was the lair of wild animals who dragged their dead quarry into the cave.

Coygan was not the only cave site where evidence relating to humans was discovered. In two other areas in the county, where caves were formed in the limestone outcrops bordering the coalfield, human remains were found. These, it was concluded, did not appear to belong to the Palaeolithic period.[2] The smaller of the finds was discovered in a cave in the stark limestone crag upon which Carreg Cennen Castle was built. Beneath a layer of stalagmites the remains of two adults and two children were found by T. C. Cantrill (c. 1907). The bones, it was initially concluded, were too recent to belong to the Palaeolithic period. Also recovered was an incisor tooth of a horse, which had a hole drilled in one end, possibly for suspension on a necklace. A re-examination of the Cantrill collection in 1980, and further work on the site located a small bone deposit in the area believed to have provided Cantrill's discoveries. Three human teeth were noted. A re-evaluation of the drilled horse tooth showed it to be similar to others, which are generally classed as belonging to the upper Palaeolithic period.

The larger and perhaps more intriguing find was made in 1813 at Craig Derwyddon near Pant-yr-Odyn on the border of the parishes of Llanfihangel Aberbythych and Llandybïe. In this area there is an impressive limestone outcrop which has been quarried for over two hundred years. The tiny quarrying communities of Pantllyn and Pentregwenlais developed around this outcrop. News of the discovery was published in

The Cambrian newspaper (14 August 1813) and drew the attention of the Swansea scientist and industrialist Lewis Weston Dillwyn. He visited Llandybïe some weeks later and gathered information which he subsequently published in his *Contribution Towards a History Of Swansea* (1840). The site was investigated twice at a later date, by Professor Rolleston in 1878 and a local landowner and antiquarian Alan Stepney Gulston of Derwydd, who published an account of the discoveries in *Archaeologia Cambrensis*, 1893. There appeared to be some dispute over the extent of the discovery. Dillwyn claimed that ten human skeletons were found in a shaped chamber. Stepney Gulston asserted that twelve was the correct number – Dillwyn having failed to record a further two located deeper in the cave. Both agreed that the skeletons – which were large – were laid out, face up in a manner consistent with a ritualistic internment although of indeterminate age, and that the chamber was man-made. The orientation of the skeletons was heads facing either west or south, with the skulls resting in each case upon a solid ledge some six inches higher that the body. The remains were possibly of Bronze Age origin.

The Mesolithic Period *c.* 8,000–*c.* 3,500 BC

Abrupt changes in climate around 10,000 years ago brought the Palaeolithic period to a fairly rapid end. The rise in temperature replaced the cold, dry conditions with a milder, more humid and wetter climate. This dramatic change had a profound effect upon the ecosystem, particularly its flora and fauna. Vegetation linked to tundra and the northern steppes receded and was replaced by extensive afforestation. Animals that thrived in the cold environment and which had provided the main source of food for early man, moved northwards and were replaced by different species. By about 8,000 BC post-glacial woodland was well advanced. As soils improved tree cover expanded – pine and birch dominated most areas. New modes of living were needed for this new environment. Not only did the climate impact upon the flora and the fauna of the region, but it also altered the physical landscape. The rising sea-level resulted in the submersion of the plain consisting of the Bristol Channel and Carmarthen Bay. Greater afforestation led the inhabitants of this era to occupy sites near the coast or where the soil was too poor to support tree cover. They lived by gathering roots, berries and shellfish, hunting small game and fishing. Mesolithic man was very much characterized by the nature of his pointed flint tools known as microliths. These would have been placed in wooden shafts and used as arrowtips, knives for cutting or sawing and harpoons for spearing fish.

It was at one time asserted that no trace of 'Mesolithic man has yet been found within the limits of modern Carmarthenshire'.[3] This view may now require modification. It is certainly possible that Mesolithic man visited the coast of Carmarthenshire as evidence has been found along the neighbouring Pembrokeshire coast. He may also have visited the interior of the county following perhaps the course of the river Tywi. Mesolithic sites have been identified in mid-Wales. There is evidence which might indicate the presence of Mesolithic occupation. A collection of flint implements recovered by A. L. Leach from the exposed submerged coast at Amroth in 1912 was probably of Bronze Age origin. However, two minute microliths which were similar to those common in the Mesolithic period (but also used during a later period) were found near the skeleton of a pig. The clearest indication is from the excavations at Coygan Camp which produced a 'Mesolithic assemblage of microlith, saw, blades and flakes', totalling twenty-one items.[4] Clearly further finds will be required before the extent of Mesolithic settlement in Carmarthenshire can be more fully evaluated, but the evidence is now much more encouraging in this direction than it once was.

The Neolithic Age c. 3500 BC–c. 2000 BC

The first significant socio-cultural and economic change to affect Wales as a whole and thereby including Carmarthenshire, was the introduction of an agricultural way of life to replace that characterized by hunter-gathering and fishing. Clearly the development of agriculture as the prime means of subsistence had a profound impact not only on the environment but more importantly on the inhabitants. The growing of crops and the rearing of animals was a far more sedentary activity than hunting. It implied a degree of organization, planning and cooperation with others as opposed to hunting which was a much more solitary activity. The production of more food meant that a larger population could be sustained. Communities developed and there is evidence of trading and basic 'manufacturing' taking place. Food in the form of grain could be stored so that climatic variations over a number of years could be evened out.

There is some debate about how these new methods were introduced into the British Isles. The traditional view which has been put by John Davies is that: 'The first of the farmers of Wales were colonists from mainland Europe who brought with them their grain and stock.'[5] Some archaeologists believe that this interpretation may not be fully supported by the evidence and that it provides far too smooth a change from a society of hunter-gatherers to one of farmers. An alternative hypothesis suggests that coastal communities – and there is clear evidence of these in Pembrokeshire and Gower – may have become aware of continental developments in farming possibly through visitors/travellers from the Iberian peninsula, and that they copied them. Archaeologists term this process acculturation. It may well be that both processes were occurring simultaneously.

Evidence relating to the Neolithic settlement of Carmarthenshire broadly falls into two categories. The first is linked to how Neolithic man tamed and survived in his environment. Farming required skills and certainly equipment, which were very different from those found in hunter-gatherer societies. Vessels made of pottery were produced to store and prepare food. Flint was the main material used for making edged tools, but there was also a tendency to refine the stone implements which were produced. Stone axes for tree felling were possibly their most prized tools. They would either be polished or ground. While the number of Neolithic stone axes discovered within the county is not great – just over a dozen or so, their distribution does provide an indication of where settlement occurred. With very few exceptions the locations of the axes were near to the valleys of the rivers Tywi and Taf. Some axes had a broad butt opposite the cutting edge, while others had a pointed butt. There are good examples from Llandeilo Fawr and Llanfair-ar-y-bryn. Besides evidence for the possible location of Neolithic communities, the axes also suggest the movement of manufactured objects within Wales. An axe fragment from Myddfai has been identified by Professor F. W. Shotton as probably a product of an axe-factory on Mynydd Rhiw, Aberdaron in Caernarfonshire.

One of the most characteristic artifacts of the Neolithic period is the flint leaf arrow-head. Examples of these had not been discovered in Carmarthenshire until comparatively recently. Four leaf arrow-heads were discovered by G. J. Wainwright in 1967 at Coygan Camp near Pendine, in the vicinity of a pit containing Neolithic pot sherds and hazelnut shells. Radio-carbon analysis of the shells gave a date of 3,050 +/- 95 BC. In June 1980 a broken but clearly recognizable leaf arrow-head was discovered near Arosfa Garreg Roman camp between Llanddeusant and the Usk Reservoir.

The second category of evidence is far more dramatic and can offer anyone interested an opportunity to visit the sites occupied by our Neolithic ancestors. This category relates to the ritual associated with the treatment of their dead and the arrangement for their burial. These monuments to the dead are by far the most impressive group of remains from this age. What has survived are megalithic (large stone) chambered tombs. There are a number of different types with essentially one common feature, namely a chamber which is sepulchral. The Cotswold-Severn type consisted of a central cist or chambered tomb, which was covered by either earth or stones which extended beyond the area of the chamber.

This is called a long barrow or long cairn. A second type of monument, widely found in west Wales, including Carmarthenshire, is a portal dolmen. In Welsh this structure is termed a *cromlech*. This consisted of three or more large upright slabs, supporting a single capstone. Unlike the Cotswold-Severn these structures were probably never covered by a mound, although many were surrounded by a low platform. There are sixteen dolmens, most in a ruinous condition, located within the county. Two of the best known are Twlc-y-filiast (kennel of the greyhound bitch) near the village of Llangynog, and Gwal-y-filiast (lair of the greyhound bitch) near Llanboidy.

Few of the sites have been carefully examined by archaeologists. The excavation of the Twlc-y-filiast site by H. N. Savory in 1953 proved to be revelatory. The *cromlech* is located about 108m. above sea-level near the head of a small stream. What at first sight appears to be a simple dolmenic chamber had a small outer compartment separated from the inner one by a low sill, where some kind of ceremonial deposit was made. The chamber was set in an oval cairn which, because of the way some of the larger stones were arranged, suggested the observance of a forecourt ritual. The cairn – an oval structure – measured about 18.5m. in length with an overall width at its widest of about 9.25m. Two prehistoric finds were made in the body of the cairn – a flint scraper and an amulet. Twlc-y-filiast is not a simple dolmen, neither can it be classed as a typical Cotswold-Severn long cairn. Savory's evaluation was that Twlc-y-filiast was a 'late monument, culturally intermediate between the Cotswold-Severn and the Irish Channel groups of chambered long cairns'.

It was thought, before the Second World War, that with only one exception (Waun-y-pwtlyn near Llangadog), all the tombs in Carmarthenshire were dolmens. In 1940 Professor Grimes noted a rectangular chamber set in a ruined oval cairn at Gelli farm, Llanfair-ar-y-bryn. The size of the chamber was, he believed, sufficient to justify its classification as a megalith rather than a Bronze Age cist. Dr Savory has suggested that Carmarthenshire in Neolithic times was a 'cultural borderland' between two primary settlement areas in south-east Wales, and the coastal areas near the Irish Channel. His excavation of the Twlc-y-filiast site revealed a number of features 'not unparalleled in Cotswold-Severn culture'. He suggested that there was evidence within the county to reinforce the view that the 'Cotswold-Severn group established a colony in the Tywi valley'.[6]

The megalithic tombs of Carmarthenshire are, given the tools and technology available during the Neolithic Age, an impressive and lasting testimony to the ingenuity and engineering skills of our ancestors. A great deal of human labour would have been required to construct these monuments which in turn would have required community cooperation.

Little is known about the nature of the societies which conducted these interments, or of who and how many were buried in each tomb. The remains may have been cremated or they may have undergone a process of excarnation – where a body is exposed to the elements and allowed to decompose before interment in the tomb. Little is known of their beliefs or their social structures. Most of the megaliths were located on low-lying land below 120m.

Two other types of Neolithic remains need to be mentioned. The first is the stone circle. There were two examples of this type of monument in Carmarthenshire. They were located at Llandysilio East (*Meini Gwyr*) and Capel Hendre (*Y Naw Carreg*). Both of these circles have unfortunately been destroyed. The *Naw Carreg* circle (nine stones – the name being given to the number of surviving stones at that time) was surveyed by the Ancient Monuments Commission after its destruction in 1915. An examination of the holes from which the stones were removed enabled a plan to be drawn.[7] The circle was found to be 18.5m. in diameter and to have contained fourteen stones of which nine remained on the site. There was a break in the circle where possibly a number of stones had been removed. The largest of the stones that were left on the site after destruction was approximately a meter in length. All the stones were of local origin, and formed of millstone grit. This may have been the circle referred to by the antiquarian Edward Lhuyd in 1696 when he visited the locality: '*Y deg karreg ar y Mynydd mawr* are so many stones pitched on end in a regular order' ('The ten stones on the Great mountain …').[8]

The second and by far the most numerous of all megalithic remains within the county are the standing stones, or in Welsh *y meini hirion*. Once again their purpose is unknown. It can be speculated that they may have had some sepulchral significance – possibly marking and recording an important grave. An alternative view is that they may have had some phallic symbolism related to fertility worship. Perhaps they were marker stones. In north Wales Emrys Bowen and Colin Gresham have shown that standing stones occur along the principal routeways into the uplands. Whatever their purpose, transporting and erecting these stones would have been a considerable feat of engineering. Some were very large. The Bryn Maen standing stone in the parish of Llan-non is one of the tallest in Carmarthenshire and rises to over 4.6m.

The Bronze Age, *c.*2,000 BC–*c.*800 BC

The transition from the Neolithic Age to the Bronze Age was prolonged rather than sudden. It may well have lasted from *c.*2,400 BC to 1,400 BC. In areas that were less exposed to the new changes, that is further away from coastal influence, old practices and methods continued well into the Bronze Age with stone tools in use until 1,400 BC. The central difference between the two ages was the introduction, manufacture and use of metal for the production of tools and weapons. Copper was found to be too soft for effective use. When tin was added to it however, the resulting alloy – bronze – was found to be much stronger and more durable. The discovery of how to manufacture bronze was made in the Near East at least 2,000 years before the first metal products reached Britain. Small quantities of metal objects were introduced into Wales from around 2,400 BC, perhaps as a result of trade, possibly by migrants. It is not certain when domestic production of bronze commenced, but if the number and location of bronze artifacts is suggestive then it would appear likely to have been after c. 2,000 BC.

The most widespread evidence from the Bronze Age in Carmarthenshire relates to the new practices which were adopted in relation to burials. The migrants who arrived in Britain are known as the Beaker-folk. This term refers to their custom of burying their dead in graves which contained decorated pottery vessels (beakers) which were of much better quality than the locally produced ware. They originated in the Iberian peninsula and came to Britain from the low-lying areas around Holland and the Rhine estuary. The relationship between the migrants and the native peoples of Carmarthenshire can only be guessed at. It is also uncertain why they chose to settle in the county. That they crossed by sea is obvious but whether their motive was trade or colonization is unclear. Their knowledge of how to produce bronze weapons would have given them a distinct military advantage, but there is no evidence of conquest and subjugation of the native inhabitants. This is not to imply that society was non-violent. The existence of defended enclosures and evidence of battles during the third millennium BC have been established along the Welsh border areas.

Society continued to be very much related to agriculture. The climate was warmer and drier than it is today. This would have been particularly significant for a county like Carmarthenshire where a great deal of land lies above 200m. An increase of temperature of 1°c could have made previously marginal land far more productive. Tools, even wooden ones, would have become more sophisticated and there was evidence of weaving and the use of wheels. There is at present no archaeological evidence within the county of any domestic Bronze Age settlement. Our knowledge of the Bronze Age settlement of Carmarthenshire therefore depends almost exclusively upon the surviving funerary monuments and the metal artifacts after which the period is named. During the last fifty years the number of sites that have been properly excavated and reported, and the number of new finds that have been discovered has increased.

In Volume 1 of the *History of Carmarthenshire* two beakers are recorded as having been discovered in the county.[9] They are from Pale Bach in the parish of Cyffig, and Cors-y-dre near the village of Llan-non. At Pale Bach fragments of a beaker were found in a cist below the gateway of a farm. The pottery shards were of a light pinkish colour and were covered in a chevron and hatching pattern which had been made with a blunt tool. Similar patterns occur on beakers from Somerset and Dorset. After reconstruction the vessel measured 15.5cm.–20.5cm. in height. Beakers were placed in contracted inhumation burials as part of a funeral rite for the dead individual. No human bones were found with the Cyffig beaker.

The Cors-y-dre beaker was discovered in 1930 by a farmer engaged in spring ploughing. Shortly after the discovery the site was investigated by Iorwerth C. Peate from the National Museum of Wales. A cist had been uncovered. On removal of the large capstone (approximately 1.6m. by 1m.) the cist was found to contain a beaker and three flint implements lying at one end of the chamber. No human remains were discovered. Peate noted that several other large slabs had been unearthed in the past in different locations within the field and that it was possible that there may have been other burials in the vicinity. The beaker was 20.5cm. high, with a rim diameter of 14cm., it varied in colour from light brown to pink and had a slightly polished surface. It was decorated with bar-chevrons on the neck, with the lower body consisting of a series of bar-chevrons applied differently to give a lattice-work effect. Peate noted that it matched beakers which had been discovered in Somerset and Wiltshire. The site of the cist, within easy distance of the sea, and parallels with beakers from the West Country, would suggest that the beaker tradition reached Carmarthenshire via the Bristol Channel. Further confirmation for the coastal distribution can be taken from the discovery of a cist containing a crouched inhumation found at Orchard Park in Laugharne in 1949.

Some sites which might have extended our knowledge of the early Bronze Age in Carmarthenshire have regrettably been either destroyed, or examined and recorded haphazardly. In the parish of St Ishmael's on the hill of Allt Cunedda two barrows were opened in 1850. These were recorded in *Archaeologia Cambrensis* in 1851. The first barrow was called Banc Benisel. It was found to contain a hexagonally-shaped stone which sealed a pit containing the skeleton of a very tall human, buried in the prime of life. According to local tradition, this was presumed to be the grave of Sawyl Benisel, King of the Britons. A large cist, covered by a cairn was exposed during the construction of the railway line between Carmarthen and Llandeilo in 1864. It was located on the floor of the Tywi valley at Maes-y-crug near Nantgaredig and may have contained a Beaker inhumation.

Very few metal objects that can be ascribed with any degree of certainty to the early Bronze Age have been found within the county. This may well be due to the fact that there were very few to begin with, possibly because they were introduced only gradually. The inhabitants would have continued to develop and refine their stone and flint implements. The presence of worked flint implements alongside the beaker burial from Llan-non might support this view. Many of these implements are very well crafted. There is a fine axe of bleached flint with a slightly expanded edge from Llanegwad. A discoidal flint knife from Capel Gwynfe near Llangadog shows evidence of 'corn gloss' resulting from continuous use during the harvesting of cereals. One of the most interesting finds was made originally in 1905, at Cilrhedyn East, but was not made public until 1949. This was a very rare mace-head, made from felspathic dolerite from the Preseli hills, dated at between c. 1,800 BC and c. 1,400 BC. A finely chipped flint spear head from Llanelli is very similar in shape to spear heads made from bronze.

Dr Savory has suggested that there were trading links between west Wales and Wessex during the early Bronze Age. The discovery that the blue stones used during the second phase of construction of Stonehenge were quarried from the rock of the Preseli hills would indicate that these links clearly existed. Whether these links spread to cultural ones is unclear. Records of the only stone circle from this period, at *Meini Gwyr*, Llandysilio East, to be examined, were destroyed during the Second World War. Indications are that the circle was enclosed by a wide low bank, and approached by a narrow entrance through the bank lined with upright slabs. These features, which were different from other stone circles in mid-Wales and south Wales bore some resemblance to Irish stone circles.

Early Bronze Age implements are uncomplicated in appearance with minimal flanges, no loops or cavities. They would appear to have been cast in very simple moulds. Of the small number of metal objects that have been found in Carmarthenshire one of the first was an early Bronze Age flat axe or chisel, discovered at the Chapel Quarries, Gors-las. It is very slightly flanged and has transverse bars on the face. More typical are the bronze flat axes from Newcastle Emlyn, Garn Wen Quarry Llanglydwen, Llanarthne and Glangwenlais quarry in Llandybïe.

Much closer emphasis upon field surveys towards the end of the twentieth century has revealed more Bronze Age monuments than were previously known. Sites which had been previously examined have also been re-evaluated. This has started to extend much further our knowledge and understanding of early Bronze Age settlement within the county. A central figure in this process has been Anthony Ward. Over a number of years he conducted a detailed survey of the Bronze Age monuments on one of the most important but previously neglected sites in south-east Carmarthenshire at Mynydd Llangyndeyrn (265m.), the watershed between the Gwendraeth Fawr and Gwendraeth Fach rivers. Ward noted that on and around the mountain there was a complex of monuments which, on the basis of variation, he suggested could be divided into two groups – burial or sepulchral monuments, and those linked to ritual and ceremonial functions. The site had been clearly occupied for a long time. Within the site there were two badly ruined megalithic chambered tombs (known as Bwrdd Arthur and Gwal-y-filiast) at the base of a small cliff, a standing stone, five cairns (possibly two others) with at least one cist, and three ring cairns. While the majority of the remains were of a sepulchral nature the three ring cairns, argued Ward could 'be designated ritual or ceremonial sites on the basis of [other] … excavated examples in Wales'.[10] This may also be the purpose of the standing stone. Most of the cairns were of early Bronze Age type while the chambered tombs were Neolithic. An explanation suggested by Ward to account for the concentration is that a social unit was using the mountain for burial and ceremonial traditions in addition to economic and perhaps settlement purposes. People in the Bronze Age may have been drawn to the site because of its commanding appearance over the locality.

Not far from Mynydd Llangyndeyrn and once again occupying a prominent position there was another group of Bronze Age cairns near the village of Carmel. Ward surveyed and reported on four major cairns including a ring cairn.[11] The cairns were spread on the summits of a ridge over a distance of 1.6km. Garn Big is the highest point on the ridge at 273m. The commanding locations would certainly suggest a deliberate choice by the builders. They may have been linked to the burials already noted at Craig Derwyddon caves. At the centre of the cairn an inverted collared urn dating to c.2,400–1,800 BC, lay on the bedrock floor of the hollow. The urn contained the cremated remains of a single adult and was characteristic of an early Bronze Age single grave.

During the transition from early to mid-Bronze Age, the practice of cremation was replacing inhumation as a means of burying the dead. Food vessels were placed alongside the burials. At Cadno mountain tumulus near Pendine fragments of pottery food vessels have been uncovered. A reconstruction of one has revealed a bowl-shaped vessel decorated with a 'twisted cord ornament'. Flint knives were found in one of the graves. The similarity of some of the vessels unearthed in Carmarthenshire and south Pembrokeshire with ones discovered in Ireland suggest that some cultural contact between the two areas was taking place.

In the middle Bronze Age proper, the practice of cremation completely replaced burial by inhumation. More significantly beakers and food vessels were no longer placed in graves. Middle Bronze Age graves are found to contain a cinerary urn and an incense cup. A central feature of the shape of these urns is the projecting rim or collar. Only a small number of urns have been recovered from burial mounds within the county. These mounds are known as round barrows. When the mound is made of loose stones and they are located at a higher elevation they are called cairns.

The earliest barrows to be effectively examined and recorded were near the hamlet of Crosshands, near Llanboidy in the upper Taf valley. The hamlet which is located at a height of around 200m is surrounded by a number of prehistoric monuments, including a ruined megalith. Cyril Fox undertook a detailed examination of the site in 1925 and excavated two barrows. In the first he discovered evidence of a cremation in a large overhanging-rimmed urn protected by a stone slab. The second barrow he concluded was similar to a type commonly seen in Cornwall and Ireland. In his evaluation of the Crosshands site Fox drew attention to the proximity of a megalithic structure (c.2,000 BC) to the barrows where the dead were buried up to c.1,150 BC. He concluded that the continuity of use of a sacred site 'suggests some tribe may, for a millennium have remained in possession of this remote area'.[12] Close to the Crosshands group, and about three miles north of the village of Llanboidy lay another group of three mounds. These contained primary and secondary burials. An urn which was recovered from one of the barrows was similar to those from the Crosshands group.

As with the earlier period all too few metal items have been recovered and recorded from the Middle and Late Bronze Ages. In general the essential characteristic of metal items from these two periods is the greater sophistication of their appearance and construction. Technological progress in both design and production was being made by these early metallurgists. Axes in particular from this period contrast markedly with the early flat axes. The characteristic axe-form of the middle Bronze Age is the palstave. This evolved from the flat axe, by the development of flanges and a stopridge. There are good examples from Capel Isaac, Cynghordy and Llangathen. The Pen-gai socket axe, which resembles a type commonly found in Ireland, is a good example from the late Bronze Age. Other items from this period found within the county are a leaf shaped sword from Cynwyl Elfed and a spear head from Llanarthne.

The number of metal items found in Carmarthenshire from this period was increased dramatically in the early 1980s with the discovery of a hoard at Gelli Felen farm near Myddfai. In total eight axes were found, while a ninth axe or axe fragment was later lost. Six of the eight axes belong to a typically south Wales type – a three-ribbed socketed axe tradition. Of the other two one indicated a broader southern British provenance, while the eighth had similarities recognized among north, east, Welsh and Marcher axes. The 'hoard' is not an uncommon feature of the late Bronze Age. The Myddfai hoard may well have represented the stock of an itinerant metal-worker. A small hoard was discovered in the Kidwelly area during the early part of the twentieth century.

Not all the items discovered are of a functional nature. A small number of decorative pieces made from gold have been discovered. At Cwrt in the parish of Llanfynydd a gold amulet was found in an urn in 1876. The gold was probably of Irish origin from the Wicklow hills. A small hoard of four gold bracelets was found at Capel Isaf, Llandeilo and have been dated to c.1,250 BC. A fragment of an encrusted urn from Cadno mountain, Pendine, is of a type that belongs to the very end of the Bronze Age (c.500 BC) and probably came to Wales via Ireland. The discovery of these items is a further indication of the connection between west Wales and Ireland. It has been suggested that traders moving between south Wales and the south of Ireland avoided navigating around the Pembrokeshire peninsula, preferring instead to land on the north Pembrokeshire coast and move their goods across land. The discovery of objects of Irish origin within the county offers tentative support for this view.

The archaeological evidence suggests that there was no sharp breach with the Neolithic period, and that some of its practices almost certainly survived into the early Bronze Age. Stone implements were being used alongside those made from bronze for many centuries after the transition. That Carmarthenshire was absorbing new cultural ideas and practices is quite clear. Trade and contact with other parts of the British Isles and the continent was taking place, although what the terms of this trade were, is unknown. While the economy is clearly related to farming there were improvements in the tools used, crops grown and animals reared, particularly cattle. The pottery that was used for domestic and burial purposes was also of a superior quality and tended to be more elaborately decorated. Technological advances in the design and casting of metal goods are visible. For the first time decorative goods made of precious metal are found. A number of sites appear to have been occupied for a prolonged period. The extent to which this continuity of use is linked to the emergence of tribal/communal groups can only be hinted at, in the absence of any firm evidence. Of the size of the population or their domestic arrangements, very little is known. What language they spoke and the main tenets of their culture also remain a mystery. Despite our increasing knowledge of this age there are clearly gaps in our understanding, some of which are unlikely ever to be filled.

The Iron Age *c.*600 BC–AD 42

Some time during the turn of the first millennium BC metallurgists in central Europe – Austria and Bavaria (Germany) – discovered how to smelt and cast small quantities of iron. The first iron products to be introduced into Britain, from the continent, arrived during the late Bronze Age. Once again there is no sharp or clear delineation between the two ages. In many places, particularly in western Britain, bronze goods would have continued to be produced for some centuries after 600 BC, before finally giving way to iron. A deteriorating climate and the move towards communalization helped delineate an age characterized by aggression and uncertainty. There is evidence that society was becoming much more organized and it is during this period that tribal groups linked to loosely defined areas start to emerge.

Demand for bronze saw a depletion of sources of raw materials and therefore alternatives were needed. Iron as a material could be produced more widely, and therefore in greater quantities, than bronze. Initially the iron tools were brittle and not as superior as bronze tools, but when refined and forged implements made from iron were harder and sharper than those previously in use. These new tools enabled the environment to be tamed more effectively – forests could be cleared and farming practised. Moreover people were increasingly more able, and prepared, to defend their land if and when necessary. There is evidence in many parts of Britain that rivalry between various tribal groups during this period resulted in conflict and warfare. It is believed that the first Celts arrived in Wales during the Iron Age, bringing with them a language which would ultimately evolve into Welsh.

Given the nature of the society that was emerging – querulous tribal groups jealously guarding their lands and striving for local ascendancy – one of the most dramatic legacies of the Iron Age are the great hill-forts. The construction of these sites, of which there may have been many phases, would have been undertaken over a long period. In terms of feats of civil engineering, the larger hill-forts in particular are very impressive achievements. The society that planned the construction would have needed to be very organized, probably hierarchical, and to have operated a clear division of labour among its members.

It is possible to identify very generally two broad groups of fort within Carmarthenshire. The first group, which is the largest (approximately forty-nine sites), consists of forts constructed on commanding locations, usually a hilltop, occasionally a coastal promontory or cliff top, sites which were carefully selected with a view to incorporating the natural features into the defences of the fort. These are sometimes supplemented by earthen ramparts or dry-stone walling. A commanding location might well have served to remind the local inhabitants of the control which the tribal hierarchy exerted over their lives. The second broad class of forts can best be described as having been constructed with no discernible relation to the local environment. Many are rectangular in shape and have earthen ramparts. In addition to forts a small number of other structures exist which are much smaller and may be fortified farmsteads.

Without doubt, the jewel among the first group of Carmarthenshire hill-forts is Garn Goch near Llangadog. There are in fact two hill-forts, 200m. apart, one significantly smaller than the other. The site has drawn the attention of antiquaries and tourists over the centuries who marvelled at its commanding location and massive stone ramparts. A. H. A. Hogg conducted a survey of the site for the Welsh National Monuments Record which was published in *Archaeologia Cambrensis* in 1974. As no archaeological excavation has taken place on the fort, there are no finds linked with the site. The dating of the site is therefore uncertain although it is clearly of Iron Age origin.

The position chosen for the larger fort is a sandstone ridge, which is one of the spurs of the Black Mountain. The northern side of the fort rises very steeply from the Tywi valley and would have posed a formidable if not impregnable obstacle to attackers. Most of the enclosure, which is roughly rectangular in shape, is over 200m. above sea-level, with the highest point rising to 233m. The fort is almost 700m. long, and at its widest is just over 150m. The natural defences are supplemented by large ramparts of dry-stone walling. Contained within the fort are a number of structures. Dominating the site is a summit cairn. This is a mass of rubble some 3m. high, piled up on a natural crag which accentuates its position. It measures 55m. by 20m. and is in effect a long cairn. There is no evidence of any burial and it is probably of Bronze Age origin. The first recorded survey of Garn Goch in 1860 noted that the summit had lost its original form partly through the actions of the Rebecca rioters 'who in 1843 erected beacons here for raising the country'.[13] Two rectangular structures of different sizes and a round-house platform, comprise the remaining visible internal structures. Near the centre of the camp there was a small pool. Three phases of fortifications have been detected. The ramparts are clearly the most impressive surviving features of Garn Goch and are at their most commanding on the western side of the fort, where they rise to over 6m. in height and 6m. in width.

The second largest hill-fort in the county lies lower down the Tywi valley at Merlin's Hill, Abergwili. It was excavated in the 1980s by the Dyfed Archaeological Trust. Two radio-carbon dates were obtained from an occupation layer which pre-dated one of the ramparts. The dates were 360 +/- 60 BC and 150 +/- BC and indicate a broadly middle Iron Age date for the main fort. Merlins's Hill lies almost in the centre of a line of hill-forts running roughly across the middle of Carmarthenshire and primarily located in the Tywi valley. It is suggested 'that the site acted as a trading centre on the interface of a territory based on the Tywi valley with its 'capital' at Garn Goch'.[14] It is also speculated that given the important location of the fort – near trade routes and close to the navigable limits of the Tywi – and even similarities with the name, that it may have been the precursor for Carmarthen.

One of the most carefully excavated and surveyed sites in the county is Coygan Camp near Laugharne. It differs from the other two forts in that its location is coastal. It is a promontory fort which utilizes the cliff face as part of its defences. The enclosed area, which has a mound in the centre, is defended by a massive rampart fronted by a ditch. Wainwright's excavations showed six cultural phases of occupation for the site spanning the Neolithic period to the Dark Ages. The fort did not appear to have been occupied continuously. It was during the fourth phase of occupation that the banks and ditches were constructed, a development Wainwright said was probably attributable to La Tène immigrants. The recovery of pottery shards which were of undoubted Iron Age origin, confirmed this conclusion. Two other promontory forts worth noting are Castell Pyr, Llanllwni and Hafod Camp, Llan-gan East.

In the second broad class of forts there are six rectangular earthworks and four which are enclosed by walls but are circular in shape. A typical example of a rectangular earthwork is Eithin Mân, Llangynog. It is located on a site that provides a very good view of the surrounding countryside including the estuaries of the Tywi and the Taf. There is a rampart and a ditch which encloses an area measuring 40m. × 28m. into which there is only one entrance. The corners are rounded and the breadth of the rampart at ground level is 5.5m. It is possible that the earthwork was influenced by methods of fortification introduced by the Romans.

In addition to what are confidently labelled Iron Age forts, there are other smaller and more numerous structures. Although constructed on a much more domestic scale, possibly for family units, in keeping with the nature of the times they were invariably defended. They have not in the past received the attention from archaeologists they deserved. Over the last twenty years this position has been slowly rectified. Our understanding of day-to-day life has been enhanced by studies of these sites. A good example in Carmarthenshire of a late Iron Age defended farmstead comes from Pen-y-coed in Llangynog, which was excavated by Ken Murphy in 1983. There were several other defended sites of possible Iron Age attribution in close proximity to Pen-y-coed. The undulating area between the river Cywyn and the Tywi estuary has good fertile soil which could be easily worked. This would have proved attractive to early Iron Age farmers and would have drawn them to this part of the county.

Within the context of the time the area was quite well populated. Fourteen defended enclosures are located within an 8km. radius of the site.

Pen-y-coed was recognizable by the presence of earthworks. Although they are in a very poor state of preservation, they are visible and mark a rectangular enclosure measuring 46m. by 26m. Within the enclosure there was the base of a round-house which provided a radio-carbon date of 160 +/- 60 BC (a second smaller round-house had been built on the site at a later date of 235 +/- AD 60). Some black pottery shards and two glass beads fused together were of late Iron Age origin. There was evidence of palisades and drains on the site. The discovery of an Iron Age beehive quern for grinding cereal and a small quantity of seed indicated a subsistence lifestyle. Detailed analysis of pollen, insects and plant macrofossils indicated that the economy of the site had a largely pastoral basis but there is limited evidence of arable land being used. Mixed farming has certainly been a feature of the rural economy in this part of the county during the last century. This system may well have been evolving during the late Iron Age.

Material evidence made from iron reflecting the social, domestic and military activities which people engaged in between *c.*600 BC and AD 45, is fairly paltry considering the number of sites identified within the county. The excavations at Coygan Camp produced only one iron object from an Iron Age layer. This was a square-sectioned nail. A total of 371 iron items, however, were found in deposits dated as Romano-British, some centuries after the end of the Iron Age. Although outside the scope of Carmarthenshire's prehistory, the quantity of artifacts is revealing. Many of these items would have been similar to those in use at the very end of the Iron Age. Large numbers of nails were found including some hobnails which were used in footwear. Clamps which were used in the construction of timber houses, in addition to the nails and a fine socketed axe, indicate the use made of iron for building purposes. A bar-share plough tip, a socketed plough-share tip and a forged hoe were clearly used for farming – the main economic activity of the community. It has been shown that these were the normal types of ploughs in the Iron Age and the Romano-British period. An assortment of knives, daggers and spear-heads represented the military equipment from this turbulent period.

There was a change in the climate towards the beginning of the Iron Age. It became rather cooler with an increase in rainfall accompanied by stronger winds. The upland areas of the county which had been occupied during the Bronze Age would have been less suited to sustaining arable farming. Under these conditions low-lying areas would have been more attractive. Improved tools and casting techniques would have made it easier for farmers to clear woodland. There is an absence of early embanked enclosures from the moorland areas of Carmarthenshire but they are common on the relatively low-lying ridges near the Tywi and Teifi valleys and in the vicinity of Carmarthen Bay. What is noticeable when examining the distribution of hill-forts within the county is the small number of what can be termed large hill-forts. These are almost entirely confined to the Tywi valley, an area of very good agricultural land and also a natural routeway into mid-Wales. There are no hill-forts of a similar size to what can be loosely termed the 'Towy group' (Savory) west of Carmarthen. It is unclear as to whether the Tywi valley was a 'frontier' zone well fortified between tribal groups, or the heartland of a tribal group. Although relatively few in number the large forts had formidable defences and had clearly been well selected. There is no evidence to date that these defences were ever used to repel any attack during this period. The preponderance of forts and enclosures in the west and south-west of the county is also very noticeable. It may well be possible to conclude that this was linked in some way to the quality of the farmland.

Romans, Saints and Princes: AD 43–1066

With the arrival of the Romans, Carmarthenshire leaves the potential uncertainty and speculativeness of the unrecorded past and embraces, albeit tentatively, the much more familiar world of recorded history. The first written references to places within the county are made by Claudius Ptolemy of Alexandria in *Geography* which was written shortly before AD 150. Ptolemy noted that at the time of the Roman conquest of Wales, the area in the south-west of the country was occupied by a tribe called the Demetæ. A derivative of this tribal name has survived into the present as Dyfed. He names two locations within the tribal territory which have been identified as being Carmarthen and Dolau Cothi. There is also a possible reference to the river Tywi. In the early part of the third century AD a traveller's road book was compiled – the *Antonine Itinerary* – which noted the Roman name for the settlement of Carmarthen as *Muridunum*. The more commonly accepted Latin spelling for Carmarthen is *Moridunum* which means 'sea fort', derived from the British '*mori*' (*môr* in Welsh) sea, and '*dunum*' latinized from the Celtic 'dunos' meaning fort. The word 'dunos' survives in Welsh as '*dinas*' – city.

The Claudian invasion of Britain was launched in May AD 43. Four years later south-eastern Britain had been subjugated and an unstable frontier established along the Fosse Way, the Roman road from Exeter to Lincoln. The fledgling Roman province came under attack almost immediately from a number of independent tribes living beyond its perimeter. One of the most formidable of these was the Silures of south-east Wales who attacked the new province in AD 47 and AD 48. The native prince Caratacus (Caradog in Welsh) who had taken refuge with the Silures following the defeat of his tribe, the Catuvellauni, may well have organized or instigated these attacks. Roman response to these attacks, and others elsewhere along the frontier, was to retaliate with force. Operations against the Welsh tribes were to be undertaken by the three legions in the west. These operations commenced in AD 47. The plan to conquer Wales and crush native resistance involved two simultaneous attacks in the north and the south. Naval forces were also deployed. It took the Romans rather longer than they probably anticipated – almost twenty years, to defeat native resistance. In AD 51 Ostorius Scapula, the Roman governor defeated the Silures. The following year the twentieth legion was in turn defeated by the Silures. It was during the governorship of Julius Frontius, who arrived in AD 74 that the resistance of the Silures and possibly the Demetæ was finally crushed.

There are no specific references to the Demetæ in the main written source of the Roman conquest of Britain, the biography of Agricola by his son-in-law Tacitus. A possible indication that the military campaign and consolidation process against the Demetæ was on quite a large scale can be drawn from the existence of two large temporary camps located at Trecastle mountain on the border between Carmarthenshire and Breconshire. These temporary structures – the smaller camp is located within the perimeter of the larger camp – would have been constructed during the course of a campaign and would have contained nothing more permanent than military tents. The site at Y Pigwn lies at over 415m. above sea-level. The larger enclosure covers 36.8 acres while the smaller one covers 23.9 acres. The extent of the site, its commanding location and the contraction of the larger camp to be replaced by a smaller one suggest that the military operations were far from insignificant in scale and may well have been prolonged. No evidence however has been found of any Roman military operation within Carmarthenshire yet the size of the newly discovered Roman fort at Llandeilo would suggest a substantial military presence was required.

By about AD 100 the conquest of Wales was complete and the Romans set about the task of consolidating their new acquisition and binding it into the imperial framework. North-east and south-east Wales were dominated by the two great legionary fortresses at Chester (*Deva*) and Caerleon (*Isca*). To the west of each legionary fortress there were auxiliary fortresses at Caernarfon (*Segontium*) in the north and Carmarthen (*Moridunum*) in the south. These military extremities formed a crude rectangle containing several other smaller auxilliary bases, linked by a well developed road system. Roman Carmarthenshire was in many ways on the very margin of the empire given that neighbouring Pembrokeshire was not under the same degree of control and was subject to occupation by Irish settlers during the third century.

Although Tacitus does not mention directly the Demetæ and their tribal lands he does offer a clue as to the attraction of conquering and occupying their territory. In the *Agricola* he notes that 'Britain yields gold, silver and other metals, to make it worth conquering'. The Romans developed a substantial gold-mining operation at Dolau Cothi in north Carmarthenshire, which was worked intermittently until the twentieth century. The other remains from the Roman period consist of civil and military settlements, the remains of roads and a small number of villas and other homesteads.

The centre of all Roman authority in west Wales was *Moridunum*. It was at the very extremity of Roman civilization in Britain and Europe. The arteries of the Roman corpus were undoubtedly its roads. In Roman times as at present, roads converged on Carmarthen. The road link from Isca entered Carmarthenshire it is assumed via the small fort of *Leucarum* (Loughor) which guarded the crossing point of the river Llwchwr. Alternatively it is possible that the route entered the county at Pontarddulais and went through Pontyberem to Carmarthen. It is likely that Carmarthen was linked by road to Llanio via Llanybydder. Recent research appears to indicate that there may have been a Roman road running westwards towards Whitland. From Carmarthen there was a road along the Tywi valley to Llandovery. The small fort at Llandovery was itself one of the hubs of the mid-Wales road network. One road went north-west to the gold mines at Dolau Cothi, another went east towards Brecon while a third ran north-east towards Castell Collen. The Roman road from Carmarthen to Brecon follows very closely the route of the present A40. Roman road building was an impressive achievement which in turn helped bind the empire together and at various times ensured its survival through facilitating the rapid deployment of soldiers to deal with full-scale rebellions and 'little local difficulties'.

Since Sir Mortimer Wheeler's *resumé* of Roman Carmarthenshire in 1935, significant progress has been made on uncovering the nature and extent of the Roman occupation of the county. Considerable archaeological work has been undertaken in the last half century. It is now more than possible (as might be expected) to revise Wheeler's observation that evidence of the Roman occupation of Carmarthenshire is 'meagre in the extreme'. Improved understanding has taken place in three areas: (i) the growth and development of *Moridunum* – its change from military to civilian use; (ii) improved understanding of the gold-mining operation at Dolau Cothi; (iii) the Romanization of the Carmarthenshire countryside.

The most important development to have occurred relates to our understanding of the evolution of *Moridunum* from a military settlement to a formalized Roman town and the cantonal capital and *civitas* of the Demetæ. The exact location of the Flavian fort and the Roman town, while known to exist when Wheeler produced his survey, were not accurately recorded. Two very significant discoveries were made in 1968. During excavations in the carpark of the Ivy Bush Hotel, by Professor Barri Jones, a ditch was uncovered which was identified with the initial fort, part of the Frontian system of conquest dating to the mid-70s AD.[1] Early Flavian pottery was found in the sump of the ditch. As a result of Jones's work the position of the fort was located quite precisely to the Spilman Street – King Street area. Outside the walls of a fort it was normal for a small township or *vicus* to develop, of traders, merchants etc., who would service the needs of the military. The large number of finds and the location of Roman remains to the east of the fort could not be effectively explained by a *vicus* alone. The second important discovery was of a massive stone revetted rampart south of the line of Richmond terrace. This proved to mark the outline of a formalized Roman town. A date for its construction based on ceramic evidence indicated the second half of the second century AD.

During the summer of 1969 Jones returned to Carmarthen and continued his excavation on a site scheduled for development as a carpark, opposite St Peter's church, and within the presumed boundary of the *civitas*. The results were dramatic. Work on the area behind the rampart revealed the existence of an east–west street or *decumanus* running through part of the site. This made it much easier to identify building plans within the 'gridded layout associated with the formal planning of the demetic capital'. Some of the buildings which were uncovered were clearly commensurate with *Moridinum*'s status as a regional capital – one building had a colonnaded portico almost 2m. wide along the edge of the street. Finds from the site consisted of painted wall plaster, window glass and the remains of a hypocaust system of underground heating. The site also revealed the remains of an even larger structure, measuring approximately 25m. by 34m. A coin recovered from the site dated it to *c.* AD 320. At least one room had been floored with tesseræ of terracotta. Two, almost mint, coins, discovered in the foundation level of the later building, from the reign of the Emperor Magnentius and his brother Decentius (AD 351–3) dated its construction fairly accurately. Even though much of the foundation had clearly been stripped of shaped stones, sufficient remained to provide a useful insight into the development of the settlement. Professor Jones concluded that there was firm evidence of urban life in the westernmost cantonal capital of Roman Britain well into the last quarter of the fourth century, and probably later. No evidence was found of any violent destruction.

Further proof – if it were needed – of the settlement's status was the examination and confirmation that the semi-circular depression in the hillside below the Park Hill housing estate at the western end of Priory Street was, as had been suspected, a Roman amphitheatre. The possibility that the site was in some way linked to Roman Carmarthen was first recognized in 1936 by the borough surveyor. His foresight in preserving the site from further encroachment ensured its survival. A brief survey in 1968 established the line of the arena wall. A much more detailed examination was undertaken in 1970. The northern *Cavea* was formed by excavating a semi-circular hollow into the hillside in the manner of a Greek theatre. Material obtained from the excavation would be used to construct the southern *Cavea*. These two sides bound an elliptical *arena* floor measuring at its widest 50m. × 30m. A small fragment of Samian ware pottery was recovered from the seating bank which was dated to the first half of the second century AD. It is estimated that the amphitheatre's seating capacity was in the region of 4,500 to 5,000.

Since the innovative work of the late 1960s and early 70s the pace of excavation has developed rapidly. Under the auspices of the Dyfed Archaeological Trust which was formed in 1975 (and more recently Cambria Archaeology) watching briefs on any developments within the known boundary of *Moridunum* and subsequent rescue excavations have expanded knowledge of the changes and developments that took place during the Roman occupation. Heather James has provided an excellent summary of the growth and development of Roman *Moridunum*. The following is based on Ms James's analysis and evaluation.[2]

Roman settlement began with the establishment of an auxiliary fort probably about 5 acres in size, in AD 75. The fort was located in the Spillman and King Street area and was called *Moridunum*. The garrison was scaled down and the fort reduced in size before being finally abandoned sometime between AD 95 and 105. There is evidence that buildings were demolished and that the withdrawal was orderly and planned. Occupation of an agricultural nature continued in the annex to the east of the fort. A small temple was located in this area and may have provided a focus for the occupation. Pottery from the site has been dated to AD 90–110. There is no archaeological evidence to date to identify a *vicus* type settlement outside the fort. Some time after AD 120 but before AD 150 a planned street system was laid out on either side of the main road on the east of the fort site. It is likely that this marks the official designation of *Moridunum* as the *civitas* or tribal administrative centre for the Demetæ. Outside the walls an amphitheatre was built in the late second century. A pattern of rectangular timber houses and workshops were identified during excavations in 1980–84 including a large building at the Church Street site from the mid-second century. On the southern side of the town a civic building, possibly a *mansio* or an inn, has been recorded. Between the second and third centuries there appears to have been a marked change in the character of the occupation as evidence from excavations in Priory Street indicates a period of abandonment.

New earth and timber defences were constructed during the late second century. Their relationship to the changes noted at the Priory Street excavations is unclear. Larger, grander and more Romanized town houses were built during the third and fourth centuries. Sometime during this period the defences were remodelled on a more substantial scale; the clay bank was widened to form a low ramp behind a stone wall fronted by a shallow ditch. Fourth-century coins and pottery and the continued maintenance of the street system suggest that urban life continued until late into the fourth century. It can be speculated that the discovery of some third and fourth-century military type fittings might suggest a military presence towards the end of Roman occupation. After the collapse of Roman rule in the early fifth century it appears that *Moridunum* continued to be occupied and that new defensive arrangements were made. A large 'V' profiled defensive ditch was discovered which cut across the Roman fort site at Spillman Street. This has been dated to the mid-sixth century.

The detailed and thorough investigations into Roman Carmarthen have provided a wealth of material and information about the first recorded urban centre in west Wales. Its administrative functions and continued claims to be the regional capital of the area remain to this day. It was the administrative centre of Dyfed and is the county town of Carmarthenshire. No other town in Wales can boast such a lineage of administrative service. Its only rival from this era is Caerwent, the *civitas* of the Silures tribe. Nowadays this is little more than a small town.

In the north of the county at Llandovery, a fort was strategically placed at the intersection of a number of roads. There has been some uncertainty as to the Roman name for the fort at Llandovery, but it is now believed to be *Alabum* which is noted in the Ravenna Cosmography. The fort is located near the hamlet of Llanfair-ar-y-bryn about a mile outside the centre of Llandovery along the road to Builth. The church of St Mary is located within the area of the fort. In extent it covers about 5.88 acres and it was excavated in 1961 and 1963. The fort does not appear to have been occupied after *c.* AD 160. Given its size the fort could have accommodated a garrison of a thousand men. The *RCAM* noted that a few remains, possibly a bath-house, had been found outside the perimeter of the fort near the river Brân.[3] Its significance was its strategic importance at a point where small valleys enter the vale of Tywi. It is possible that its decommission as a military site may in some way be linked to the ending of gold-mining at Dolau Cothi.

Archaeologists had long suspected that there might be another fort between Llandovery and Carmarthen. Roman forts were often located a day's march apart (roughly 15 miles). In the spring of 2003 the exciting discovery of this previously unknown fort was made in the grounds of Dinefwr Park, Llandeilo following a ground radar survey of the site. The survey revealed the classic rectangular outline of a typical Roman fort. However, archaeologists were particularly intrigued by the fact that there appeared to be two overlapping forts – a larger one of eight acres and a smaller one of approximately three and a half acres. Preliminary investigations were made in the summer of 2005. These showed that the larger fort was the earlier of the two and was dated to the later part of the first century AD – late 70s – and that military occupation lasted until AD 120–30. The size of the larger fort would indicate a base large enough to house a legionary detachment (perhaps two thousand men). A force of this size would suggest that the resistance of the Demetæ may well have been far more determined than previously thought. Once the initial campaigning and pacification phase was over, a smaller garrison fort was built which was possibly occupied by an auxiliary unit or cohort comprising about five hundred foot soldiers. One of the most important discoveries on the site was the existence of a small *vicus* near the north-east entrance of the smaller fort.

It is a matter of conjecture as to the significance of the existence of gold within the territory of the Demetæ and the determination by the Romans to occupy their territory. This may have been as Tacitus asserted one of the main benefits of conquest and the real imperative behind the military campaign. The fact that the site was occupied very early after the conquest might be taken to support this theory. It is likely that the Romans were aware of mining operations in this area before their occupation. The location of Iron Age type hut circles close to the site and some evidence of pre-Roman mining could be taken to support this view. What is clear is that the focus of Roman interest in this area was the gold-bearing quartz found in the northern part of Carmarthenshire, in the hills around Dolau Cothi, near the confluence of the Twrch and Cothi rivers. The Roman site at Dolau Cothi is now considered to be the location identified as *Louentinum* in Ptolemy's *Geography*.

Greater understanding of mining operations in other parts of the empire has shed light on how the Romans conducted their mining activities. It is now fairly clear that sophisticated and, in the context of the time, very advanced methods were used based on a hydraulic technique. A considerable quantity of water, under pressure, was needed. Mining operations were located in the hillside bordering the east bank of the Cothi in the parish of Cynwyl Gaeo. Roman miners quarried out the gold-bearing ore from the hill-side using an open-cast method of mining. Large volumes of water would be used to prospect for the quartz veins. It has been calculated that the miners removed 500,000 tonnes of rock from the surface. More water was used to process the ore, by sifting and washing the crushed quartz. It was initially thought that the water was brought to the site by means of a single aqueduct. The aqueduct was partly cut into the rock and partly constructed of wooden troughs. From the point on the Cothi where the water was diverted into the aqueduct, to the mine, was a distance of 7 miles. Near the mine the water was fed into two large rock-cut tanks and a reservoir from which the water was released to the processing area by means of sluice gates. The discovery by archaeologists of further aqueducts in the Cothi valley and an entirely new system which provided water for the mine in the Annell valley has confirmed the importance of the mine to the imperial economy. When it was no longer possible to use the hydraulic method because the increased height of the opencast mines limited the quantities of water that could be channelled into the tanks, the miners continued their excavations underground. The underground workings were discovered when mining resumed on the site during the mid-nineteenth century.

While intensive fieldwork during the late 1960s shed considerable light upon the scale and nature of the mining operation, little was known of the settlement attached to the mine. That there was a site was evident from chance finds of pottery and coins in the vicinity of the village of Pumsaint, and the discovery of a bathhouse near Ynysau Uchaf farm on the south side of the Cothi in 1831. An opportunity to mount an excavation near the Dolaucothi Arms Hotel in 1972 unearthed part of the settlement. Jones and Little discovered the site of a small Roman fort which covered 4.7 acres. It proved to be of a standard Roman type. The main building which could be identified was a granary. Finds from the site suggested that it was built around *c.* AD 75–80 very shortly after the Frontian invasion. Structural changes were recorded during the late Flavian-Trajanic period. In the early part of the second century the fort was reduced in size by almost a half. The barracks and the granary were demolished to make way for workshops which contained a small furnace. It is unlikely that occupancy of the fort lasted beyond *c.* AD 150, although it is possible that the area continued to be inhabited, as third century finds have been identified near the mine.

Outside the urban centre of *Moridunum* and the forts at Pumsaint and Llandovery what influence did the Romans have on the local population? What did the Romans do for Carmarthenshire? Their military and civilian presence would certainly have stimulated aspects of the economy – trade (food, utensils, cloth), construction, metal-working and mining are obvious sectors to have developed under their patronage and benefitted from *pax Romana*. The first embryonic road network was laid out. Much of the construction work would have been carried out by Roman engineers possibly supervising local workers and slaves. Central-heating appears for the first time in the county. During over three centuries of occupation it is not unreasonable to expect considerable evidence of Romanization. The reality is that there is very little to suggest the existence of a thriving and vibrant Romano-British society for this period. Only time will tell whether this is waiting to be discovered. Detailed work on a site known as Llangynog II of a house platform has revealed no evidence from the Roman period. Radio-carbon dates taken from the platform indicate that the site was occupied around the end of the first and early part of the second century AD. It was tentatively speculated that the site was abandoned as a result of the gradual Romanization of the area and that the occupants left to find a new site on which to establish a more Romanized farmstead.

There are three sites within the county which have provided positive evidence of Roman structures that are not linked to a military presence. The site at Abercyfar, two miles south of Carmarthen is now lost. Documentary evidence from the late eighteenth century records the discovery on the site of a 'remarkably fine tessellated pavement, with a prodigious quantity of silver and copper coins of the lower empire'. This might suggest a villa. The second site at Cwm-brwyn, three miles north-west of Laugharne was excavated by J. Ward in 1906. Cwm-brwyn is a small earthwork enclosing a Roman farmstead. Against the western rampart and facing the gate there was a long narrow building (33.5m. × 7.3m.). It had a slate roof and glass windows. Some of the rooms were heated by a hypocaust system. A small number of datable finds were recovered, one of the most significant being a bronze coin of Carausius (AD 287–93). The third site is potentially the most exciting of all. Llys Brychan, Llangadog, has been known for a long time but was excavated only in 1961. Within the confines of a small excavation site traces of three rooms were unearthed and clearly many more remain unexposed. There was evidence of an under-floor heating system and many floor tiles were recovered. About sixty fragments of painted wall plaster were found – mainly green and red with sophisticated patterns. While it was not possible to date the structure accurately, it was concluded that by Welsh standards this was a fairly prosperous villa.

Michael Jarrett suggests that Llys Brychan is the first important villa to be recorded in the territory of the Demetæ.[4] The other sites are farmsteads enclosed by rath-like earthworks which may have belonged to a local aristocracy. Llys Brychan on the other hand might well have been the home of a Demetic notable. He argues that the absence of military bases west of Carmarthen does not indicate that the Demetæ were thought unimportant, rather it indicates that they accepted Roman rule. It may have been the case that the Romans made them an offer they found difficult to refuse: support the Silures in their resistance to the occupation and risk destruction and slavery, or accept the suzerainty of the Romans and the potential benefits of peace and prosperity. Sizeable military forces (as located at Y Pigwn) on the borders of their territory may have swayed the uncertain, to acquiesce to Roman rule. There was a military presence in Carmarthenshire but it appears to have been on a relatively small scale.

A great number of Roman finds have been discovered within the county which have helped date the sites from which they were recovered with accuracy. They span many aspects of Roman life – civil and military, domestic and social, cultural and religious. Few are unique within the context of Roman Britain. A small number, however, are worthy of note. One of the most important hoards of Roman gold objects dating to the second or third century AD was discovered near the village of Pumsaint towards the end of the eighteenth and the beginning of the nineteenth centuries. The hoard consisted of two chains with wheel-clasps and crescent pendants, and two snake-armlets, one inset with jewels. It is uncertain whether these were manufactured at the site or were imported into the locality. The Kyngadle saucepan is a bronze patella with strainer and base plate. In itself it is not unique. What sets it apart is its decoration. It is pierced with a triskele of Celtic origin. This piece is a remarkable fusion of Roman design married to native manufacture and art. It is dated to the late third century AD, when Celtic art was less evident. The patella was discovered some years before 1839 at Coygan Camp in the parish of Llansadyrnin. It contained coins from the reign of Carausius (AD 287–93) which helped to date it.

The end of Roman rule in Carmarthenshire occurred during the early part of the fifth century. Barbarian attacks on Rome prompted the withdrawal of garrisons and legions to protect the heart of the empire. In historical terms the next three centuries are known as the Dark Ages on account of the paucity of written historical information surrounding the political and social structures then operating. The few tantalizing glimpses into this period suggest an age mired in violence and conflict as successive power-brokers fought to establish their control over particular localities. There is however archaeological evidence in the county, from the 'Dark Ages', and a small number of monuments and memorials have survived. Coygan Camp was certainly occupied during the late Roman period and possibly beyond. Its inhabitants, on the basis of archaeological evidence, farmed the land and produced materials from wood, leather and wool. The discovery of many weapons attests to a need to protect the community. With the withdrawal of the legions and the end of *pax Romana*, Roman civilization was brought to an end although their language survived for many years. A large inscribed stone from Llansadyrnin perhaps dating from the early sixth century bears the Latin inscription *TOTAVAL FILIUS DOTHO RANTI*. This is a memorial possibly to the most important man in the district. Two important developments which occured in the post-Roman period were the consolidation of Christianity which had been introduced in the latter years of the Roman empire, and the emergence of small Welsh kingdoms.

That Christianity was introduced by the Romans into Britain is now accepted. When Christianity reached the borders of the future Carmarthenshire is much less certain. During the political vacuum which characterized the ending of Roman rule it was at one time considered that the church which emerged in the western part of Britain – 'the Celtic church' – was a separate entity from the mainstream church in the rest of western Europe. It was argued that it evolved its own identity in particular different services, organization and an 'austere spirituality'. The church does appear to have been cut off from the mainstream Christian tradition and its peripheral location may have accounted for its particular evolution and its missionary approaches, but it would be wrong to consider it as entirely separate. Given the desire neatly to package and homogenize eras in history, the post-Roman period is frequently referred to as the 'Age of the Saints'. This implies a period of asceticism, spirituality and devotion. An alternative label for these centuries is the 'Dark Ages'. In a way both are appropriate. Christianity was established but any conclusions made are at best tentative. Regarding the spread of Christianity, this age was clearly linked with several key figures who became central to our culture. That these men and women who were canonized, inspired cults and followers is also a credible assumption. Documentary confirmation of their activities is however very patchy and was frequently produced several centuries (mainly in the eleventh and twelfth centuries) after they died.

Evidence of their locations and the extent of their influence is sought in studies of place names. The preponderance of places starting with *llan* in Carmarthenshire is all too frequently cited as evidence of the county's long tradition of Christianity stretching back to the Age of the Saints. Originally, *llan* meant an enclosure and only much later did it come to mean a church. Many village names with the prefix *llan* have clearly no religious links, for example as in Llanfynydd. Others however do have a Christian link, and some can trace their origins to the middle of the first millennium. Two individual cults have strong links with the county – those of St David and St Teilo – while there are also many churches dedicated to the children of Brychan.

St David (*c.*520–*c.*588), our patron saint, has links with the area but there is no evidence to suggest that any of the churches dedicated to him were in fact founded by him. There are eight Carmarthenshire churches dedicated to St David and they cover most of the county from Pendine to Cenarth Mawr, Castelldwyran to Llandyfeisant. More closely linked with the county is the cult of St Teilo. Llandeilo Fawr is considered to be the site of a tenth-century reference to the altar of Teilo and the presumed location of the centre of the cult. It is very likely that there was a religious community attached to the church, with its own scriptorium and library. One of the most important early Welsh manuscripts from this period, the magnificently illustrated 'Book of Teilo' was in all probability produced at this religious community, possibly around 740. It is now located in Lichfield cathedral and is known as the 'Book of St Chad'. There may well have been an itinerant bishop linked with the cult. In geographic terms the cult was closely linked to the Tywi valley. Llandeilo Abercywyn and Llandeilo Rwnws also directly bear his name. A final group of churches is linked to the children of Brychan. These include his reputed sons, St

Cynog (Llangynog), St Cledwyn (Llanglydwen) and St Dingad (Llandingat) and among his daughters St Tybïe (Llandybïe). W. N. Yates, who carefully re-evaluated this period, concludes that there is no evidence to suggest that Celtic saints actually founded churches dedicated to them. Yet he considered the term 'Age of the Saints' to be a perfectly valid descriptor if it implied a period when Wales was undergoing conversion to Christianity and the church was in its infancy.[5] A small number of Christian memorials support the view that Christianity was advancing during this time. One of the most important inscribed stones in the county is the richly carved cross of Eiudon which was originally located at Llanfynydd. This outstanding example of a stone carved column was the shaft which would have supported a wheel head cross.

South-west Wales before and during Roman occupation was the tribal land of the Demetæ. There is no reason to suggest that the members of the tribe did not continue to inhabit the area following the departure of the Romans. Their land was mainly situated between the rivers Tywi and Teifi and extended westwards towards St Bride's Bay. It may well have included initially the area known as Ystrad Tywi. In cultural terms the Celtic roots of the Demetæ were closer to the Irish than to their Brythonic cousins in the rest of Wales and Cornwall. There are a number of memorials from this period which offer an indication of the ethnicity and culture of the population. Three memorial stones from Eglwys Gymyn, Llandawke and Llanwinio bear dual inscriptions in Latin and the Irish ogam script. These stones offer a glimpse into a society that was clearly at some level literate in lettering its memorials, and was also bilingual – Latin and Irish. The memorial from Llanwinio also bears a cross on the flat upper surface which was probably a later addition. One of the first figures linked with the post-Roman period in Carmarthenshire is Vortigern (Gwrtheyrn in Welsh) a notorious pagan ruler from the fifth century who ruled over lands near Radnorshire. From a number of sources, among them the works of Bede and the Saxon Chronicle, it emerges that he sought the help of Saxon chieftains to repel an invasion of hostile tribes from the north. He was denounced by his fellow British rulers for introducing the marauding Saxons into Britain. His significance for Carmarthenshire is his link with Craig Gwrtheyrn hillfort in the parish of Llanfihangel-ar-arth. According to the writer Nennius (AD 796) this stronghold of the Demetæ was his last refuge. There is some dispute over this assertion.

One of the most evocative names from this period is Merlin, or in Welsh – Myrddin. His name has been very closely linked with Carmarthen in its Welsh form Caerfyrddin. The legend of Merlin and his relationship with another 'mythical' figure – Arthur – has been well recorded in literature and legend. Merlin's oak which stood in Carmarthen was a visible reminder, until it was removed, of this enduring tradition. There are, however, considerable doubts as to whether such a person ever existed. The origin of the link with Carmarthen can be traced back to Geoffrey of Monmouth's *History of the Kings of Britain* (*c.*1136). Geoffrey created the name Merlin from the Welsh Merddin, which later became Myrddin, and hinted that there was a clear link between Merlin and Caerfyrddin. The link is entirely spurious, since the origin of Caerfyrddin is from the Latin *Moridunum*. As Professor Jarman noted: 'Caer-fyrddin was soon converted by popular fancy into the name of an imaginary eponymous personage, thought to have been the founder of the fortress in the distant past.'[6] In early Welsh literature from this period there is a tradition of a wild man who lived in the woods and was vested with supernatural powers enabling him to foretell the future. It would appear that Geoffrey fused a number of myths before adding his own particular gloss to the tale. *The Black Book of Carmarthen* (*c.*1250) contains many poems relating to heroes from Dark Age Britain. Three of the poems deal with the legend of Myrddin and his prophecies.

Nennius is an informative source about the polities of this period. He wrote about the arrival of the Celtic leader Cunedda Wledig and his eight sons from northern England to north Wales. One of the sons Ceredig was responsible for setting the boundary – the river Teifi, between his lands – Ceredigion and those of Dyfed and Ystrad Tywi. The lands of the future county of Carmarthenshire were at this time divided into two parts by a line running north from the Tywi estuary to the river Teifi. To the east of the line was the territory of Ystrad Tywi which formed part of the patrimony of the kings of Ceredigion, of whom the most powerful was Seisyll and his descendants. West of the line was Dyfed. The writer Gildas is scathing in his remarks about Vortipor, the king of Dyfed whom he describes as the tyrant of the Demetæ. Vortipor is the only ruler from this era who is confirmed archaeologically by a stone monument. This monument originally stood outside the entrance to Castelldwyran churchyard in the west of the county. The inscription is bilingual, in Latin and the Irish ogam script. The Latin text reads *MEMORIA VOTEPORIGIS PROTICTORIS* which translates as 'in memory of Vortipor the protector'. The other interesting feature is a wheeled cross located above the word *memoria* which probably indicates a Christian burial.

From the end of the fifth century the line of the royal house of Dyfed is unbroken down to Hywel Dda. The death in 814 of Tryffin ap Rhain without a male heir contributed to a period of instability compounded by sea-borne incursions by Viking raiders. The emergence of Rhodri Mawr (*c.*844–78) as ruler of Gwynedd marked the end of the small native Welsh states. Following Rhodri's death in 878 his lands south of the river Dyfi – Seisyllwg (Ceredigion and Ystrad Tywi) – passed to one of his younger sons, Cadell (d.910). His elder brother Anarawd invaded south Wales and attacked much of Ystrad Tywi. Cadell recovered his possessions and went on to found a dynasty which would have a significant impact on south Wales. On his death he left his lands to his two sons Hywel and Clydog. His son Hywel ap Cadell through the good fortune of inheritance and marriage and his diplomatic skills created a united kingdom of Deheubarth and was acknowledged as 'king of all Wales'. In a more localized context Sir J. E. Lloyd noted that: 'An important step had been taken towards the formation of the county of Carmarthen; henceforth the Gwili and Clawdd Mawr, the 'great dyke' of the uplands, were no longer inter-tribal barriers'.[7]

Hywel ap Cadell is more widely known in Welsh history as Hywel Dda (Hywel the Good). On the death of his brother Clydog in 920 he succeeded to the whole of his father's lands. A judicious dynastic marriage to Elen the daughter of Llywarch, last prince of Dyfed, brought him the lands of his father-in-law as a dowry. Following the death of his cousin Idwal Foel, ruler of Gwynedd and Powys, he took possession of those territories. With the exceptions of Morgannwg and Gwent he established himself as ruler over most of Wales. Hywel maintained good relations with the King of Wessex, Athelstan, and paid homage to him. It appears that Hywel admired many aspects of the rule of his predecessor King Alfred, and sought to emulate them in his own conduct and in his own realm. In 928 he embarked on a pilgrimage to Rome. His status in Welsh history depends primarily on his attempt to codify the myriad of ancient laws, customs and traditions which prevailed in his kingdom. According to tradition, these were framed at his command during a great assembly held at *Tŷ Gwyn ar Daf* – Whitland. Representatives from each commote in his kingdom attended, although when it occurred is unclear. A date of sometime between 942 and Hywel's death in 950 is the best estimate. He instructed that three copies of the laws were to be made. One would accompany him during his progress around his realm, one would be located in Dinefwr and the third in Aberffraw. His wisdom, vision, and the excellence of his laws set him apart from most other rulers in Wales during this period.

The laws provide an insight into the nature of the society they were attempting to regulate. This was very much a rural society with the population living in small scattered communities. Their economy was based on subsistence farming, both arable and pastoral. It is fairly safe to conclude that in our county there were no large settlements – the *civitas* of Carmarthen had been abandoned by its civil population. That this society was organized is supported not only by the laws but by the marginalia inserted by an unknown scribe in the Book of St Chad (*c.*800). Why they should have been produced is unclear – possibly a documentary record in a venerated manuscript provided a distinctive cachet for important local information. And some of this information was local to the Llandeilo area where it is believed the manuscript was produced. One insert has been identified as coinciding with the northern boundary of Cantref Mawr. There is a reference known as Chad 6 to the *maenor* of *Med Diminih* which has been identified as Meddynfych in the parish of Llandybïe. The *maenor* is the Welsh equivalent of manor which consisted of a group of small settlements y *taeogdrefi* and was essentially an early administrative unit, dealing with issues relating to obligations, dues and crops. Meddynfych may have been the site of the *maenor*'s *llys* (court) and was some distance from the *llan*. Chad 6 gives a list of places which provide the measure of the *maenor* which, although extensive, is not coterminous with the later parish of Llandybïe. It contained seven small townships. These entries suggest a stable society that was much better organized than was once assumed.[8]

Hywel's death plunged his realm into chaotic infighting among his heirs. His son Owain emerged as ruler of Deheubarth while Gwynedd reverted to the descendants of Anarawd. During the early eleventh century the balance of political power in Wales swung towards the north. Confirmation of this is evident in the rise of Gruffydd ap Llywelyn as ruler of Gwynedd and Powys in 1039. His aim was to try and annex Deheubarth. The great-great-grandson of Hywel Dda, Hywel ab Edwin, proved to be a doughty opponent until 1044 when he was killed resisting Gruffydd. He was succeeded by Gruffydd ap Rhydderch who sought valiantly to keep Deheubarth independent. Gruffudd ap Llywelyn enlisted the support of the English in his attempt to seal victory. In 1055 Deheubarth finally succumbed to the superior might of Gruffydd who succeeded in his goal of uniting the whole of Wales. His triumph was short lived and his many enemies, aided by the English, plotted his downfall. There followed another turbulent period for the two kingdoms. In the south, Rhys ap Tewdwr, a descendant of Hywel Dda, took possession of Deheubarth. These events were largely overshadowed by the drama being played out across the border in England. In 1066 Harold had been killed by an invading army led by the ruthless and ambitious William, Duke of Normandy. The portents for maintaining any long-term independence against the Normans were not auspicious.

III

Conquest, Settlement and Revolt: *c*. 1066–1485

The period covered by this chapter is very significant in the history of what would ultimately become the county of Carmarthenshire. A number of key developments occur. In 1066 there was no geographical or administrative area known as Carmarthenshire. Following the Edwardian conquest of Wales in the late thirteenth century a miniature county bearing this name was created. A pattern of settlements was established which formed the basis of the main pre-industrial communities in the area. The town and borough of Carmarthen emerged as the undisputed military, administrative and economic centre of the region. Finally, as a result of various local wars and disputes, a substantial portion of land in this area was annexed by the English Crown. This would make the eventual reorganization of the area under the Tudors much easier to achieve.

In the years immediately following the invasion of England by William the Conqueror in 1066 no real threat was posed to the native rulers of west Wales. Wales was peripheral to the ambitions of the Normans. Such a situation was unlikely to survive the subjugation of England. Norman infiltration of Wales was largely due to native rulers attempting to enlist the support of the invaders to settle their own bloody squabbles. Once they became involved in Wales they were reluctant to withdraw. The position of Rhys ap Tewdwr who became ruler of Deheubarth in 1075 was challenged by local rivals on a number of occasions. His decisive victory over his Welsh enemies at the battle of Mynydd Carn (1081) proved to have significant long-term consequences for the area. In the same year William the Conqueror visited Wales. While it is unclear whether the two men met, it is known that Rhys was recognized by William as the undisputed ruler of Deheubarth. This recognition, however, was guaranteed on condition of the payment of an annual tribute of £40 to the English crown. His submission to the Norman king provoked outrage among some Welsh noblemen. Rhys ap Tewdwr was the last Welsh prince to rule by hereditary right over the area which now includes Carmarthenshire. Following the Conqueror's death the Normans launched a number of incursions into central Wales. Rhys was killed in 1093 while trying to stem the tide of the Norman invasion. It is evident that the sovereignty guaranteed to Rhys did not extend to his sons. For ambitious Norman barons, Deheubarth was at their mercy. If the Welsh sought to disagree then disputes would be settled by force.

A key feature in accounting for the military success of the Normans was their castle building programme. Castles were the predominant instrument of conquest, consolidation and defence at this time. Initially these were temporary structures of the motte and bailey type – earth ditches and mounds defended by wooden palisades and towers. They afforded security for garrisons when controlling hostile areas. While many were later abandoned a small number were converted into stone castles. These formed the nuclei of settlements which grew up in the shadow of the castle walls. Native castles and strongholds were also seized and incorporated where appropriate into the Norman defence structure. Location was all important in the construction of these castles. Coastal sites, and sites which commanded river crossings were favoured. The first castle to be built in the area by William Fitzbaldwin in 1093, was placed to command a crossing over the river Tywi. It is recorded as Rhyd-y-gors. No physical remains of this castle survive. It may have been located on the banks of the Tywi about a mile south of Carmarthen. This castle had a chequered history with the garrison withdrawing in 1096 following the death of Fitzbaldwin, only to be re-established shortly after Henry I became king. It was finally abandoned in 1106 and a new castle was built on its present site in 1109, by Walter of Gloucester. The site was on an imposing bluff overlooking the river Tywi which at that point was tidal. When Gerald of Wales visited the town on 20 March 1188 he observed that 'this ancient town is enclosed by brick walls, parts of which still stand'. He was probably referring to the Roman fortifications which may initially have been incorporated by the Normans as part of their defences.

There is very little evidence of military or civilian occupation of the site near which the new castle was built. The former Roman town of Moridunum had been abandoned with one exception. A small religious community or *clas* had been established near the Roman town to honour Teulyddog a disciple of St Teilo. The community was presided over by an abbot and its importance can be gauged by its designation as one of the seven 'bishop-houses' of Dyfed. It fared badly under the Normans who had very little time for domestic saints or their followers. They introduced a new foundation, an Augustinian priory. These two communities – the one military and the other ecclesiastical – would coexist as two distinct administrative units for four centuries. The castle and its settlement was called New Carmarthen in order to distinguish it from Old Carmarthen centred around the priory.

In addition to Carmarthen, nine other castles were built or rebuilt over the course of the next century and a half. Dryslwyn (*c.*1190), Dinefwr

(c. 1274) and Carreg Cennen (c. 1274) were built by the native Welsh, while Kidwelly (1106), Llandovery (1113), Laugharne (c. 1116), Llansteffan (c. 1146), and Newcastle Emlyn (c. 1240), were of Norman origin. Besides these, there were many temporary mottes which were never strengthened into stone castles. The castles are mainly concentrated on the coast or extend along the Tywi valley. Their locations are a combination of the spectacular and the functional. Most witnessed short periods of violence interspersed by many decades of peace.

Not only did the Normans wish to impose their military control over the region, they also sought to impose a cultural hegemony. A key element in this strategy was religion. The Celtic church was viewed as the main bond linking together native Welsh culture. Change was needed. During the twelfth century offshoots of the various monastic orders were introduced into the area. In 1106 Henry I established his justicer, the powerful Bishop Roger of Salisbury, at Kidwelly and the building of the castle and town was probably started shortly after that date. A church was established in the same year – St Mary's – and was given to Sherborne Abbey in Dorset. They set up a small Benedictine priory. The Benedictines also gained a foothold in the north of the county when, sometime before 1126, Richard Fitzpons bestowed the rectory of Llandingat to the Benedictine Priory of Great Malvern in Worcestershire. A small cell was established which lasted for about three quarters of a century before being dissolved. A Cistercian abbey moved to Tŷ Gwyn ar Daf in c. 1151 from Haverfordwest. At St Clears a small priory for one or two monks was founded and bestowed to the Parisian Cluniac priory of St Martin des Champs. In the next century, possibly in 1284, a small Franciscan friary was built on land outside the borough.

Following the death in battle of Rhys ap Tewdwr the claims of his sons to his lands were ignored. One of the sons, Gruffydd ap Rhys, after a period in Ireland returned to the Tywi valley and was well received by the local people. An attempt to capture him led to a revolt. Gruffydd and his followers attacked the recently built castle at Llandovery in 1116, but despite destroying the outer defences were unable to scale the keep. As news of his partial success spread he gained more supporters. Carmarthen castle was attacked but again they failed to capture the keep. The Normans regrouped and Gruffydd retreated northwards into the more inaccessible areas of Ystrad Tywi. When Henry I died in 1135 Gruffydd was lord of only a single commote – Caeo in Cantref Mawr. The power struggle in England over the succession between Stephen and Matilda presented the Welsh with an unexpected opportunity to recover lost lands. Gruffydd had married Gwenllian the daughter of Gruffydd ap Cynan, ruler of Gwynedd and had six sons – Anarawd, Cadell, Maredudd, Morgan, Maelgwn and Rhys. While her husband was in the north in 1136 negotiating with her relations, the formidable Gwenllian and her sons Morgan and Maelgwn attacked Kidwelly castle. The attack failed and Gwenllian and Morgan were killed while Maelgwn was captured. Although the castle at Kidwelly held out, Gruffydd gained some satisfaction from defeating a combined force of Normans, English and Flemings at Crug Mawr on the outskirts of the town. According to a contemporary chronicler (in *Brut y Tywysogyon*) 3,000 Normans were killed in this battle. This was Gruffydd's last important victory before his death in 1137. In the same year the castle at Carmarthen was destroyed and over the next twelve years the surrounding area was brought under the control of Gruffydd's sons Anarawd, Cadell, Maredudd and Rhys. Cadell rebuilt the defences of Carmarthen castle and a number of other bases were also fortified. Of the four brothers it was

Carreg Cennen Castle, Cantref Bychan, built *c*. 1274

Rhys – Lord Rhys – who emerged to become one of the most important resistance leaders in the struggle against Anglo-Norman oppression.

Rhys ap Gruffydd – Lord Rhys

When Rhys ap Gruffydd (*c.* 1132–97) succeeded his brother Maredudd as ruler of Deheubarth in 1155 his inheritance denoted more of a geographical than a political area. Although a relatively young man he had already helped his elder brothers in their military campaigns. He was certainly no novice to the brutal and treacherous internecine warfare that characterized tribal relations in Wales during this century. At the age of fourteen he is recorded as taking part in the storming of Llansteffan castle. The accession of Henry II (1154–89) to the English throne introduced a much more formidable foe than the rather ineffectual Stephen. Henry's victory over Owain Gwynedd brought Rhys into the political frame. The two men met in 1158. Henry allowed Rhys to retain Cantref Mawr and another unspecified *cantref*. Significantly the Norman barons who had been dispossessed by the Welsh during the previous reign were reinstated. The Clares and Cliffords returned to west Wales. At a stroke Rhys's lands were considerably reduced. To exacerbate the sense of humiliation, Henry did not honour the promise of an additional *cantref*. An attack on his lands from Cantref Bychan led Rhys to retaliate which, in turn, precipitated a swift royal response. Confronted by a royal expedition Rhys submitted to Henry, who, satisfied that affairs in Wales were in some sort of order, turned his attention to France.

Rhys seized the opportunity presented by Henry's absence to try and reassert his authority. His attack on Carmarthen castle drew an immediate reaction from the Crown, and a large relief force was dispatched. During the years 1159–62 Rhys proved to be more of an irritant than a serious threat to Norman rule. When Henry once again turned his attention to his troublesome Celtic neighbour and visited south Wales in 1163, Rhys was compelled to pay homage to the Crown at Pencader and hand over his son Maredudd as a hostage. Rhys accompanied Henry to England where, along with other Welsh rulers, notably Owain Gwynedd, they paid homage to him at Woodstock. Following this act of contrition, Cantref Mawr and Dinefwr were restored to Rhys. His return home was a case of back in Wales and back in business. There followed a period of sustained aggression against all and sundry – marcher lords and native rulers – which resulted in Rhys's ascent to become the most powerful figure in Wales following the death of Owain Gwynedd in 1170. He commenced his activities by attacking Ceredigion, where the murderer of one of his nephews had fled to seek refuge from Earl Roger of Hereford. The whole region with the exception of the castle at Cardigan came under his control. His lands now extended to the river Dyfi and bordered Owain Gwynedd's territory. On this occasion the response of the crown did not dislodge Rhys. Henry's expedition in 1165 was abortive and his withdrawal presented Rhys with a great opportunity to complete the conquest of Ceredigion. Henry's frustration was vented on his Welsh hostages and he ordered that Maredudd and others be blinded. Rhys attacked and finally captured the stronghold of Cardigan in November 1165. Cilgerran and Llandovery castles fell in swift succession. Emlyn and Cantref Bychan were brought under his control and the power of the Clare and Clifford families was broken. Rhys's success emboldened him and he sought to extend his jurisdiction into Brecknock. This proved to be an assault too far. In the king's absence in France his justiciar persuaded Rhys to call off his campaign. The dramatic change in Rhys's fortunes was in no small measure helped by the difficulties facing Henry II, particularly his quarrel with Thomas Becket, Archbishop of Canterbury. In Wales the momentum of the Norman expansion slowed as Henry diverted his attention towards Ireland. The emergence of a powerful military and political figure in an area of inherent instability, may well be the reason behind the *volte-face* in royal policy in 1171–2. From being a threat, Rhys was now viewed as a potential ally and stabilizing force. He was confirmed by the king as ruler of his territories and was well received by Henry at Laugharne. While the respect each had for the other might have been grudging, the outcome was that Rhys was appointed justiciar for the whole of south Wales. This marked the summit of his power, which effectively remained unchallenged for the next twenty years.

Consolidating his territories and, if possible, extending his influence were two of Rhys's priorities. Deheubarth was a vulnerable kingdom. The existence within its borders of Norman castles and colonies (Carmarthen, St Clears, Kidwelly) provided a constant reminder of the realities of the post-conquest period. Rhys adopted a variety of stratagems. Marriage alliances were made with other native rulers and Norman lords. The good-will of the crown was cultivated with great success. Defences were strengthened, Cardigan castle was rebuilt in stone in 1171 and similar work was undertaken at Dinefwr and Llandovery. It would be wrong to dismiss Rhys as simply another powerful medieval warlord whose only motive was self-aggrandizement. His support for native Welsh culture is clearly recorded in his patronage of the Cardigan 'eisteddfod' of 1176. Rhys entertained and welcomed Gerald of Wales and Archbishop Baldwin during their tour through Wales in 1188 to recruit volunteers for a crusade. His attitude to the Church was one of benevolence and he tolerated the Norman foundations. The only new religious community founded in the area during his rule owed much to his support. A house of Premonstratensian canons was established in a secluded and isolated lakeside site at Talley. Administrative reforms were introduced – the texts of Welsh laws were assembled in book form, and money rents replaced food-renders. To ensure the security of his territory, particularly his frontiers, he built a number of castles modelled on the Norman motte and bailey type such as those at Ammanford and Aberdyfi. His confidence and awareness of his status is visible in the title he assumed for himself – rightful prince of south Wales. Professor R. R. Davies concludes that Rhys's achievement was nothing short of astounding: 'he had reconstituted the kingdom of Deheubarth and made it the premier Welsh kingdom.'[1]

The death of Henry II in 1189 severed the personal bond between Rhys and the English Crown. An indication of the strength of these ties can be gauged from Rhys's dispatch of soldiers to help besiege Tutbury where Earl Ferrars was defying the Crown. Freed from any commitment to temper his expansionary zeal, Rhys attacked the foreign colonies which he had reluctantly recognized while Henry was alive. His sudden assault against Laugharne and Llansteffan resulted in their surrender without any resistance. Fissures however were appearing in the noble house of Dinefwr. These were clearly visible in the latter years of Rhys's rule. Their appearance was not due to external factors, more a consequence of domestic feuds. The endemic weakness of noble families in medieval Wales – too many over ambitious sons and heirs – afflicted the house of Dinefwr with a vengeance. Rhys fathered by a conservative estimate eighteen children. Four sons who had reached adulthood – Gruffydd, Rhys (Gryg), Maelgwn and Hywel (Sais) – displayed an unhealthy and ultimately disastrous sibling rivalry. In 1189 blind Maredudd persuaded his father that Maelgwn was a threat and that he should be imprisoned in Dinefwr castle. Rhys attacked and captured St Clears and its adjoining commotes and granted then to Hywel Sais. In 1190 the great Norman citadel of Kidwelly was finally taken. Displaying no loyalty to his father Rhys Gryg seized Dinefwr and Llandovery. Rhys himself suffered the indignity of being imprisoned by his own sons in 1194. Regaining his freedom he seized his errant sons, and in a display of vigour moved against the de Breos family in mid-Wales, taking the castle of Radnor before securing a truce. This was his last great campaign, before his death in April 1197. A recent biographer neatly summed up the essence of his career: 'he was an astute politician, a zealous reformer, a sensitive patron of the arts, a "tribal" patriarch of princes, an enlightened religious benefactor, a builder of castles and a warrior of distinction but above all he was the architect of peaceful coexistence'.[2] In a survey published by *The Sunday Times* (2000) 'the Richest of the Rich in British history', Rhys's wealth, in contemporary terms was estimated at £4.3 billion, placing him 95th out of 200.

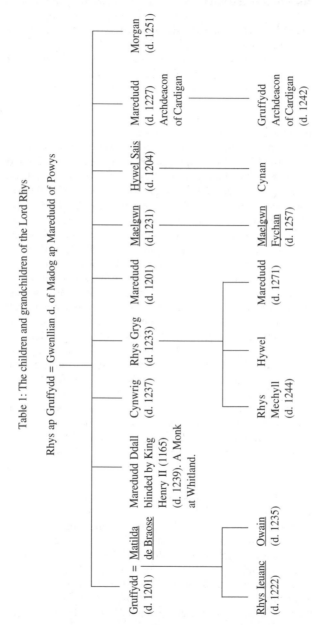

Table 1: The children and grandchildren of the Lord Rhys

Rhys ap Gruffydd = Gwenllian d. of Madog ap Maredudd of Powys

Gruffydd = <u>Matilda</u>
(d. 1201)   <u>de Braose</u>

Maredudd Ddall
blinded by King
Henry II (1165)
(d. 1239). A Monk
at Whitland.

Cynwrig
(d. 1237)

Rhys Gryg
(d. 1233)

Maredudd
(d. 1201)

<u>Maelgwn</u>
(d.1231)

<u>Hywel Sais</u>
(d. 1204)

Maredudd
(d. 1227)
Archdeacon
of Cardigan

Morgan
(d. 1251)

<u>Rhys Ieuanc</u>
(d. 1222)

<u>Owain</u>
(d. 1235)

Rhys
Mechyll
(d. 1244)

Hywel

Maredudd
(d. 1271)

<u>Maelgwn</u>
<u>Fychan</u>
(d. 1257)

Cynan

Gruffydd
Archdeacon
of Cardigan
(d. 1242)

Key—Buried at Strata Florida.

The Decline of Deheubarth

The death of the family patriarch in 1197 sparked a round of brutal internal feuding among his quarrelsome sons and their heirs. In the long term Deheubarth was the undisputed loser and the Anglo-Normans the victors of this domestic bloodletting. Hywel Sais was killed by followers of his brother Maelgwn in 1204. When it suited their purposes they involved the English in their disputes. Gruffydd ap Rhys was captured and handed over to the English. The heart of the problem was how to divide Rhys's lands in an equitable and acceptable manner between the various heirs. This proved to be fiendishly difficult. A settlement was finally imposed upon the main heirs by Llywelyn ab Iorwerth of Gwynedd the main ruler in Wales after Lord Rhys's death. He summoned them to Aberdyfi in 1216 and compelled them to accept a partition. Maelgwn was given the three cantrefs of Emlyn, Cemais and Gwarthaf and the castles of Carmarthen and Cilgerran, in addition he was handed the commotes of Ceredigion, Gwinionydd and Mabwnion, the two commotes of Ystrad Tywi, Mallaen in Cantref Mawr and Hirfryn in Cantref Bychan along with the castle of Llandovery and the maenor of Myddfai. The two sons of Gruffydd ap Rhys, Rhys and Owain were handed the remainder of Ceredigion along with the castle of Cardigan. All of Cantref Mawr except Mallaen, Cantref Bychan south of Myddfai, along with Kidwelly and Carnwyllion were alloted to Rhys Gryg. An insight into the new ruler's court is provided in medieval manuscripts from this period which identify among other features his court physicians. They are named as Rhiwallon and his sons, Gruffudd, Einion and Cadwgan who are according to tradition the Physicians of Myddfai.

Over the course of the thirteenth century the once mighty Deheubarth was reduced to a collection of fractious mini-principalities under the yoke of English power. The early years of the reign of Henry III (1216–72) were very unstable with friction continuing between native rulers and the English Crown. A key event in this period was the capture of Carmarthen by Earl William for the English in 1223. The town with its castle, bridge and dependant territory became a centre of English influence, which the native Welsh were unable to recover. Appointing a sheriff was a portentous development. During the thirteenth century the power of Dinefwr was eclipsed by the house of Gwynedd, to whom it played a supporting role. Between 1240 and 1256 there was a clear attempt to reassert royal power in Wales. In 1240–1 Carmarthen and its lands came into the possession of the Crown. Henry III's officials established an inquiry into the nature and extent of 'royal rights in the honour of Carmarthen'.[3] The period between the death of Llywelyn ab Iorwerth

(1240) and the emergence of Llywelyn ap Gruffudd in *c.* 1251 was one of instability. There was intense rivalry between Rhys Gryg's son Maredudd and his brother Rhys Mechyll and later between him and his nephew Rhys Fychan of Dinefwr. Rhys Fychan appeared to have had a very favourable relationship with the Crown through which he secured the restoration of prime family assets. In 1248 he seems to have recovered Carreg Cennen and later Dinefwr. Maredudd was not entirely comfortable with his nephew's connections. Llywelyn negotiated a secret pact with Maredudd ap Rhys Gryg and Rhys Fychan in 1250. This was to pave the way for a concerted effort to challenge English power in Wales.

In 1256 Maredudd accompanied Llywelyn on his victorious expedition and he was present at the great victory over the English in 1257. To check Llywelyn's progress English forces were mobilized and sent to the Tywi valley. At Coed Llathen and Y Cymerau the invaders suffered what contemporary chroniclers described as one of the most devastating defeats inflicted on the English by the Welsh in the thirteenth century. More than three thousand knights and men at arms were killed. The location of this great victory however is unclear but it is assumed to be near the confluence of the Tywi and the Cothi. Llywelyn's control over native Wales was established during these years. Maredudd's dislike of Rhys Fychan, whom the English appear to have been grooming as a protégé, led him to waver in his support for Llywellyn. Maredudd was restored to his family's lands in Ystrad Tywi and Rhys Fychan was returned to his castle and lands at Dinefwr.

Maredudd ap Rhys Gryg took part in the general homage sworn to Llywelyn early in 1258 but later in the year transferred his allegiance to the English Crown. His treachery led to his arrest and trial. He was the first native lord to be charged and tried for treason by his peers. A council of native lords found him guilty and he was imprisoned for a time in Criccieth castle. Following the imposition of severe terms he was reconciled to Llywelyn in 1261. His services to the royal cause were rewarded by the deliberate retention of his homage by the king in the Treaty of Montgomery (1267). English control over Carmarthen and the miniature 'county' attached to it served as an important bridgehead for the eventual consolidation of their power in this unstable area. Maredudd ap Rhys Gryg and his great rival Rhys Fychan both died within weeks of each other in August 1271. They were succeeded by their sons Rhys ap Maredudd and Rhys Wyndod.

The Edwardian Conquest

The Edwardian conquest made a huge impact on the future of the area. Edward I (1272–1307) was determined to destroy the power of Llywelyn and his family. In the south the lordship of Carmarthen was restored to the Crown in 1279. Royal authority was once again very firmly established in the Tywi valley. The royal grip over the area was further tightened in 1281 when Robert de Tibetot was appointed justice of south Wales and the King's representative in Carmarthen. Another round of conflict erupted in the Tywi valley in 1282. Rhys Wyndod and his brothers broke into revolt to support a rising in north Wales. They captured the castles of Llandovery and Carreg Cennen (now under royal control). A hard-fought battle near Llandeilo did halt the Crown's attempts to suppress the rebels. The turning point in the fortunes of Wales and of Carmarthenshire came when Llywelyn was killed in December 1282. In the wake of his death, defeated Welsh noblemen and dynasties were disinherited and their lands brought under the control of the English Crown. The Crown emerged as the largest and by some way the most powerful landowner in south-west Wales. To those who had assisted him in battle or remained loyal through the war, Edward provided rewards. Cantref Bychan was given to John Giffard in 1282–3. Rhys ap Maredudd of Dryslwyn the grandson of Rhys Gryg was one of only two native Welsh noblemen to remain loyal to Edward, even when his lands in the vale of Tywi were attacked by Llywelyn. As a reward he was allowed to extend his control over the whole of Cantref Mawr and two commotes in Ceredigion.

For the future of Carmarthenshire the Edwardian settlement is particularly important. As the largest landowner in the area Edward reorganized his territories. In the Statute of Wales (Rhuddlan) 1284, Edward set out the new structure of government in his conquered territories, with the shire as the main administrative unit. The small 'county' which had been attached to Carmarthen was further extended and consolidated with newly acquired lands. Carmarthen castle became the centre of the Crown's administration in the area and a sheriff was appointed with a legal and administrative role. During the reorganization of Henry VIII's reign, this would become the basis for the enlarged shire of the modern era. An additional part of the Crown's strategy to support its legal and administrative initiatives, was to establish plantation settlements of English colonists in the newly occupied lands. Two small boroughs were founded in the Welsh heartland at Dryslwyn (1287) and Newtown (1298) in the shadow of the former stronghold of the native princes of Dinefwr. Burgesses in these new boroughs would be given special privileges regarding trading and legal rights. In the long term neither of these two settlements were successful in stimulating urban communities.

The defeat of the last independent Welsh prince and the imposition of English rule over large tracts of Wales were traumatic events. Welsh reaction to them came from a rather unexpected quarter. Rhys ap Maredudd, whose loyalty had appeared secure, rebelled in June 1286. The probable cause of his revolt was a personality clash between him and the justice of south Wales, Robert de Tibetot. After initial success in capturing the castles of Llandovery, Dinefwr and Carreg Cennen a massive force of 11,000 soldiers was assembled by the Crown to crush the revolt. Against such overwhelming odds Rhys's stronghold at Dryslwyn was taken and the castles at Llandovery, Dinefwr and Carreg Cennen were recaptured. Rhys escaped and managed to evade his pursuers until 1292, when he was caught and executed. An immediate outcome of the revolt was that Rhys's lands were nominally attached to Carmarthen which only served to strengthen the Crown's position in the new shire.

The Growth of Carmarthen

Following the establishment of the castle in Carmarthen a small community grew up under its protection. Its existence was precarious and the inhabitants suffered periodically from the vicissitudes of conflict between Welsh and Anglo-Norman forces. The fledgling community and its defenders were attacked, burnt and besieged at various times in 1116, 1146, 1159, 1196 and 1214. Following each assault the castle and its garrison recovered. Measures were taken between 1229 and 1232 to strengthen the castle's defences. This added protection contributed to the emergence of a thriving community. Much of the activity of the civilian population would be closely linked to servicing the garrison and ministering to its economic and recreational needs. Carmarthen was granted a number of royal charters which specified the rights and obligations of the inhabitants with particular reference to their commercial activities. In 1257 the town was granted borough status. Its leading citizens became burgesses and they were able to benefit from English laws and customs. One of these allowed the property of a deceased burgess to be passed to an heir in its entirety without having to be divided among all heirs as was the Welsh custom. Clearly the new borough was being shaped quite deliberately as a foreign enclave. Its attractive economic and commercial privileges were part of a sustained policy to tempt the native population towards the benefits of the new order.

Carmarthen's pre-eminence as a military garrison was more than matched by its importance as an ecclesiastical centre and an administrative base. The value of the religious communities is emphasized by their educational, literary and cultural work. One of earliest Welsh manuscripts produced during the medieval period, the mid-thirteenth-century *Llyfr Du Caerfyrddin* (The Black Book of Carmarthen) is linked very closely with the priory. It remains, however, an open question as to whether or not it was produced there. Carmarthen castle was the administrative centre not only for the royal lands in Carmarthen but also for those in Cardigan. An indication of how important contemporaries considered it to be can be gauged from the fact that it was the only Welsh town included in the map of Britain produced by Matthew Paris in 1240. What ultimately drove the expansion of the town was its economic and commercial domination. Its position as a port on the main arterial route in the region gave it a significant advantage over neighbouring boroughs. The granting of the right to hold fairs in the area now known as Nott's Square drew in buyers and sellers from a wide area. Shops and commercial premises were licensed by the town officials. An indication of the size of the town is given in a royal survey conducted in 1268 which lists 123 burgesses in the borough and 167 burgage tenements on which houses were built.[4] Trading links with other parts of Britain and the continent were a factor in driving forward the borough's growth. Wool was exported to the Iberian peninsula, Gascony and Calais. Flemish merchants purchased Welsh wool in Calais.

Following the destruction of parts of the town during the Glyn Dŵr rebellion (1403 and 1405), a rebuilding programme using stone in place of timber was carried out. The town walls of New Carmarthen were strengthened and expanded to incorporate new areas into the borough. As New Carmarthen expanded its relations with Old Carmarthen were frequently acrimonious and a healthy rivalry persisted between the two settlements throughout the period.

Fourteenth-century Carmarthenshire – 'the Palsied Years'

Wales, according to Professor R.R. Davies, was little more than a geographical expression in the fourteenth century.[5] The trauma of the post-conquest period was deeply embedded in the national and local psyche. In many ways the hallmarks of this period are repression, pestilence and resentment. However in other ways there was economic recovery and a reluctant stoicism among the descendants of the noble families to make the best of what was a fairly bad lot. The future county was an agglomeration of two main administrative structures. First there was the lesser county of Carmarthenshire which was part of the principality, this was extended by the addition of Cantref Mawr following the defeat of Rhys ap Maredudd and the confiscation of his lands. The remoter areas

of Cantref Mawr were known as the Welshry since most of the population were native Welsh. Second there were the various marcher lordships
– Cantref Bychan, Is-cennen, Kidwelly, Ystlwyf, Laugharne, Emlyn and
St Clears. The most powerful marcher lord in the middle of the century in
south-west Wales was John of Gaunt, Duke of Lancaster, a younger son
of Edward III. His control of Kidwelly was further strengthened when Is-
cennen was handed over to his charge.

The attitude of the English rulers to the native Welsh was one of deep
suspicion. There was a clear reluctance to appoint Welshmen to any
position of power and influence within the principality. Their propensity
to revolt meant that they had to be kept on a very tight leash. English
suspicions were not entirely unfounded. Carmarthenshire was considered to have a ready pool of tough, experienced fighters, ideal recruits
for the numerous military campaigns waged by the English at this time.
Many Carmarthenshire men enrolled for military service with the Crown.
Displaying scant loyalty to their fellow-Celts, recruits from the county
fought at Bannockburn (1314). Up to 1,200 men from the Lancastrian
lands in Kidwelly, Is-cennen and Carnwyllion were arrayed for royal
service in 1346 and fought at the Battle of Crécy. Others were present at
the siege of Calais. Of the few native Welshmen who successfully broke
into the upper echelons of power, the most prominent by far was Sir Rhys
ap Gruffudd of Llansadwrn. Sir Rhys inherited extensive estates in
Cantref Mawr and Cardiganshire and during the first decade of the
century was appointed to a number of minor but lucrative offices in
south-west Wales. He was astute enough to realize that real power could
only be gained by allying himself to one of the powerful noble families in
England. His support of the Despensers led to his appointment as deputy
to the royal justice in south Wales and he was made a sheriff of
Carmarthenshire. Rhys's career almost foundered during the Edward II
abdication crisis in 1327, when, following his support of the disfavoured
king, he narrowly escaped capture. After a brief period overseas he
rebuilt his influence. The new King Edward III recognized his great
skills as a military commander and organizer. He was present at Crécy,
following which he was knighted. In the context of fourteenth-century
Carmarthenshire his career is unique. His descendant was an equally
important figure, Sir Rhys ap Thomas.

If Carmarthen was without rival as the administrative and military capital
of south-west Wales in the early fourteenth century, it was also tightening
its economic grip on the region. In 1326 the town and port was recognized
as a staple. This meant that it was one of only fourteen ports in royal
territories able to export goods. Royal officials would collect taxes on exports
at staple ports. Under the shelter of this monopoly status it assumed a
commanding position in the highly lucrative wool trade. During the 1350s it

has been estimated that over 525 stones (3,341 kg.) of fleeces were exported annually from the port. An indication of the great wealth being generated within the borough can be gleaned from the fact that one local merchant, John Owen, was making £450 per annum in the 1390s.

The greatest natural disaster to befall the county in the fourteenth century was the Black Death or the bubonic plague, which swept through Europe in the 1340s. Although records regarding its impact on the county are rather patchy it is possible to gain some insight into its effects. The plague reached Carmarthen in March 1349 possibly entering the borough through the port. Among the first victims of the plague were the officials of the staple. The incidence of the plague was greater in built-up areas where human contact was a regular occurrence. At Llan-llwch eleven of the twelve *gafol-men* are recorded as dying from the plague. Local records indicate that many holdings were vacant and administrative positions unfilled. Those fortunate enough to survive found their services at a premium.

Carmarthenshire and the Glyn Dŵr Rebellion

As the fourteenth century drew to a close the sense of injustice felt by many native Welsh people particularly in the *cantrefi* of Carmarthenshire had not diminished. These resentments were deep rooted. Tensions between the inhabitants of the Welshry and the foreign burgesses in the boroughs occasionally spilled over into violence. Those who ruled were viewed as rapacious exploiters. John of Gaunt, Lord of Kidwelly, was particularly active in enforcing the payment of monies due to him. This festering native resentment was fuelled by the bards who were such a prominent feature of the cultural life of the local nobility. They prophesied the appearance of a deliverer who would cast off the chains of English servility and restore Welsh independence. Few could imagine that a dispute over land between two neighbours in Rhuthun would presage a national revolt the like of which had not been seen in over a century, and which would last for well over a decade. The instigator of the rebellion was a remarkable individual, able, gifted, shrewd and with a sense of vision and political acumen absent from Wales since the days of Llywelyn the Last. Moreover he was able to exploit the political crisis in England for his own purposes, and added an international dimension, largely missing from previous uprisings to his struggle. Owain Glyn Dŵr had the blood of three native dynasties coursing through his veins – Gwynedd, Powys and Deheubarth. He was therefore assured a measure of support from north, mid and south-west Wales. His revolt has elevated him to iconic status in the nation's history. Over the course of the rebellion

Carmarthenshire would figure prominently in the ebb and flow of the military action.

The proclamation of Owain Glyn Dŵr as Prince of Wales in September 1400 was a momentous event. While Glyn Dŵr did not turn his attention to south Wales until 1403 there was clearly a degree of support for his cause in the area. Henry Dwnn of Kidwelly, an old friend of Glyn Dŵr, was urged in a letter to join the rebellion. Fearing the collapse of royal authority in the south west Henry IV visited Llandovery and Carmarthen castles in October 1401 and arranged the strengthening of their garrisons. At Llandovery, Llywelyn ap Gruffudd Fychan, whose sons were with Owain, was hanged, as a salutary reminder to anyone contemplating joining the revolt, of how swift and brutal the response of the Crown would be. The next time Carmarthen figured in the revolt Owain's stock was rising rapidly. He was able to capitalize on disaffection with the king to forge an alliance with powerful English barons – the Mortimers and the Percys. South-west Wales was an area into which Glyn Dŵr had not made any significant inroads. He rectified this situation in the summer of 1403. Owain's arrival in Carmarthenshire was the catalyst for a widespread revolt in July 1403. Most of the area's castles were threatened. The twelve days during which Owain campaigned around Carmarthen are among the best documented periods of the whole revolt. A series of ten letters written by royal officials survive, which give a very interesting if one-sided account of events from or about the theatre of operations.

Owain arrived in the Tywi valley on 3 July with an army possibly numbering 8,000 men. He proceeded to attack and burn the town of Llandeilo. On his way to Carmarthen, the administrative linchpin of royal government in south-west Wales, it appears the castle of Dryslwyn surrendered to him without a fight. The defenders of the regional capital were far more determined, possibly because they had more to lose as the borough was by some measure the wealthiest area in a rather impoverished region. Carmarthen town and castle were attacked on 5 July. Against overwhelming odds the small garrison was defeated. A letter from the constable of Dinefwr castle Jankyn Havard on 7 July to John Fairford, a royal official, captures the element of fear permeating the ranks of the royal administration:

> I do now write that Owain Glyndwr, Henry Dwnn, Rhys ap Gruffudd ap Llywellyn, Rhys Gethin, have won the town and castle of Carmarthen, and Wigmore constable of the castle has yielded up the castle of Carmarthen to Owain: and has burned the town, and slain the men of the town more than 50 men; and they be in purpose to Cydweli; and to besiege as he has ordained at the castle that I keep, and that is a great peril for me,

and all that be within; for they have made their vow that they will have us all dead therein.[6]

Following the capture of Carmarthen the constable of Newcastle Emlyn crossed over to support the rebels. The sources indicate some uncertainty as to what Owain was proposing next – moving towards Kidwelly, as Havard suggested, or turning west towards St Clears. Holding the Crown line on the Pembrokeshire border was a determined and able soldier – Thomas, Lord Carew. Owain was unable to negotiate terms with Carew, and it appears that his force of 8,000 was somewhat divided. A detachment had been left at Carmarthen to share out the plunder, while a larger body of 700 men were sent to the north of Carmarthen to secure a line of communication. They were ambushed and defeated. Following this reversal Owain left the area. The appearance of the king in late September was designed to provide moral and material support for the royal defenders, many of whom were rewarded handsomely for their loyalty to the crown. Henry made very little attempt to subdue the area before returning to England. The absence of Owain did not quench the spirit of revolt among his followers. Owain's international connections appeared to be paying dividends. When Henry Dwnn attacked the castle and borough of Kidwelly he was assisted by a force of French and Bretons who had landed in Carmarthen Bay. Although Dwnn failed to take the castle, it was fairly clear that beyond the boroughs and castles support for the revolt remained undiminished. Dwnn's activities were a timely reminder of the precariousness of the royal writ in the area. The Duke of York was appointed lieutenant of south Wales and was dispatched to Carmarthen with over a thousand soldiers. An uneasy peace was maintained for the next eighteen months.

In 1404 Owain concluded a formal alliance with France. His new ally offered military support for the revolt and this duly arrived at Milford Haven in August 1405. Owain met the French with a force of 10,000 and the combined armies moved eastwards towards Carmarthen. Once again the centre of royal government was captured by Glyn Dŵr and his men. Owain proceeded to Worcester but failed to engage his enemies. The momentum of the revolt was slowing and the tide was turning against the rebels. Despite the occasional dramatic gesture such as another attack by Henry Dwnn on Kidwelly, this was very much the endgame of the rising in the county. Although the revolt would continue until 1413 to all intents and purposes the rebellion as far as Carmarthenshire was concerned was over.

The Wars of the Roses

The deposition of Richard II in 1399 without a direct heir led to the start of a protracted dispute over the succession. Henry Bolingbroke who seized the throne as Henry IV (1399–1413) was descended through his father, John of Gaunt, from Edward III. A rival claim came from the family of the Earl of March also descended from one of Edward III's sons. March's grandson, Richard Plantagenet, Duke of York was Lord Protector of England during the long minority of Henry VI (1422–61, 1470–71). The dispute over the succession was characterized by a series of intermittent and bloody power struggles, labelled the Wars of the Roses which continued until 1485. Those in the county who were brave or foolish enough to commit themselves during this long drawn out struggle mainly favoured the Lancastrians' cause. One exception to this was the Dwnn family of Kidwelly who sided with the Yorkists. The longevity of Owain Glyn Dŵr's revolt was in part due to this dynastic instability and Henry IV's preoccupation with securing his own position in England. During the long minority of Henry VI there were a number of attempts to overthrow the king.

In the early decades of the fifteenth century most Welsh people were trying to adjust to life following the collapse of Owain Glyn Dŵr's revolt. The revolt had an impact upon Wales and the future county of Carmarthenshire in a number of ways. The periods of campaigning and fighting although brief did result in considerable destruction – Llandeilo, Carmarthen and Kidwelly all bore the scars of conflict. In 1401 Henry IV imposed very severe penal laws on the Welsh. These confirmed their status as second-class citizens compared to the English. Welshmen were prevented form acquiring land in England or in any of the English boroughs in Wales. They were also to be denied appointment to any major domestic office. Although exceptions were made, these were not typical. The simmering resentment in the wake of yet another defeat helped stimulate a corpus of anti-English literature which prophesied the emergence of a new national saviour. One of the key literary figures of this period was Lewis Glyn Cothi, whose patron Gruffudd ap Nicolas was the scion of Carmarthenshire's premier family, the noble house of Dinefwr.

The mid-years of the fifteenth century were among the most turbulent in the power struggle for the English Crown. Gruffudd ap Nicolas and his family, as Lancastrian supporters, were exempted in 1444 from the penal laws imposed on their compatriots. Gruffudd had been a sheriff of Carmarthen and had held other minor appointments. In 1452 the Lancastrian Jasper Tudor was created Earl of Pembroke and as such held Llansteffan castle and lordship. When the Duke of York assumed the office of constable of Carmarthen in 1455 Gruffudd was dismissed. York was himself replaced in 1457 by Jasper Tudor. The Lancastrian supporters from the county accompanied Jasper to confront the Earl of March during the crisis of 1461 but were convincingly defeated at the battle of Mortimer's Cross. Jasper's father was killed but he and the sons of Gruffudd ap Nicolas escaped. March, who was aided by the Dwnns, assumed the crown as Edward IV. In an attempt to minimize the threat from Gruffudd's family, Carreg Cennen castle, which they had been fortifying, was ordered to be demolished and work commenced to demilitarize it in 1462. With the Yorkists in the ascendancy the Dwnn family's fortunes were boosted.[7] They were given the lordship of Laugharne as a reward for their loyalty. When Richard III took the throne from his young nephew Edward V in 1483, the Duke of Buckingham was given Carmarthen, Dinefwr and Llansteffan castles. The ambitious Buckingham was soon plotting to put Jasper's nephew Henry Tudor on the throne. Buckingham was executed following the abortive attempt but significantly Rhys ap Thomas who was now head of the Dinefwr family did not lend his support. Richard III rewarded his inactivity. How long would this last? Only time would tell.

IV

Upheaval, Strife and Stability: 1485–1750

Tudor Carmarthenshire: 1485–1603

The events of 1485, which saw the crown change hands in dramatic and violent fashion, resulted in a new king, determined to consolidate a new dynasty, on the English throne. Henry Tudor with his strong Welsh connections was helped in his enterprise by Rhys ap Thomas of Dinefwr, the most powerful local magnate in the area which would become Carmarthenshire. The Tudor age left an indelible mark, even stain, on the political, administrative and cultural life of the area. Henry's invasion and the role played by Rhys ap Thomas is surrounded by myth, much of it embroidered by an anonymous family history from the seventeenth century. Rhys was born in 1449 and spent part of his youth in France. Initially in the 'Wars of the Roses' he supported the Lancastrian cause but was enticed with the offer of rewards to switch his allegiance to the Yorkist Edward IV (1461–83). Following the seizure of the throne by Richard III (1483–85) he continued his nominal support for the Yorkists. Contact was established however between Rhys and Henry Tudor through an exchange of letters. Henry clearly assumed that Rhys would support him in his attempt to become king. A great deal was at stake with failure almost certainly resulting in death. In the circumstances, Rhys was understandably cautious. When Henry landed at Dale on 7 August 1485 he was anxious regarding Rhys's likely course of action. Rhys did set off from Carmarthen along the Tywi valley, with a significant force of men – possibly numbering 4,000. They joined with Henry Tudor at Newtown in mid-Wales on 12 August.

Rhys was offered as an inducement a number of rewards he would have found difficult to refuse. The stakes were very high. In backing Henry he was committing treason, risking his own life and the future of his family. The support he gave Henry – both moral and material – did help secure the victory that had been prophesied by the bards. Following the battle of Bosworth, Rhys was knighted and appointed constable and steward of the lordship of Brecon, chamberlain of South Wales, and steward of the lordship of Builth. He continued to support the new king against the various imposters, and captured Lord Audeley at Blackheath in 1497. Following the death of Jasper Tudor in 1495 Rhys added the justiceship of South Wales to his collection of offices and in 1505 he was made a Knight of the Garter. His power and status within the county was unrivalled and he was the virtual ruler of south Wales. He had several residences in Carmarthenshire; at Abermarlais, Derwydd and Newcastle Emlyn. On his death in 1525 he was buried in a splendid tomb in the church of the Grey Friars at Carmarthen which following the friary's dissolution was relocated to its present site in St Peter's church.

The spectacular rise in the fortunes of the house of Dinefwr during the reign of the first Tudor monarch was matched by an equally spectacular fall from grace in the reign of his successor Henry VIII. Rhys was succeeded by his seventeen-year-old grandson and heir Rhys ap Griffith. Henry VIII was deeply suspicious of potentially over-mighty subjects, and the young Rhys ap Griffith appeared to fit this profile. He was young, powerful and well connected through his marriage to Katherine Howard, the Duke of Norfolk's sister. It is probable that his youth prevented him from succeeding to his grandfather's offices, which were given to Lord Ferrers. Mutual antipathy between the two men erupted into violence in Carmarthen in June 1529. Rhys was arrested and tried before the Court of Star Chamber and following the intervention of Cardinal Wolsey he was released. He was rearrested within a year and imprisoned in the Tower of London where he was executed in November 1531. His estates were confiscated the following year under a bill of attainder. The charge against Rhys was that he had conspired with two others to seek help from James V of Scotland in order to support his claim to the title prince of Wales. What truth there was in this accusation is difficult to establish. Henry VIII was moving towards breaking with Rome and was keen to marry Anne Boleyn, Norfolk's niece. Relations between Anne and Rhys's wife were by all accounts difficult. A heady cocktail of indiscretion, dynastic needs and petty jealousies may in the end have sealed Rhys's fate. At the time of his execution, Rhys's personal property was estimated at £30,000. Most of the estates were sold by the crown fairly soon after 1531. Some property was restored in 1554–5 to Rhys's son Griffith Rice (the family had adopted an Anglicized surname). In 1560 he received back the manor of Newton near Llandeilo, which contained the family seat.

During the second half of the reign of Henry VIII two very significant events took place which had a lasting impact on Carmarthenshire. First and foremost were the Acts of Union, 1536 and 1542. These two Acts united the existing principality of Wales with the marcher lordships and confirmed that English law would apply in the new shires which were created. Only the English language was to be used in the new law courts established by the Act. Under the terms of the initial Act in 1536 the lordships, towns, parishes, commotes, hundreds and cantrefs of Llandovery, Abermarlais, Kidwelly, Is-cennen, Carnwyllion, Newcastle Emlyn and Abergwili were joined to the existing county of Carmarthen to form an enlarged shire. Llansteffan and Laugharne were included in Pembrokeshire. This rather anomalous situation was reversed in the 1542 Act when they formed part of the hundred of Derllys and were added to Carmarthenshire. It is from this date that the area now known as the county of Carmarthenshire came into existence, as a political, social and economic unit.

In addition to the administrative reorganization, Wales was guaranteed parliamentary representation for the first time. Carmarthen was given one shire member and one member to represent the borough. An innovative feature of the Act was the system of contributory boroughs. This extended the system of representation to include other ancient boroughs in order to contribute towards the payment of the member. During the Tudor period the parliamentary returns indicate that at one time or another Kidwelly, Llanelli, Newton, Dryslwyn, Laugharne, Llandovery, Llandeilo, St Clears and Newcastle Emlyn helped elect the borough member for Carmarthen. This arrangement ended in 1604 when Carmarthen was made into a county borough and was given the sole right of electing a member of parliament.

Local government was also caught up in the spirit of reform. Carmarthen's economic pre-eminence was clearly established. This had been confirmed by the granting of a number of charters over the centuries. There emerged in effect two distinct administrative areas. Old Carmarthen was centred on the priory and had its own privileges, markets, fairs and courts. New Carmarthen, based on the castle and surrounding area, also had rights enshrined in royal charters. Tension and rivalry between the two Carmarthens often spilled over into violence. With the dissolution of the priory in 1536, there was an opportunity to resolve this unusual arrangement. In 1546 a new charter was granted which removed the distinction between Old and New Carmarthen. The area formerly known as Old Carmarthen was taken from the hundred of Derllys and added to New Carmarthen to create a unified borough. In the process the distinction between 'old' and 'new' disappeared.

The second event of Henry VIII's reign was more infamous than memorable, namely the dissolution of the monasteries. Between 1536 and 1540 the government of Henry VIII inaugurated the biggest land acquisition programme since the Norman conquest, while concurrently unleashing the greatest organized assault on the cultural fabric of Britain ever witnessed. Henry needed money to defend his breach with Rome. The monasteries owned vast tracts of land, and held in trust priceless artistic and cultural artifacts. They offered hospitality to travellers, alms to the poor and education to the children of the well-to-do. The monastic houses in Carmarthenshire were at Talley, Whitland, Kidwelly Priory and Carmarthen Priory and Friary. While the monastic chapel in Kidwelly survived, the other communities were suppressed. The buildings were for the most part stripped of valuable furnishings: lead, plate, glass and later dressed stone. Over the next twenty or so years the properties and in many instances the rights attached to them were sold off to landowners with surplus cash and a keen eye for a bargain. Tithes were appropriated by laymen and the church suffered as a consequence through a reduction of income. Appointments to livings were now frequently in the gift of lay-men. At the time of the dissolution the religious community in Talley consisted of eight canons and its monastic revenue was assessed at £136. Following the dissolution part of the church was used for parish purposes. In attempting to avert closure, Carmarthen Priory argued that it should be kept open as it provided hospitality for both rich and poor travellers. Its appeals fell on deaf ears. Sir William Thomas of Aberglasney acquired a lease of Carmarthen Priory along with the rectory of Llanllwni and the chapel of Llanfihangel Rhos-y-corn in 1537 at a rent of £43 0s 4d. Later the priory was sold by the crown to Richard Andrew and Nicholas Temple.

The closure of the Franciscan friary in Carmarthen prompted the mayor and aldermen of the borough of New Carmarthen to petition the king to establish a grammar school in the town. Their action may well have been motivated by the loss of educational facilities resulting from the dissolution. The petitioners noted that the former friary was falling into disrepair as there was 'not a foot of lead left on it'. They considered it a great shame that such a building in 'such a barren country', should not be put to good use for the benefit of all. The Crown was offered £40 for the property. After some delay a school opened in 1543 under the charge of master Thomas Lloyd, chantor of St Davids. The school did not long survive the death of Thomas Lloyd in 1547. That a town of the size and importance of Carmarthen was without a school was of some concern to many in the borough. The value of this short-lived school ultimately led to a more successful foundation in 1576 when the Queen Elizabeth Grammar School was opened.

The vast upheaval unleashed by the break with Rome saw the gradual introduction of Protestantism into Wales. Although the pace of change speeded up during the reign of Edward VI (1547–53), the whole process came to a dramatic halt in the reign of Mary Tudor (1553–8). As a Catholic she was determined to restore the old religion. In 1548 Robert Ferrar was appointed bishop of St Davids. When Mary acceded to the throne in 1553, Ferrar was already in prison in London, on charges that he had abused his authority and was not sufficiently active in suppressing Catholicism in his diocese. During Mary's reign Ferrar was removed as bishop and was accused of heresy. He was sent from London to Carmarthen and was brought before the new bishop, Henry Morgan. Ferrar refused to acknowledge the authority of the court. He was excommunicated and was burnt at the stake in the market place in Carmarthen on 30 March 1555 – one of only three Protestant martyrs from Wales. The restoration of Protestantism by Elizabeth I (1558–1603) was enforced by means of penal laws. There is very little evidence of recusancy in the county during her reign. That Catholic worship continued in secret is almost certainly the case. In 1590 Morgan Jones JP was accused before the Court of Star Chamber of being a papist and of harbouring Catholic priests. A few years later Jones was again brought before the Star Chamber, on a charge that he was showing 'unlawful affection for Recusants'. The complainant was Sir John Vaughan of Golden Grove.

The language clauses of the Act of Union with their bias against the Welsh language have drawn many hostile comments over the years. Unwittingly the religious changes, which formed the context against which the reorganization was undertaken, helped preserve the Welsh language. The insistence that parishioners have access to religious works in a form they could understand virtually guaranteed the survival of Welsh as a living language. Richard Davies, bishop of St Davids, played a key role in securing an Act in 1563 ordering the translation of the scriptures into Welsh. While at the bishop's palace, Abergwili, Davies helped translate the New Testament into Welsh in 1567. He was the first of a long and distinguished line of religious writers, either working in or coming from Carmarthenshire.

The emergence of the gentry as an important social class was accelerated during the Tudor period. This was due to the many opportunities which were made available in local and central administration, land acquisition and the application of English law. One family which did extremely well out of the upheavals of Henry VIII's reign was the Jones family of Abermarlais. This was achieved in two ways. First they took advantage of the disposal of monastic lands. In 1543 Sir Thomas Jones leased the site and demesne lands of Talley Abbey along with several rectories and granges. Second they gained from the Act of attainder passed on Rhys ap Griffith. In 1545 Jones was granted for the sum of £737 9s 10d the lordship and manor of Llansadwrn, with all ap Griffith's property in Maenordeilo, Llansadwrn and Llandeilo Fawr including the mansion at Abermarlais.[1] Of greater significance for the subsequent history of the county was the rise of the Vaughans of Golden Grove. Hugh Vaughan was appointed as administrator of Rhys ap Griffith's lands and he took the opportunity to acquire leases on these estates. Occasionally less dubious methods were used. Sir John Vaughan of Golden Grove was brought before the Court of Star Chamber during Elizabeth's reign. He was accused of inviting John Thomas of Llangadog, who was described as a gentleman, to a feast. Thomas was made drunk and compelled to sign away all his hereditary lands in Llangadog. These energetic and ambitious men took leading roles in administering the county as high sheriffs, lord and deputy lieutenants and JPs. When parliaments were summoned, the members were drawn from their ranks. The Act of Union abolished gavelkind, whereby an estate was divided equally among the heirs on an owner's death. It was replaced by primogeniture where everything passed to the first born son. Landed estates could now be consolidated and bequeathed in their entirety.

What sort of place was Tudor Carmarthenshire? We are fortunate in having available a variety of sources covering many aspects of life within the county. These consist of official records and documents as well as private observations and published works. It is possible therefore to provide a fairly reliable general view of the county and its inhabitants during this period. Leland's *Itinerary* (compiled 1536–9) is one of the earliest topographical records available for Tudor Carmarthenshire. Despite being a rather incomplete survey it does provide valuable information. His account of the southern coastal part of the county is particularly useful. He described old and new Kidwelly:

> The old town is prettily walled and hath hard by the wall a castle. The old Town is near all desolated, but the castle is well kept up. In the new town is only a church of our lady and by is the cell of the Black Monks of Sherborne. The castle is very fair and double walled. I saw three gates and over one of them was the ruin of a fair town hall. A piece of the new town was lately burned. The new town is three times as big as the old.[2]

Estimates of the population of the town of Carmarthen suggest that it totalled about a thousand people in 1500. There were 325 houses in the town in 1566 and contemporaries stress its well-established market and the flourishing nature of its port. George Owen of Henllys observed that the town of Carmarthen was 'the largest town in Wales, fair and in good estate. The rest of the town poor ... many unruly and querulous people there.' The violent nature of the town is borne out in official documents. One account relates to a dispute involving the carrying of maces in old Carmarthen by the mayor of new Carmarthen. This was considered an affront and led to a riot. Of the other boroughs and towns Laugharne is described in 1566 as a village of ninety houses but despite its small size there were merchants living there supported by a thriving coastal trade. Llanelli by contrast had only twelve houses. Leland considered

Llandovery as 'a poor market, it hath but one street and that poorly built of thatched houses'.

The economic activity in the county is well described. Leland notes coal mining taking place in the Gwendraeth Valley and around Llanelli, ring coles and stone coles (see p. 124). In addition he adds that the county produced cattle, fowls and sea-fish. The agricultural nature of the economy is clearly highlighted as being very important. This is borne out by George Owen who comments: 'The soil, a great shire, much good land: the people tall and personable.' He suggests that an important factor in Carmarthen's prosperity was the grain trade. In addition to these generalized accounts the Port Books from this period provide a detailed insight into the maritime trade conducted between the county and other parts of Wales, Britain and Europe. In 1566 the Port Books record exports from Carmarthen consisting of cloth (frieze), lead ore, coal and barley.[3] Most of these items were shipped along the channel to Gloucester and Bristol. Imports included linen, soap, barley malt, Gascony wine, hops, salt, woad and alum (for the cloth trade). Trade was by no means confined to Britain. Ships carried goods back and forth between the French ports of Bordeaux and La Rochelle and even Portugal. Although the port of Carmarthen was busy, the number and size of the ships were relatively small. There were six ships recorded in 1566, the largest of which was the *Nightingale* of 50 tonnes berth and a crew of twelve. The diversity of commercial activity within the town of Carmarthen is indicated by the different guilds and corporations which were set up in the town. In the reign of Queen Elizabeth I there were corporations for tanners, shoemakers, tailors, saddlers, weavers, tuckers, glovers and hatters. These guilds rigidly controlled entry into a trade and sought to regulate the quality of products. An apprenticeship usually lasted seven years following which a comfortable living was almost certain. Periodically various decrees and orders were issued by the council in the Guildhall. The Book of Ordinances, which recorded council decisions, noted in 1569 that the bailiffs were expressly forbidden from collecting tolls on any grain, food or hides entering or leaving the town.[4]

Stuart Carmarthenshire: 1603–1714

The accession of James I (1603–25) and the Stuart dynasty would ultimately herald a return to a much more turbulent and divisive period than the stability enjoyed for the most part under the Tudors. Initially the Stuarts were accepted with benign indifference. Carmarthenshire's squires had done rather well under the Tudors and their loyalty to church and state was well established. They considered their interests to be at one with those of the Crown. The Civil War which dominated the 1640s had its origins in a combination of contentious religious policy, autocratic royal government and financial crises. Between 1603 and the outbreak of the Civil War in 1642 relations between the Crown and a substantial number of its leading citizens represented by parliament deteriorated to a point of no return, where negotiations were abandoned in favour of armed conflict.

The Elizabethan settlement which established the Anglican Church was making good progress in Carmarthenshire by the time James I became king. There is little evidence that Puritanism was making much headway within the county. However its emphasis on strict morality and self-discipline did strike a chord with many churchmen. James's reluctance to persecute Catholics did raise doubts regarding his commitment to the church of which he was head. The most eminent cleric within the county during this period was Rhys Prichard (1579–1644) of Llandovery. Vicar Prichard was an ardent churchman who was a popular preacher and a poet whose *Canwyll y Cymry* (The Welsh People's Candle) was an attempt to produce a moral guidance, in verse form, which could be understood by ordinary people. Prichard was a close ally and friend of William Laud, one of the central figures in the events which preceded the outbreak of the Civil War. Laud was appointed bishop of St Davids in 1621 and during his five years in the diocese he recognized the importance of the Welsh language, and appointed Prichard chancellor of St Davids cathedral. When Laud was appointed Archbishop of Canterbury he became a central ally of Charles I. His 'high church' religious policy offended many Puritans and helped precipitate the Civil War. Prichard warned against moral laxity in his poetry and some Puritans believed that he was sympathetic to their cause. In reality Prichard was wholly committed to the Anglican Church and backed the royalist side during the Civil War.

During the Stuart period the Vaughans of Golden Grove established themselves as Carmarthenshire's most important family. John Vaughan (1572–1634), a close associate of the royal family, was appointed comptroller of Charles, Prince of Wales's household. In 1628 he was elevated to the peerage as Earl of Carbery – the county's first home-grown aristocrat. Along with his four brothers and various nephews, John Vaughan dominated the various offices and parliamentary representation of the county during the reigns of James I and Charles I. The most remarkable of the brothers was Sir William Vaughan (1577–1641). He was well educated, deeply cultured and possessed a social conscience. His remedy for what he considered to be the bleak prospects facing farmers in his county was colonization. In 1616 he obtained a lease for land in Newfoundland and founded the small colony of Cambriol. It was during his time at the colony that he wrote *The Golden Fleece*, his best-known work. A combination of a hostile climate and unfriendly neighbours contributed to the failure of the experiment, and the abandonment of the settlement some time around 1637.

When the Civil War broke out in 1642 it was not unexpected. The county families of Carmarthenshire were committed initially, in varying degrees to supporting the royalist cause. For most the priority was simply to retain their estates. Many walked a fine line between the two sides, none more so than Richard Vaughan of Golden Grove, the second Earl of Carbery. He was nominated in March 1642 by the House of Commons as lord lieutenant of the Carmarthenshire militia. When hostilities started the king appointed him commander of the royalist forces in west Wales. He was promptly impeached by the House of Commons. His brother Sir Henry Vaughan was commissioned to assist him on 26 October 1643 with the rank of sergeant major general. The clergy of the county also lined up behind the crown. They were uneasy with the Puritan trends discernable on the parliamentary side. Vicar Prichard gave, by his own account significant financial support to the royalists, to the extent that he had to 'shift and borrow' to meet his curate's wages and pay his tax bill. The recorder of the borough of Carmarthen was described as being 'very violent in promoting the King's cause'. Raising funds for the royalist cause was the motive behind the former mayor of Carmarthen (1641), George Oakley's decision to buy a large herd of Pembrokeshire cattle and drive them to Worcester, where they were sold and the profit used to buy weapons for the garrison in Carmarthen.

The history of the Civil War campaigns in Carmarthenshire is both complex and fragmentary. Between 1642 and 1646 the pendulum of war swung between the two sides. The only parliamentary outpost in west Wales was based in south Pembrokeshire and was under the command of Rowland Laugharne. Laugharne's stronghold at Pembroke was isolated from the main parliamentary forces but was supplied and reinforced by sea and was therefore very difficult to dislodge. Carbery was impeached by parliament in 1643 and removed from the lord-lieutenancy of Carmarthenshire. It was decided in the summer of 1643, following the capture of Bristol by the royalists, to launch an attack to deal once and for all with the Pembrokeshire parliamentarians. With little effort the royalists under Carbery's command succeeded in capturing the towns of Tenby and Haverfordwest, forcing parliamentary forces back to Pembroke where they regrouped. Laugharne was an able commander and a skilful soldier. Following the re-supply by sea of the garrison, he planned a spring offensive for 1644.

Leading royalists in Carmarthenshire drafted a 'Protestation' on 11 January 1644 pledging their support to raise trained bands and horses, to attack Pembroke. Among the signatories were Rice Rudd (Aberglasney), Rowland Gwynn (Taliaris) David Gwynn (Glan-brân) and Henry Middleton

(Middleton Hall). Despite their display of unity and resistance, Laugharne managed to turn the tables on the cavaliers. Haverfordwest and Tenby were recovered and Carbery was forced to withdraw back into Carmarthenshire. Laugharne was now poised to seize the greatest prize in west Wales, the town of Carmarthen. Although the garrison of the town was not very large it is clear that the defences had been strengthened by the erection of a 'mud wall'.

The situation on the ground appeared confused. Major Butler at Llandovery sent his assessment of the royalist position in a letter to Colonel Herbert Price (11 April 1644): 'The rebels intend speedily to be at Carmarthen if not prevented. Many of the men pressed by the parliament will go over to the king if an opportunity is offered. Lord Carbery has ordered a rate of £4,000 to be collected.' The view of John Vaughan from Trawscoed was much less optimistic. Also writing to Colonel Price (10 April 1644) he suggested that the royalists in Cardiganshire and Carmarthenshire were 'like to yield themselves to the first danger, or to fall in with the first protection, being very impotent for resistance in themselves'. The town fell without much opposition in April 1644. In the wake of the defeat Carbery resigned his command. Contemporaries suspected the hand of treachery in the fall of Carmarthen and the finger of suspicion pointed clearly in the direction of the Earl of Carbery.

Sir Charles Gerard, an able and ruthless professional soldier, took over command of the royalist forces from Carbery. He moved quickly to restore the situation, setting out from Chepstow. A contemporary account notes: 'He advanced into Carmarthenshire and took Kidwelly, a strong haven town, where he left a good garrison, and then fell on the town and Castle of Carmarthen, which he presently mastered, and there he placed a good garrison, under Colonel Lovelace, and left a garrison at Abermarlais.' In addition he re-took Laugharne, Cardigan, Newcastle Emlyn and Haverfordwest. By the summer of 1644 Rowland Laugharne was virtually back where he started from in January. Hugh Carrow complained that the royalist forces consisted for the most part of 'Papists and Irish rebels' who 'frequently vow the slaughter and destruction of all true protestants' in the three counties. It is likely that Gerrard was responsible for improving the defences of Carmarthen by constructing a substantial bulwark after he entered the town in June 1644. These defences are unique in Wales and incorporated continental ideas relating to military engineering – ditches, bastions and salients.

Beyond Carmarthenshire the royalists suffered the first of a number of major setbacks from which ultimately they would not recover. The victory of the parliamentary forces at Marston Moor in July 1644 was significant. As a consequence of the defeat the royalists lost control of northern England. Gerard was recalled from Wales to help shore up

Prince Rupert's army. Laugharne, by now a major general, once again sensed an opportunity to confront the cavaliers in Carmarthenshire from his base in Pembroke. He advanced cautiously and was determined to consolidate his hold on Pembrokeshire while establishing bridgeheads in Cardiganshire and Carmarthenshire. The castles of Haverfordwest, Cardigan and Laugharne were under parliamentary control by the end of 1644.

What turned out to be the last act for the royalist cause in Carmarthenshire was also its greatest victory. The northernmost outpost of the royalist cause in the county was the garrison at Newcastle Emlyn. Laugharne and his forces laid siege to the castle in the spring of 1645. According to a royalist account, General Gerard received intelligence that all the Pembrokeshire rebels and their allies were involved in the siege. Using the element of surprise he was determined to relieve the castle. In a remarkable feat of military endurance, Gerard and his forces marched a hundred miles in a week 'through a country from whence he had no kind of assistance, either of men, money or provisions: yet came upon the rebels so unexpectedly (by marching in small bodies, several ways) that till they took some prisoners, they did not believe he was in the field'. The relief of Newcastle Emlyn turned into something of a rout – 150 rebels were killed in the town, besides those killed in the pursuit and 486 prisoners were captured, including 20 commanders, 120 horses, some artillery and 700 arms. The royalists described their victory of April 1645 as 'this great defeat at Emlyn'. An account from the defeated Parliamentarians stated that the royalists 'imprison, plunder and abuse the well-affected townsmen'.[5] Gerard followed up his success by capturing Haverfordwest and Cardigan. Before he could deliver the killer blow to Laugharne's local force, the royalists nationally lost the battle of Naseby (June 1645). This was as much a psychological defeat as a military one. Sir William Vaughan of Derwydd who had taken a sizeable detachment from the county to join the king, was captured. Following Naseby, Gerard left Wales and Carmarthenshire's royalists to their fate.

After three years of conflict, war weariness, financial cost and defeatism, morale among Carmarthenshire's gentry for continuing the struggle was very low. There were many willing to agree with the sentiment expressed by Colonel Howell Gwynn of Glan-brân: 'Heigh God, heigh Devil, I will be for the strongest side.' It was now fairly clear that parliament's forces had gained the ascendancy. The royalists were keen to secure their estates from forfeiture. Laugharne, following his victory at Colby Moor near Haverfordwest, was once again poised to march on Carmarthen. He had under his command an army of 600 cavalry and 2,000 infantry. The gentry of Carmarthenshire sent Laugharne a letter on 5 September offering to negotiate the cessation of hostilities. Among the signatories were Rowland Gwynn, the Earl of Carbery, Rice Rudd and Henry Middelton. After negotiations they agreed to declare for king and parliament. On 12 October 1645, Laugharne wrote to the speaker of the House of Commons to inform him that: 'At nine o'clock in the morning 1,500 clubmen of the county marched out at one gate and I entered at the other.'[6] With the surrender of Carmarthen, the first Civil War in the county ended rather tamely.

The outbreak of the second Civil War in the spring of 1648 was in many ways due to unpopular policies enforced by parliament and their Puritan allies. In west Wales a remarkable feature when hostilities resumed was the abandonment of the parliamentary cause by its leading lights, Laugharne, Poyer and Powell who crossed over to support the Crown. The reluctance of the leading families in Carmarthenshire to commit themselves to the king may well be due to the influence exerted by Carbery over his fellow landowners. A letter sent to London informed parliament that: 'The Earl of Carbery, formerly a commander in the King's army, and others who have once been engaged against the Parliament, do declare and engage their honour that they will neither join with the malignants nor assist them: neither shall any of their friends, as far as they can persuade or hinder them.'[7]

Most of the fighting in west Wales focused on Pembrokeshire. Parliamentary forces passed through the county *en route* for Pembroke. There were several minor skirmishes in and around the Tywi valley. Bridges were destroyed by the royalists at Pontargothi and Llandeilo. Colonel Fleming, a parliamentary commander, was ambushed and captured near Llangathen. A royalist garrison was installed at Newcastle Emlyn. A dispatch sent from Carmarthen on 3 May 1648 by T. Sands, a parliamentary soldier, conveys a sense of panic among ordinary people at the arrival of the military: 'The Welsh people being more afraid than hurt conceived that they should receive strange cruelties from the soldiers of parliament, whereupon they quiet left their dwellings, and drove all their cattle into the mountains.' He hints that popular sympathy may well be with the king: 'malignants flock daily to the enemy'. An unusual but very effective tactic was adopted to slow the roundhead advance: 'Numerous smiths in several towns have cut up their bellows, broken down their smithies, and made all their materials unserviceable. So that we cannot get a horse shod not in twenty or thirty miles riding'.[8]

The gravity of the situation in west Wales led parliament to dispatch its leading commander, Oliver Cromwell to the area. Cromwell is reputed to have stayed in several gentry houses in Carmarthenshire on his way to Pembroke. There is a strong tradition that he visited the Plas in Llandybïe, and even called at Golden Grove. Interesting as they are, confirmation of these tales is rather elusive. The fall of Pembroke in July

1648 brought to an end a period of conflict unknown in the county since the early 1400s. There were few winners at any level of the social hierarchy. Impoverished landowners and peasant refugees all welcomed the end of the conflict. With the fighting over, retribution was the order of the day.

At the start of the war parliament was determined that those who took up arms for the Crown would be made to suffer. These enemies were labelled 'delinquents' and 'malignants'. It ordered that the estates of its leading opponents be sequestered. Carbery was ordered to pay a fine of £160 and in 1645 his assessment as a delinquent amounted to £4,500. Following the intervention of a number of leading parliamentarians such as Laugharne and the Earl of Essex on his behalf in 1646 he was pardoned and his assessment cancelled. This lenient treatment of such a high profile royalist could be interpreted as a *quid pro quo* for surrendering Carmarthen without much of a struggle in 1644. In 1645 a Committee of Compounding was set up and it sent sequestration commissioners to calculate the payment due from the delinquents. The commissioners in Carmarthen in 1647 expressed their frustration in trying to seize property from those whom it had identified as delinquents. An act was passed in 1648 which specified the amounts to be raised by each county in the form of fines. Carmarthen had to pay £4,000. Among those fined were the following: Sir Rice Rudd of Aberglasney (£581), Sir George Vaughan of Pen-bre (£2,609), Henry Middleton of Llanarthne (£120), Sir Francis Lloyd of Dan-yr-Allt (£1,053). In Carmarthenshire the work of sequestration was largely carried out by men from other counties. The level and scope of the retribution did not endear the gentry to parliament. Parliament was resigned to the fact that support for the Puritans was likely to be superficial at best. A strained relationship lasted throughout the Commonwealth and there was a clear reluctance to allow the gentry of Carmarthenshire to determine who would represent them in parliament.

In January 1649 the Commonwealth was established and later that month Charles I (1625–49) was executed. Various Commonwealth governments ruled until 1660 when Charles II was restored. The basis of their authority was the army and the gentry had to contribute to its upkeep. Samuel Hughes of Llwyn-y-brain's contribution to an extraordinary tax 'for the new raised force for the use of the Commonwealth' was £5 11s 6d In the localities government was placed in the hands of County committees. There was a shortage of loyal parliamentarians to serve on these committees as most of the prominent county families had backed the Crown during the Civil War. The nucleus of the Carmarthenshire committee consisted of former cavaliers who had negotiated the surrender of the county in October 1645. These in effect were the governing families of the county. A notable exception was Carbery who was too deeply compromised and effectively withdrew (albeit temporarily) from public life. Sir Edward Vaughan of Tor-y-coed (Carbery's cousin) served on the committee along with Sir Rice Rudd, Rowland Gwynn of Taliaris and Howell Gwynn of Glan-brân. It is unlikely that parliament placed too much trust in the group, but it was compelled to work with it in order to preserve some semblance of continuity in local administration.

Following its victory parliament attempted to deal with what it considered to be a central problem it had identified in Wales. This was the distinct lack of spiritual enlightenment in the country, which it believed only Puritanism could provide. Its solution was to pass in 1650 the Act for the Better Propagation and Preaching of the Gospel in Wales. It was envisaged that the Act would remain in force for a period of three years and would then expire having hopefully completed its work successfully. Seventy one commissioners were appointed under the terms of the Act. Not one of them came from Carmarthenshire. To support the commissioners twenty-five Puritan ministers known as 'approvers' were selected to fill any church ordered vacant by the commissioners. A purge was launched by the Puritans against clergy who were slack or negligent in their pastoral and spiritual duties. Clergy were ejected from eighteen parishes from Pen-bre to Myddfai. The majority of these individuals were probably guilty of nothing more than supporting the Crown and displaying a measure of indifference towards Puritanism.

To ensure that the Propagation Act was carried out and to overcome the shortage of Puritan ministers in Wales, the commissioners were compelled to rely heavily on itinerant preachers to spread the Lord's word. Early in 1654 commissioners for the Approbation of Public Preachers (known as Triers) were appointed. They sought to organize preachers and to fill vacant parishes. In Carmarthenshire they approved fourteen new ministers. While some were competent, most were mediocre. Among them however was a man destined to become one of the most important religious figures in seventeenth-century Wales. According to Professor Glanmor Williams, in the teeth of enmity on the part of Church and state, no one 'held his ground more firmly or shone more brightly in the surrounding gloom than Stephen Hughes'.[9]

Stephen Hughes (1622–88) was born in Carmarthen. He was the son of a prosperous merchant who was mayor of Carmarthen in 1650. Hughes was installed as rector of Merthyr but was presented with the living of Meidrim in 1654. The scale of his activities was impressive. He was keen to improve educational opportunities and was disappointed that no schools had been set up in the county under the Propagation Act. He is best remembered for his publishing activities, particularly his efforts in promoting religious works in the Welsh language. Hughes was largely responsible for publishing the works of Vicar Prichard especially 'Canwyll y Cymry' (1681). With the restoration of the monarchy in 1660 and the Anglican reaction against the Puritans, Stephen Hughes was ejected from Meidrim and was subject to the punitive measures of the Clarendon Code. He remained active as a minister and preacher and was responsible for all the Independent churches within Carmarthenshire. In 1672 he published a 2000-copy edition of the Welsh New Testament. Hughes was supported by William Thomas, Bishop of St Davids from 1677 to 1683. An important contact was established in the early 1670s when he met Thomas Gouge who formed the Welsh Trust, an organization whose aim was to help the less fortunate and to disseminate Christian beliefs through education. By the time of his death Hughes had established a reputation as a minister, preacher, publisher, teacher and author. Welsh dissent was gathering its own momentum. He is perhaps appropriately labelled 'Apostol Sir Gâr' ('The Apostle of Carmarthenshire').

After Carbery's retirement from military service, his seat at Golden Grove became something of a centre of learning in the county. From 1644 to 1655 Carbery provided support in the moral and material sense to the leading Anglican theologian Jeremy Taylor (1613–67). While enjoying Carbery's hospitality as the family chaplain, and the quiet seclusion of the Tywi valley, Taylor produced some of his best devotional work. *Liberty of Prophesying* (1646) is an eloquent plea for religious toleration and freedom of conscience. Other important works written during his stay were *Holy Exemplar* a life of Christ, *Holy Living* (1650) and *Holy Dying* (1651). He named a collection of 522 sermons for the Christian year and a manual of devotions *Golden Grove* as a tribute to his friend and protector. He was thrown into prison by Cromwell for publishing this work. In addition to his writings Taylor also focused on education. Along with William Nicholson, the ejected vicar of Llandeilo and Thomas Wyatt his assistant, Taylor ran an academy preparing young men for university, at Newton Hall, Llanfihangel Aberbythych.

The death of Cromwell and the reluctance of his son to continue as Lord Protector led to the restoration of the monarchy in 1660. It is possible to gauge the reaction of the townspeople of Carmarthen to this news from an entry in the Corporation Order Book: 'This yeare, May 1660, King Charles the 2nd returned, and his health was drunk in wine from the conduits in Carmarthen.' Following the celebrations it is likely that many in the county would wish to draw a veil over the Commonwealth period. Carbery emerged from his 'retirement' and was rewarded handsomely for his loyalty to the Crown. He was appointed a privy councillor, a member of the Committee of the Mint and steward of several castles. The most prestigious of his appointments however was the presidency of the Council of Wales and the Marches, a position which carried an annual salary of £400.

His family also resumed its dominant position within the administration of the county. They monopolized the parliamentary representation of both borough and county for much of the remaining Stuart period. Francis Jones memorably summed up this period of Vaughan ascendancy over Carmarthenshire's affairs as 'government by pedigree'. The one blot on this imposing landscape was Carbery's removal as lord president in 1672 following the accusation that he had cruelly mistreated his servants and tenants at Dryslwyn by cropping their ears and cutting out their tongues.

In political terms the Restoration period saw the emergence of the two party system during the exclusion crisis (1679) when the Whigs sought to exclude Charles's Catholic brother and heir James, from succeeding to the throne. The Tories, who supported the hereditary succession, defended his right. Within Carmarthenshire the Vaughans acted as a coherent bloc to exert their influence and preserve their interests. They held the county seat from 1661 to 1689, and the borough seat from 1661 until 1725. There were several other county families with incomes reaching or approaching £1,000 a year whose political claims could not be passed over. Of these Williams of Edwinsford, Mansel of Muddlescombe and initially Jones of Abermarlais were the most significant. Sir Rice Rudd of Aberglasney ended the Vaughan sequence of representing the county when he was returned in 1689. Even the Dynevor family was slowly recovering its fortune and influence. Rudd was succeeded as MP for Carmarthenshire in 1701 by Griffith Rice of Newton, the first member of the family to sit in the Commons since the Tudor period.

Land was the basis of gentry wealth and many were developing their estates during the relative tranquility of the Restoration period. Several contemporary commentators note the abundance of corn and cattle the county produced. Richard Blome in his *Britannia* (1673) informed readers that 'Carmarthenshire, esteemed by some the strongest county in South Wales, and generally of a fertile soil, bearing good crops, hath rich meadows which feed store cattle and is well clothed with wood, the inhabitants are plentifully served with foul and fish, especially salmon in great abundance.' This view is confirmed by Thomas Dineley who accompanied the Duke of Beaufort on his progress through Wales in 1684. Dineley wrote that the soil was particularly rich and that the main commodities were cattle, salmon and pit-coal. There is evidence that improved methods of farming were being contemplated. William Vaughan in *The Golden Fleece* advised farmers to add manure and marl to the land to counter loss of fertility through over-cultivation. It is unlikely that his well intentioned advice was widely adopted. What is clear is that many farmers, particularly those in upland areas, were appreciating the value of using lime as a fertilizer and were prepared to travel quite long distances to obtain it.

The Restoration of the monarchy and the established Church unleashed an Anglican reaction against the Puritans. Retribution was enforced through the punitive measures of the Clarendon Code. Puritan ministers such as Stephen Hughes were ejected from their livings and were prevented under the terms of the Five Mile Act from living near a borough or keeping a school. While it is difficult to assess the actual numbers of Nonconformists within Carmarthenshire in the 1660s it is unlikely that there were many. At great personal risk some itinerant preachers did endeavour to serve the few dissenting communities in the county. William Jones established a Baptist community at Rhydwilym in 1668, in the west of the county. One of the earliest meeting houses for the Baptists was Capel y Graig in Newcastle Emlyn, first used in 1668. Dissenters received some relief in 1672 when Charles II issued the Declaration of Indulgence suspending penal laws against Nonconformists. Licences were granted to Nonconformist preachers. Three Independents and three Baptists were licensed to preach and establish meeting-houses. Stephen Hughes obtained a licence to preach in Llansteffan and Pencader, while the Baptist Robert Morgan obtained licences in Llangennech and Llan-non. According to a religious census held in 1676 to assess the extent of Nonconformity the figure of adherents for Carmarthenshire was 179. While the veracity of these figures has been seriously questioned, even allowing for an underestimation and taking into account omissions (Llanelli was not included) they are low. This was a very unpropitious beginning for a religious movement which would make such a great impact on the county over the next two centuries.

With the accession of the Catholic King James II in 1685 a renewal of the sectarian strife of the 1630s and 1640s was a distinct possibility, with the additional element of popery to ferment the brew. James was determined to reverse the religious policies of the previous 130 years and restore Catholicism. He hoped to subvert the democratic process by securing the return of a pliant parliament. Part of his strategy involved replacing existing borough charters with those that favoured his supporters. In 1686 a new charter was sent to Carmarthen and most of the council were removed from municipal office. The new officials were nearly all members of families who had been loyal to the Crown during the Civil War. Henry, Duke of Beaufort, the president of the Council of Wales and the Marches was appointed recorder of Carmarthen.

The new Common Council included Sir Rice Williams of Edwinsford, Rowland Gwynne and Sir Edward Mansel. Williams was emerging as the only prominent landowner in the county prepared to support the new king. Hopkin Rees the sheriff was also removed from his office. Two years later James renewed the charter granted by Henry VIII and ordered the purge of an additional six members of the Common Council. Sir Rice Williams was elected mayor of Carmarthen in 1688. The birth of a son to James meant that his avowedly Protestant daughters Mary and Anne, moved down the order of succession. Contemplating the prospect of a Catholic heir was too much for a number of powerful Protestant grandees and plans were drawn up to depose the king. James's unceremonious removal during the Glorious Revolution of 1688 was well received by the Carmarthenshire gentry who had no appetite for the former ruler's despotic tendencies. The only significant casualty was the replacement of Rice Williams as mayor of Carmarthen.

Following the Glorious Revolution religious dissent began to spread slowly across the county. Under the protection of the Toleration Act (1690) Protestant Nonconformists were given the freedom to worship in public. Dissenting meeting-houses and chapels were built which replaced the private houses formerly used for worship. These served large but relatively poor rural communities. By 1715 many Independent and Baptist chapels had been built, and ministers supplemented their incomes by holding schools.

Early Hanoverian Carmarthenshire: 1714–c.1750

On the death of Queen Anne in 1714 the crown passed to her distant German relative, George Elector of Hanover. George I (1714–27) was a Protestant, unlike Anne's half brother the Catholic James Edward Stuart. James had been excluded from the succession much to the opposition of his Jacobite supporters. These in the main were Tories, committed to upholding the principle of the hereditary succession. The arrival of the Hanoverians coincided with the start of the long Whig ascendancy as they were the new ruler's principal backers.

The succession was determined by the need to ensure the survival of the Protestant Church. A monarch's religion took precedence over his nationality. What therefore was the condition of the established Church in the early eighteenth century? In Carmarthenshire and the diocese of St Davids there is a considerable volume of evidence relating to the state of the Church. Two valuable sources are the churchwardens' presentments for Bishop George Bull's primary visitation in 1705[10] and Erasmus Saunders's *A View of the State of Religion in the Diocese of S. Davids* (1721). The reports presented to Bull are particularly useful as they provide a wealth of information regarding individual parishes in the county. There were clearly hard-working, diligent, resident vicars, who conducted regular services and discharged an educational as well as a pastoral role. The churches in Llandyfaelog, Llanarthne, Llanegwad, Llanfihangel Aberbythych and St Clears were all well maintained. Church schools were held in the parishes of Llangyndeyrn, Meidrim, Llandovery, Kidwelly and Llanddarog. Well organized parishes were more than countered by those that were seriously deficient in some way. Non-residency was considered a problem in Llanfihangel-ar-arth, Llanddowror, Llandeilo and Llan-non. The vicars of Llansadwrn, Llanfihangel Abercywyn, Llanfallteg and Abergwili all held other benefices. Poor maintenance of church buildings was an urgent issue in Talley: 'Our parish church is part of the demolished monastery; the walls and roof thereof are not in good repair, the windows have had no glass on them in our memory.' Llangennech had no chalice and no flagon, and 'we do want decent seats in our church'. In Laugharne the churchwardens informed Bishop Bull that 'the walls, windows, and ye church floor in indifferent repair; the bells much out of repairs'.

Erasmus Saunders began his book at the insistence of Bishop Bull. Both men were concerned with the deterioration of religious life in the diocese. Saunders was a devoted Anglican who painted a dark picture of ruined churches, of the non-residence and pluralism of the clergy and of the ignorance of the unbeneficed priests. He attributed all these problems to the poverty of the church, and argued that this had been brought about by the alienation of tithes by lay proprietors – a consequence of the dissolution of the monasteries. His passion permeates the text: 'I can scarce without tears, but not at all without a most astonishing concern and pity, behold the venerable ruins I have been describing … so great are the Desolations in this Country; so many of our Churches are in actual Ruins; so many more are ready to fall, and almost all are robb'd and pillag'd by a sweeping Alienation of all the Tythes and Glebes are belonging to them'.[11] Taking the sum of £50 a year as a viable living, Saunders lists all the parishes in the diocese. The majority generated less than £50. In the deanery of Kidwelly ten parishes were listed. Only two of these were above the £50 threshold. The value of the living of Llangyndeyrn is given as a mere £6 13s 4d.

If the darkest hour is just before dawn then the church was about to emerge from the gloom. Carmarthenshire occupied a pivotal role in facilitating the slow recovery of the fortunes of the Church in Wales. In addition, an education movement was started in the county that became the envy of other denominations and even countries. Griffith Jones (1683–1761) played a central role in both. He is a leading candidate as the most influential Welshman of this period. Jones was educated at Carmarthen Grammar School and was ordained by Bishop Bull in 1708. His remarkable preaching ability drew large crowds to his services in Laugharne. He soon came to the attention of rich and influential laymen who shared his concern regarding the condition of the Anglican Church. In 1716 he was appointed rector of Llanddowror by his friend and patron Sir John Philipps. Philipps was a generous and supportive man who devoted a great deal of energy to the Society for the Promotion of Christian Knowledge (SPCK). Griffith Jones sought to instil new vigour and enthusiasm into the Anglican church and his evangelistic approach is often credited with paving the way for the mid-eighteenth-century 'revival'.

Griffith Jones is best known for his educational work, which he saw as a key component in reversing the decline of the Church. He was appalled at the level of ignorance of the Bible when an outbreak of the plague visited his parish in 1730–1. A school was opened at Llanddowror around 1731–2. This was a success and other schools were set up in neighbouring parishes. Thus Circulating Schools came into existence. The essence of the movement was that itinerant teachers visited parishes to set up schools. They normally stayed for up to three months before moving on to the next location, leaving the schools hopefully to continue under their own momentum. The focus was on teaching pupils to read the Bible. Tuition was free and was open to adults and children. School classes were conducted through the medium of Welsh and at times suitable to working adults and children. Funds for the scheme were obtained from subscriptions, and Bibles from the SPCK. A periodical, *Welch Piety*, which detailed the progress of the movement was sent to subscribers. The remarkable success of the movement is borne out by the large numbers of schools set up not only in Carmarthenshire but throughout Wales. An estimation of the number of pupils taught during the thirty years that Griffith Jones was involved with the movement is over 150,000. Towards the end of his life he stayed in the house of his most faithful friend and supporter Madam Bevan of Laugharne who was entrusted to continue the work.

The early years of Hanoverian rule saw an upsurge in writing and printing books in Welsh. Most of these were devotional works of one sort or another. Sixty per cent of all books published in Wales between 1660 and 1730 (a total of 330 out of 545) appeared during the two decades 1710–30. The Welsh Trust and the SPCK were very active in supporting these ventures. In response to this literary renaissance the first printing press in Wales was set up at Adpar near Newcastle Emlyn, by Isaac Carter in 1718. Others followed across the county. The first book printed in Carmarthen was *Llun Agrippa*, published in 1723. Of the authors of Welsh books (*c.*1660–1730) whose names are known, twenty of the 140 came from Carmarthenshire. This was the second highest total in Wales. Not all the authors were clerics or academics. William Lewes of Llangeler was a gentleman sheep-farmer who was also a keen antiquary and genealogist in his spare time. He translated *Maddeuant i'r Edifairiol* (1725–6) and *Dwy Daith i Gaersalem* (1728).

Party politics during the period 1714–50 was rather frustrating for the Tories. They had clearly backed the wrong horse in choosing to support the Stuarts, and were paying dearly for this. They were excluded from government for the entire duration of the reigns of the first two Georges. Under the influence of the third earl of Carbery Carmarthenshire was a Whig stronghold in a predominantly Tory Wales. His death in 1713 ended the male line and the title became extinct. He was succeeded by his daughter

Anne who married the second Duke of Bolton. Party labels during this period became somewhat blurred. In the 1722 county election both candidates were Whig and though Edward Rice of Newton was backed by the traditional Whig interests, both he and his opponent Sir Nicholas Williams of Edwinsford were supported by Tories as well as Whigs. The contest was acrimonious and frequently violent. After a bitter campaign Rice was declared the winner by five votes (593 to 588) following the April poll. Williams immediately challenged the result by petitioning the House of Commons. After a protracted inquiry the seat was finally awarded to Williams in November 1724, two and a half years after the election.

Williams had little opportunity to establish himself in parliament. At the 1727 election he faced a formidable challenge. His opponent on this occasion was his near neighbour in the north of the county, Richard Gwynne of Taliaris. Gwynne was a committed Tory and an active member of the Society of Sea Serjeants as its president 1733–52. The society was suspected by many contemporaries of being a front organization for the Jacobites, an accusation hotly denied by the members who claimed that it was nothing more sinister than an annual dining and social gathering at different coastal locations. What is clear is that the society contained West Wales's leading Jacobites and Tories. Using the connections which the society afforded, Gwynne was supported by Sir Edward Mansel of Strade. The poll saw Williams returned by the fairly close margin of 693 to 591. P. D. G. Thomas believes that the society was clearly something more than a convivial dining club: 'Even if proof of their sedition is lacking it cannot be a coincidence that the Society was disbanded soon after the accession of George III in 1760.'[12] George was the first Hanoverian born and bred in Britain, a consideration which possibly reconciled hard-line Jacobites to the dynasty. There were no further challenges to Williams who remained as the county member until his death in July 1745. The subsequent by-election saw the return of the Golden Grove interest to county politics. Their new member was John Vaughan of Derwydd a second cousin to the Duchess of Bolton. When she died in 1751 he inherited the Golden Grove estate.

The stability of the first half of the eighteenth century did provide an opportunity for the economy of the county to develop and diversify slowly. While the pace of change would accelerate after 1750, the ground was prepared in the first half of the century. A measure of prosperity among the gentry, coupled to limited educational opportunities and access to professions among Nonconformists, led many to channel their energies and entrepreneurial talents into trade, commerce and industrial activity. These will be considered more fully in Chapter VI.

V

Society, Politics and Culture: *c*.1750–1914

Population

The most important social development in Carmarthenshire during the period 1750–1914 was the remarkable growth in population. If the demographic impact was dramatic, it was by no means equitably distributed throughout the county nor evenly spread across the period. The headline figures conceal real variations within the county regarding patterns of redistribution. In general there are three variations. Some parishes expanded steadily before enduring several decades of depopulation. Others expanded slowly then experienced rapid growth during the last quarter of the nineteenth century. A third group grew slowly during the opening decades of the nineteenth century and then stagnated until the outbreak of the war. The population of the county is estimated at 62,000 in 1750. The first census in 1801 revealed a figure of 67,317. During the period 1801–41 the population of Carmarthenshire increased by 50 per cent. Over the next half century, 1841–91, the total growth was a more modest 23 per cent. During the first two censuses of the twentieth century the pace of growth once again speeded up, to record a 23 per cent increase. In 1911, 160,430 people lived in Carmarthenshire.

The initial reason for the increase in population during the period 1750–1841 was a sharp decline in the death rate, particularly the infant mortality rate, while the continuing high birth rate produced the net surplus. Diseases such as smallpox effectively disappeared from the county. Towards the end of the century inward migration to the industrial areas in the south-east of the county helped sustain population growth. Within Carmarthenshire there was some very significant redistribution of population. The overall change in population for the parish of Llanelli during the period 1801–91 was 978 per cent, for Llangennech 526 per cent and for Pen-bre 343%. These figures reflect substantial inward migration by workers from rural areas, attracted by good wages and regular employment in the iron and tinplate works and the coal mines. Parishes such as Cil-y-cwm, Myddfai, Llanfynydd and Llanddeusant on the other hand, are fairly representative of those rural parishes that experienced a net decrease in population over the period 1801–91.

Carmarthenshire's towns were emerging as centres of culture, commerce and change. Two stand head and shoulders above the others. Carmarthen remained throughout the period the judicial, administrative and social heart of the county. It was also an educational centre with its teacher training college, Presbyterian college and grammar school. In 1810 the first edition of the *Carmarthen Journal* was published to disseminate both local and national news for the expanding middle classes. Yet its population remained static at almost exactly 10,000 for the whole of the period 1831–1914. The narrow streets of the borough contained over 300 retail outlets to service the needs of the surrounding area. Its heart was the bustling livestock and produce market. To service the financial and commercial needs of the town the first bank was founded in 1791 and by 1834 two more had opened for business. Behind its genteel façade however, there was a dark and seamier underside to Carmarthen. The town had expanded during the eighteenth century in a rapid and unstructured way. Life for the borough's inhabitants living in the narrow mean streets close to the castle was difficult and dangerous. The civic fathers were well aware of the situation and sought to improve the town by demolishing areas of poor housing. An insight into conditions in the town is provided in a petition of 1792 requesting a parliamentary act to bring about improvements. According to the petition:

> The town is ill supplied with water whereby the inhabitants are liable to great mischief in cases of fire – that the streets, lanes and public passages within the said borough and liberties and precincts thereof are very ill paved and cleansed and incommodious to passengers by the reason of various nuisances, annoyances and obstructions: and many disorders and irregularities are frequently committed in the night time for want of the said streets and other places being properly lighted and watched.[1]

There were frequent outbreaks of lawlessness, triggered by adverse economic or political circumstances. Very occasionally these erupted into serious disturbances (as in 1755, 1757, 1831 and 1843), linked to the notorious Carmarthen 'town mob'. To try and curb this lawlessness and maintain order, one of the first police forces in Wales was set up in the borough in 1836. The small force reached the strength of twelve in 1857 when it became popularly known as the 'Carmarthen Shilling' – twelve coppers.

In the east of the county the growth of Llanelli was extraordinarily rapid. Its population of 4,193 in 1831 had soared to 36,520 by 1921. Whereas Carmarthen was considered a rather reserved county town, Llanelli was a brash and vibrant community whose initial growth was largely due to inward migration. A busy port and a renowned tinplate industry supported a thousand businesses by 1914. Two of the best known were the Buckley and Felinfoel breweries and the internationally famous Stepney Spare Wheel Motor Ltd (first developed in 1904). The inaugural meeting of the town's rugby club took place on 11 November 1875 and its first competitive game was held on 1 January 1876. The 'Scarlets', as the team was affectionately known by its devoted followers, would become one of the most famous rugby clubs in the world. In recognition of its growth, Llanelli was designated an urban district council in 1894 and attained full borough status in 1913.

Both towns were keen to display their civic pride, and were justifiably proud of their wealth and status. Yet beyond the central commercial districts and the avenues of genteel housing were tucked away far less salubrious areas. These were inhabited by the poor, some of whom formed an underclass existing on the margins of Victorian society. In Carmarthen the poorest housing stock was concentrated towards the eastern end of the town around Priory Street and Oak Lane. The worst of the town's slums were in the Dan-y-Banc and Kidwelly Fach area just below the gaol. Before advances in public health there was little sanitation and it was not uncommon for up to twenty families to share a communal toilet. These were fertile breeding grounds for disease, particularly cholera. An epidemic in the summer of 1849 resulted in the deaths of 102 people. Following this outbreak schemes were initiated in the 1850s to clean up these areas. Two reservoirs were built between 1853 and 1858 and improved drainage and sewerage systems were laid.

Other established county towns such as Llandeilo, Llandovery and Newcastle Emlyn experienced mixed fortunes during the period. Malkin remarked that the streets of Llandovery were 'filthy and disgusting'.[2] Yet within a generation improvements were occurring. Within their boundaries a new middle class of bankers, solicitors, merchants, auctioneers, doctors, entrepreneurs and of course shopkeepers was emerging. Socially dynamic and with a keen eye regarding their status they built new town houses, subscribed to parks and hospitals and helped administer local government. Ammanford was the newest of the urban communities. Its growth was nothing short of spectacular. In 1851 Cross Inn was part of the parish of Llandybïe. Its fifty-nine houses accommodated 282 people. By 1902 large scale anthracite mining and tinplate production had transformed a small hamlet into the confident urban community of Ammanford. The population of Ammanford Urban District in 1911 was 6,074. Rapid progress did not come without a price. The *Carmarthen Journal* (31 January 1890) published a prize winning essay by *Le Pont de*

L'Amman on the progress of Ammanford during 1889 which highlighted a serious problem:

> The Amman is a very dirty river at present, owing to the refuse thrown into it in the tinworks in Cwmaman and Brynaman and several other works which are built on its banks. This refuse, especially vitriol from the tinworks is deadly to trout and other fish which used to be abundant. Butter which is obtained from cows which drink water from the river, is not what it used to be either in quality or quantity.

The prevalence of diseases such as diphtheria, typhoid, polio and tuberculosis was accentuated by the very basic sanitation, inadequate diets and only the most rudimentary of health care facilities. Many families experienced the trauma of childhood deaths as the young and vulnerable succumbed to a range of illnesses. The death rate in the county in 1908 was 17.1 per 1,000, significantly higher than the figure for England and Wales which stood at 14.7. An important recent study of aspects of the social structure of the county is Russell Davies's *Secret Sins: Sex, Violence and Society in Carmarthenshire 1870–1920*, dissected carefully the various social layers and issues impacting upon them. He explored and exposed the various misconceptions relating to preconceived notions surrounding the quality of life in Carmarthenshire. The traditional view of a respectable society with strong family values, where the father worked and mothers were the bedrock of domestic life was shown to be something of a caricature. Those with mental illnesses, the elderly and young pregnant mothers were more likely to be cared for in the towns than in the countryside, where traditional values were considered to be more firmly rooted. The highest rates of illegitimacy were in rural Carmarthenshire where practices such as *'caru yn y gwely'* (courting in bed) were well established. 'Prostitution, back-street abortions and infanticide were far more frequent than historians have allowed'.[3] Although vicious assaults and murder were not unknown, most of the crime recorded in the last half of the nineteenth century involved drunkenness, petty theft and infringements of the game laws. While clearly Nonconformity, the form of worship favoured by most Christians in the county, provided firm moral guidance, it was not averse to supporting direct action in pursuit of causes which it deemed to be justifiable, such as the tithe dispute. The society that emerges from Dr Davies's researches is a complex amalgam of the modern and the traditional, where superstitious practices such as sin-eating co-exist with what at the time was the very latest industrial technology.

Society

In 1750 the social structure of Carmarthenshire society had hardly altered in centuries. During the course of the period 1750–1914 however, the changes would be nothing short of seismic. County society in the middle of the eighteenth century was rigidly hierarchical and roundly class based. Economic and political power along with status was almost entirely linked to the ownership of land. For most of the period under consideration in this chapter the county's social landscape was dominated by the twin peaks of the Dynevor and Golden Grove families. Below them in rank and status were numerous other families.

In terms of lineage, the premier family in 1750 was Dynevor. Its power and influence had risen and fallen in spectacular fashion during the reigns of the first two Tudor monarchs. After 1750 the family experienced a considerable reversal of its fortunes. George Rice is sometimes described as 'the second founder of his house'. He secured a title for the family through his marriage to the only daughter and heiress of William, second Baron Talbot. Lord Talbot also obtained a barony, and took the name of his son-in-law's estate – Dynevor. His grandson, George Talbot became the third Baron Dynevor.

Golden Grove was the seat of the wealthiest family in the county. In 1751 with the Earldom of Carbery extinct John Vaughan was bequeathed the land and possessions, following the death of his relative Anne, Duchess of Bolton. He became lord of twenty five manors and managed a diverse and financially productive estate totalling some fifty thousand acres. Vaughan interests spanned agriculture, forestry, mining and smelting. The exit of the Vaughans and the entry of the Cawdors into Carmarthenshire society, occurred in dramatic circumstances. On his death in 1804 John Vaughan (grandson of the previous John Vaughan) bequeathed his estate not to his near relations, but to a friend, John Campbell of Stackpole Court in Pembrokeshire. Whatever the reason for this curious decision, a family of Scottish ancestry descended from Macbeth, with hardly any Carmarthenshire associations, almost overnight became joint leaders of county society. Their association would last until well into the last quarter of the twentieth century when they sold their estate to a pension fund and decamped back to their ancestral home in Scotland.

Below these aristocratic families there were a number of others possessing ancient and well connected pedigrees. Among these were the Philippses of Cwmgwili, the Williams family of Edwinsford and the Stepneys of Llanelli. Of some concern to many gentry families was the continuation of their line and if possible the expansion of their estates. Marriage was a far more serious business than love, compatibility and companionship alone. It was on the one hand a contract for securing the line while on the other snaring an heiress could restore where necessary financial solvency or expand the patrimony. A number of Carmarthenshire families married their heiresses to English husbands and the slow process of Anglicization continued remorselessly. Research by Professor David Howell has revealed that of forty-nine prominent families living in the county between 1702 and 1760 only seventeen (28.6 per cent) of them saw the estates survive in the direct male line. Nineteen (38.8 per cent) passed via heiresses and a further fifteen (30.6 per cent) passed via indirect succession with the outcome in one case unclear.

Marriage to 'outsiders' was clearly one way by which county society was regenerated. Another was the arrival of newcomers with no previous ties to the county, who purchased an estate or set up a business and settled. These social migrants – many drawn by the beauty of the county, as much as by its commercial opportunities, did occasionally make a lasting impact. William Chambers started Llanelly Pottery, William Du Buisson whose family were Huguenot émigrés developed the estate of Glyn-hir near Llandybïe. The most celebrated of these *arrivistes* however was William Paxton.

William Paxton made a fortune in the service of the East India Company. In 1786 he bought the Middleton Hall estate near Llanarthne and set about transforming the mansion and the grounds into a stunning arrangement of lakes and formal gardens. His refurbished mansion offered a chalybeate spring and hot and cold baths as attractions to his guests. The most visible and enduring of his structures was the folly now known as Paxton's Tower, completed *c.*1808 to commemorate Nelson's victory at Trafalgar. He was described by contemporaries as a 'generous, public-spirited and kindly man'. As a newcomer he was anxious to win the acceptance and friendship of his neighbours. He readily contributed large sums to local causes and charities. This largesse contributed to his appointment as mayor of Carmarthen in 1802. During his period in office he replaced the defective wooden conduits with iron pipes and provided the borough with a much needed reliable water-supply. Paxton failed however to gain the acceptance of the Carmarthenshire gentry, who effectively thwarted his political ambitions. This resulted in one of the county's most famous elections, the '*Lecsiwn Fawr*' (Great Election) of 1802. Clearly wealth and the best of civic intentions could not automatically buy social and political acceptance.

With few exceptions the bulk of a landlord's estate would be rented out to tenant-farmers. Holdings varied in size from around 150 down to 10 acres. The norm for a farm during the nineteenth century was probably around 40 to 50 acres. Larger farmers employed several servants some of whom lived with the family. The rapidly expanding population during the early part of this period placed many pressures on the largely rural population of the county. Nowhere was this more acute than among the landless labourers who until the development of industry in the nineteenth century eked out a miserable existence at subsistence level. Rural society was an intricate nexus of social and economic relationships over which the landlords for much of the period reigned supreme. It remained predominantly a deferential society where the tugging of the forelock and the doffing of the cap signified a combination of respect and inferiority. It tended to be both socially and economically conservative. Old ways and traditions lasted well into the twentieth century.

During the nineteenth century there appeared a fairly constant stream of official information which proved to be a gold mine for social historians. In 1873 the government published *The Return of the Owners of Land* – sometimes called the 'second Doomsday book'. All who owned land were required to register their holding, and the income they received from any rentals. John Bateman in 1876 published an analysis based on these figures. For Carmarthenshire he identified 8,021 individuals who owned land. Heading the list was the Earl of Cawdor who owned 33,782 acres with a gross estimated annual rental of £20,780 18s. Mary Williams of Talley whose 2 acres were worth £1 12s was one of the 5,168 cottagers who owned between them a mere 2,286 acres at the other end of the landownership table. The élite of the property owners were the 'great landowners', those who owned estates with a minimum acreage of 3,000 and a minimum rental of £3,000. There were thirteen such individuals in Carmarthenshire including A. J. Gulston (Derwydd), J. W. M. Gwynn-Hughes (Tre-gib), Sir J. H. Williams-Drummond (Edwinsford) and C. W. Mansel-Lewis and Sir J. S. Cowell-Stepney of Llanelli. They owned between them 30.9 per cent of the county. While this statistic would appear to be very high, by contemporary standards it was the lowest among the Welsh counties and was well below the national total of 41.3 per cent. In Carmarthenshire landownership was spread among more individuals than in almost any other Welsh county. This could well explain the independent minded nature of those who lived in the countryside since they were largely beholden to no one – beyond the reach of squire and master.

For the upper echelons of county society duty and pleasure existed side by side. The county's landowners served as justices of the peace and very occasionally kept the parliamentary seats warm for the scions of Dynevor and Golden Grove. Many served on the town corporation of Carmarthen and were mayors of the borough. Most, dutifully, took their turns as high sheriffs and deputy lieutenants of the county. Following the Poor Law Amendment Act of 1834 they filled the roles of guardians, and with the introduction of county councils in 1888, they were invariably returned to sit as members. As these posts were unpaid, only 'gentlemen' with unearned income could realistically aspire to them. Those inclined to military life, but perhaps not wishing to risk life and limb in colonial or foreign wars would join the militia – as officers.

Table 2: The Great Landowners of Carmarthenshire, 1873

Name of Owner	Address of Owner	Size of Estate	Gross Estimated Rental
Lord Ashburnham	Sussex	5,685	£3548 7s
Lord Cawdor	Golden Grove	33,782	£20,780
A. H. S. Davies	Pentre, Pembs	3,702	£3,118
Sir J. H. Williams -Drummond	Edwinsford	6,900	£5,096
Lord Dynevor	Llandeilo	7,208	£7,253
A. J. Gulston	Derwydd	6,744	£10,976
J. W. M.Gwynne -Hughes	Tre-gib	6,797	£3,990
A. H. C.Jones	Carmarthen	7,662	£4,610
Morgan Jones	Llanmilo	11,031	£5,867
C. W. Mansel-Lewis	Stradey	3,139	£4,265
David Pugh	Llandeilo	6,198	£3,569
H. L. Puxley	Llethr Llesti	6,522	£4,969
Sir J. S. Cowell -Stepney	Llanelli	9,841	£7,047

The social life of the upper classes was based around country pursuits such as hunting, shooting and riding. Those who could, might spend part of each year in London or Bath for the social season. A revealing insight into the activities of the Carmarthenshire gentry during its golden age – the middle of the nineteenth century – is given in the journals of Agnes Hermione Jennings of Gelli-deg. She records archery competitions at Llandeilo, magic lantern and croquet parties, visits to Tenby, Plas Llansteffan, Aberglasney, Dirleton, Iscoed, Edwinsford, Pantglas and Stradey. Hunt balls were held in the Assembly Rooms at Carmarthen as were various musical recitals. These activities were in addition to lengthy interludes in London during which, in March 1866, she was presented at court to Queen Victoria.

The income to support the lifestyle of the gentry was running out for many families. A number of smaller estates were burdened by debt. Rental incomes during the agricultural depression of the last quarter of the nineteenth century were declining. Many estates were mortgaged to the hilt. During the first decade of the twentieth century increasing numbers of properties were being sold. John Francis of Carmarthen noted in 1911 that 'It has become very general to break up the large estates'. This process would be accelerated by higher levels of tax, land value duties

Herbert Eccles, excavations at Coygan Cave, 1913
(courtesy of Carmarthenshire County Museum).

Gwal-y-filiast, Cromlech, Llanboidy
(author's collection).

The tomb of Rhys ap Thomas, St Peters
Church, Carmarthen.

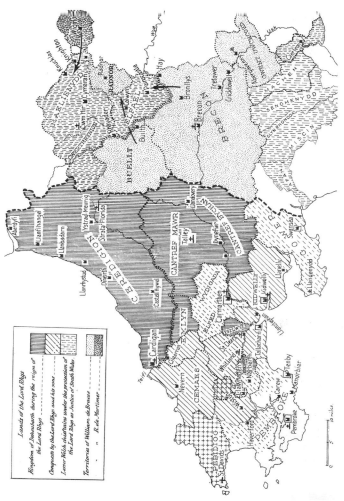

South Wales in the later half of the 12th century: lands of the Lord Rhys of Deheubarth.

Selected extracts from the Felons Register, Carmarthen Gaol
(courtesy of Carmarthenshire County Archive).

The Quay at Carmarthen, *c*.1850, by D. Cox
(author's collection).

Schreyer, the great American trick cyclist and high diver,
entertaining crowds in Carmarthen, 1905
(courtesy of Carmarthenshire County Museum).

Carmarthen Market, blanket stall, by J. F. Lloyd
(courtesy of Carmarthenshire County Museum).

Water carrier, Burry Port *c*.1910
(courtesy of Carmarthenshire County Archive).

Building Allt-y-ferin Church *c*.1852
(courtesy of Carmarthenshire County Museum).

Gardeners working at Golden Grove, by C. F. Allen, 1871
(courtesy of Carmarthenshire County Museum).

Tinplate stamping works Llanelly *c.*1898
(courtesy of Carmarthenshire County Museum).

Richard Vaughan, 2nd Earl of Carbery (1600–1687).
Attributed to William Dobson
(courtesy of Carmarthenshire County Museum).

Emlyn Colliery, Pen-y-groes, c.1930.

Supermarine Spitfires of 92 Squadron at dispersal point, RAF Pen-bre, 1940 (RAF Museum, Hendon).

The Great Glasshouse, designed by Norman Foster, National Botanic Gardens of Wales, Llanarthne (National Botanic Gardens of Wales).

Jim Griffiths (right) with his brother Amanwy (second from left) seated on Bardic Chairs won by Amanwy

Gwynfor Evans being shouldered by supporters following his victory in the
Carmarthenshire by-election 1966.

The Boat House, *Laugharne*, by Gordon Stuart RCA
(author's collection).

Dan the Mill, Milking by Aneurin Jones RCA (author's collection).

and death duties proposed by Lloyd George in 1909, and the impact of the Great War which resulted in so many heirs being killed.

In very marked contrast with the life of the gentry was that of the peasantry. They were an amorphous group comprising small tenant farmers and landless labourers. The economic condition of farm-labourers and servants was one of extreme poverty for most of the period. A young farm-servant living in on a farm (*y gwas bach*) could be employed in 1846 for £7 a year. They were usually hired on an annual basis in November of each year at hiring fairs. In Carmarthen, young boys between the ages of ten and thirteen would stand in line in Lammas Street hoping to catch the eye of a farmer. Their lodging would be provided by the farmer and this frequently meant sleeping in a outhouse. Meals would be shared with the family.

When a labourer got married in his mid-twenties he might build a *tŷ unnos* or move to a tied cottage. The exteriors of these cottages with their whitewashed walls, thatched roofs and a hint of rustic charm suggested an Arcadian idyll. The reality was very different as Thomas Campbell Foster, *The Times* correspondent, discovered on his way to Newcastle Emlyn in 1843:

> On my way I entered several farm labourers' cottages by the roadside, out of curiosity to see the actual condition of the people, and found them mud hovels, the floors of mud and full of holes, without chairs or tables, generally half filled with peat packed up in every corner, the only articles of furniture being a wretched sort of bedstead and a kettle. Beds there were none: nothing but loose straw and filthy rugs upon them. Peat fires on the floors in the corner, filling the cottages with smoke, and three or four children huddled around them. Nearly all the cottages were the same. In the most miserable parts of St Giles, in no part of England, did I witness such abject and wretched poverty.[4]

If the social and economic conditions of the farm-labourers were impoverished then that of their employers if they were small farmers – tenants or freeholders – were frequently little better. What the farmers did have was a measure of status and independence within their communities which set them apart from those they employed and the non-farming cottagers. Although the prospects of taking over a holding was one of unremitting toil trying to make ends meet, acquiring a tenancy was the aspirational goal of many labourers.

The pressures of a rapidly rising population in the period 1801–41, allied to economic recession in the countryside, resulted in a potentially combustible situation. In January 1843 an industrial recession led to a fall in farm incomes. The price that Carmarthenshire farmers were receiving for corn was 60 per cent lower than in 1840. Meat and dairy products such as salted butter and cheese were also selling at lower prices. The prevailing economic problems were exacerbated by a number of additional factors. In 1834 a new system of dealing with the poor was introduced. It established a network of workhouses to dispense poor relief. The cost of operating the system was largely borne by landowners through the poor rate. Much more contentious was the annual tithe farmers were required to pay to the church or lay tithe holder. The amount paid in kind (produce) was a tenth of the farm's annual production. In 1836 the Tithe Commutation Act introduced a fixed charge based on average prices preceding the change. As prices fell after 1836 the fixed charge increased to well beyond the traditional 10 per cent. In addition to the financial aspect, the mainly Nonconformist farmers objected to supporting what they saw as an alien church. The evidence of Mary Thomas from Llanelli to a commission of inquiry in 1843 provides a valuable insight into the hardships faced by farmers with the tithe during this period. She was the only woman out of 264 witnesses listed in the commission's index:

> Dr Lawrence is a good master, and will take what rent I can get together by rent-day, and trust me for any little matter I cannot make up for a while and I have never failed him yet. But last time, when I had the tithe to pay, I could only make up seven sovereigns which I took to Squire Thomas's agent on tithe day, but he refused to take them and trust me for a week or two for the rest, till I could sell something. I thought that very hard, for it is very hard times with us, for our stock is getting very low. I have nursed sixteen children and never owed a farthing ... but we are now worse off a deal than ever. Yet my husband has not spent sixpence on beer these twenty years, nor can I or the children go to church or chapel for the want of decent clothing. We perhaps might have gone on, but now this tithe comes so heavy; six or seven pounds is a deal of money.[5]

A final burden were the tolls farmers had to pay when using the turnpike roads that crossed the county. As regular users taking produce to markets or journeying to lime kilns to buy fertilizer they suffered more than most from the expansion of the turnpike trust network during the period after 1815.

Additional tensions were felt within the closely knit rural communities as the relationship between landlord and tenant underwent change. To the increasing Anglicization of the gentry which had been taking place slowly since Tudor times were added religious and political differences.

The phenomenal growth of Nonconformity among the farmers and their servants also spawned political radicalism. Predominantly English-speaking, Anglican Tory squires were finding themselves increasingly at odds with their 'Welsh', chapel, radical tenants. Edward Crompton Lloyd Hall a solicitor and local squire from Newcastle Emlyn noted that 'the men feel that they cannot be worse off and therefore become reckless in exhibiting the real state of their feelings towards their landlords and others to whom in more prosperous times they were accustomed to crouch like the slaves of Jamaica'. Rising rents and a perception – often misplaced – that the gentry were wholly unsympathetic to their plight drove many to take matters into their own hands. Local magistrates commented that the practice of the *ceffyl pren* (wooden horse) when a wrong-doer was carried around either in person or in effigy, was becoming increasingly common during the 1830s.

These tensions and stresses, or as they have been described 'the growing pains of a new society', erupted into the most famous outbreak of mass law-breaking during the last two centuries. While the Rebecca Riots are linked with west Wales their heartland was Carmarthenshire. The initial outbreak occurred on 13 May 1839 at Efail-wen. A large crowd of local people, said to be between three to four hundred strong, some armed with guns, many with blackened faces, others wearing women's clothes, assembled at 10.30 p.m. Most were local tenant farmers and labourers. They proceeded to destroy a new toll-gate put up by the Whitland Trust's toll contractor Thomas Bullin. Rebecca had made her first dramatic appearance. An attack on a neighboring gate at Maes-gwyn and a return visit to Efail-wen marked the end of Rebecca's first outing. It was during the second attack at Efail-wen that the leader of the rioters, possibly Thomas Rees (Twm Carnabwth), was addressed as 'Beca'. While the young Friedrich Engels dismissed the riots as a 'harmless masquerade' the authorities took a far more serious view of events. Significantly the local magistrates decided that the destroyed gates should not be rebuilt. Rebecca had won a remarkable victory. Direct action from an oppressed community had succeeded. There was no subsequent activity for three years.

Professor David Williams stated that the Rebecca Riots really broke out in the winter of 1842 'and their cause was poverty. It was distress and semi-starvation which led the country people to march under the banners of Rebecca.' This was a case of 'violence born of despair'.[6] The resumption of the rioting coincided with a renewed industrial depression. What was different in the years 1842–3 was the scale and ferocity of the attacks. Although it is unclear why the Rebecca Riots were so called, the most likely explanation is that they were named after a scriptural reference in Genesis 24:60 which contains the words 'Rebecca' and 'gates'.

The verse concludes: 'let thy seed possess the gates of those which hate them.' There was no one master-mind orchestrating the attacks. They were essentially localized and spontaneous. As in 1839 the erection of a new gate started the trouble. On 18 November 1842 a gate outside St Clears was destroyed. In the following months the activities of 'Beca' spread along the Tywi valley and into neighbouring counties. 'Rebecca the redresser' of grievances did not confine her activities to toll-gate destruction. Her greatest display of strength was the daylight procession in Carmarthen in June 1843. A large crowd of about 300 on horseback and 2,000 on foot led by a rider disguised in women's clothes marched through the town. However, the orderly procession was joined by unruly elements from the poorer parts of Carmarthen. They proceeded to ransack the workhouse. Complete destruction was averted only by the timely arrival of the 4th Light Dragoons. Less overt forms of protest were also used. Many landlords and vicars were the recipients of threatening letters. The following was sent to William Peel of Taliaris:

> In my journey of doing good to the Poor and distressed farmers I took notice of you as one who not careful enough of your tenantry do by your oppressing and arbitrary power make them to languish under your hand … I do warn you in time to mind yourself for as sure as this letter will come to your hand I and my dutiful daughters from 5 to 10 hundred of us will visit your habitation at Taliaris in a few days and you will do well to prepare a secure place for your soul we will do well with your body your flesh we will give to the Glansevin hounds … Down the rent and all will be good.[7]

Salmon weirs and the property of unpopular landlords were attacked and threats made against collectors and payers of the hated poor rate. On the night of 12 September 1843 Edward Adams of Middleton Hall on returning from the Quarter Sessions found his hay ricks on fire and the plantation around his mansion full of armed men.

The failure of the authorities to contain what was effectively a community revolt was arousing national interest. *The Times* sent a correspondent, Thomas Campbell Foster, to the area in June 1843. From the outset his even-handed and balanced reporting won the respect of the peasantry who allowed him to attend their meetings. In July 1843 he wrote 'the whole country appears to be of one mind, and it is difficult to fight against a united people'. Foster's reports ultimately helped determine the response of the government. Given the enormous emphasis the Victorians placed on the sanctity of property it was hardly surprising that the authorities should act swiftly and forcefully in countering the disturbances. By the end of June 1843 a detachment of yeomanry was based in St Clears and marines were billeted in Newcastle Emlyn. Among the places where small garrisons were located were the towns of Carmarthen and Llanelli down to smaller communities such as Meinciau, Llansawel and Cross Hands. One hundred and fifty Metropolitan policemen were dispatched from London to support the large number of special constables, sworn in by the magistrates. In October a royal proclamation was issued offering £500 rewards for information leading to the conviction of rioters.

Far from desisting from their activities the rioters widened the scope of their operations. The industrialized areas in the south-east of the county saw significant attacks on toll-gates and property in the summer of 1843. Tenant-farmers were joined by colliers who were suffering wage reductions and unemployment. It was in the areas around Pontyberem and Llanelli that John Jones (Shoni Sgubor Fawr) and David Davies (Dai'r Cantwr) conducted their criminal activities, notably extortion under the guise of Rebecca. Shoni and Dai were hunted down by the authorities and eventually transported. Rioters were using increasing levels of violence on their targets. In August 1843 the Furnace Lodge and Sandy lime-kiln gates at Llanelli were pulled down and burnt, and one of the keepers received a severe beating and a shotgun blast in the face. On 6 September following a gun battle near Pontarddulais several rioters were arrested and ultimately transported. Three days later at nearby Hendy an elderly toll-house keeper, Sarah Williams, became the only fatality of the riots when she was shot in the chest. The increasing use of fire-arms was an ominous departure and was worrying many of the farmers.

The riots ended almost as quickly as they had flared up. Many meetings were held across the county to air the farmers' grievances and to petition the authorities. One of the largest was held at Mynydd Sylen the open moorland between Llan-non and Pontyberem on 25 August 1843. It is estimated that over three thousand people attended. The decision of the government to set up a commission of inquiry did help defuse the situation and afforded the farmers an opportunity of airing their grievances and ending their protests without loss of face. The commissioners under the chairmanship of Thomas Frankland Lewis began taking evidence in Carmarthen on 30 October. Their balanced and sympathetic report was published on 6 March 1844. As a consequence of the report the government moved with great speed and introduced legislation to limit the number of turnpike trusts operating in each county. The speedy passage of the bill through both houses of parliament was largely due to the efforts of Lord Cawdor. It received the royal assent on 9 August 1844.

The expansion of industry removed the pressure on jobs in the rural areas. The thinning of the rural population, particularly after the railways were opened, saw a gradual increase in the wages of farm-labourers. Weekly wage rates in Carmarthenshire of around 12s in 1870 had increased to 16s per week on average, by 1898. Although living costs were also rising they did not entirely cancel out the wage increases. In some respects conditions were improving in the second half of the nineteenth century while in others very little had changed.

Resentment against the tithe which had been such a prominent factor during the Rebecca Riots resurfaced in the late 1880s. Disturbances broke out in the vale of Clwyd in the summer of 1886. Initially there was no activity in Carmarthenshire. Lord Dynevor shrewdly observed the dangers of the tithe question to landowners: 'All our tenants are Dissenters. The attack on the Tithe and the Church is most taken with them and advocated from all the Dissenting Pulpits.' That winter a number of meetings were held across the county at Llangynnwr, Llandovery, Llanddeusant, Llanelli, Llanwrda, Llanedi and Myddfai. An anti-tithe meeting at Y Betws, addressed by the Revd J. Towyn Jones asked the ecclesiastical commissioners to reduce the tithe by 20 per cent. The request from Henllan Amgoed vestry was for a 25 per cent reduction. Evidence of Nonconformist backing for the campaign (as Lord Dynevor had pointed out) is confirmed by a meeting of Carmarthenshire Independents at Elim near Carmarthen (17 November 1886): 'we rejoice at the reality, progress and spread of the anti-tithe movement all across the principality.' Faced with the possibility of unrest, the reaction of Mr Gwynn Hughes of Tregib was perhaps typical. At a meeting in Llansadwrn he promised to grant his tenants an abatement from his portion of the tithe of 12.5 per cent. According to the *Carmarthen Journal*: 'Conflict with the powers has thus been avoided in this parish.' There were more significant disturbances in 1888 following the refusal of a number of Nonconformists to pay what they considered to be an unjust charge. At a distraint sale held at the farm of Mr Thomas Jones of Whitland, a prominent local Nonconformist and deacon who had not paid any tithe for two years, a crowd of 700 people turned up to express their solidarity with the law-breaker. Later that summer at Pencader two mares were taken by bailiffs from the farm of David Jones and sold to realize the amount of unpaid tithe – £10, which with costs came to £25. At the sale twenty constables were present to control a large crowd, carrying banners and an effigy of a surpliced clergyman.

The Tithe Act of 1891 went some way to dealing with the Nonconformist grievances. In a broader sense the issue was part of the more complex series of relationships and tensions that continued to exist in the countryside between landlords and their tenants. Fuelled by the Nonconformist press these were grouped together as 'The Land Question'. The Royal Commission on Land in Wales and Monmouthshire

(1896), which had been set up to examine the problems of rural Wales, was divided on how best to resolve the land question. Although conditions were improving, real poverty remained. Miss Kate Jenkins observed that in the parish of Llangadog: 'The Welsh farmer would inhabit houses no English farmer would live in.'[8] Liberal politics was one way to deal with these problems. Another was to abandon the countryside.

Politics

The theatre of politics in the county during the last two and a half centuries was frequently violent, often dramatic and seldom lost its capacity to shock and awe. The period outlined in this chapter, 1750–1914, covers the pre-democratic era down to the virtual doorstep of democracy. For the purposes of this evaluation the period is subdivided into the pre-democratic age (1750–1830) and the period of emerging democracy (c. 1831–1914). In terms of national politics 1750 marked the start of the last decade of the long political supremacy of the Whig party which ended with the accession of George III in 1760.

Before the age of democracy the fortunes of Carmarthenshire's two constituencies – the county and the borough of Carmarthen – were in 1750 very much at the whim of the great landed families and their allies. The county franchise was given to men who owned land with a minimum value of 40s – 'the forty shilling freeholders'. Those eligible to vote numbered around a thousand men. Although by modern standards the figure is tiny, in eighteenth-century terms it was sufficiently large to make direct control by one family very difficult. In Carmarthen the right to vote was exercised by the freemen or burgesses of the borough. This type of borough where the franchise was traditionally small was usually described as a pocket borough. The relatively high number of voters in Carmarthen numbering well over a hundred was too large to bribe directly. It was difficult for one family to establish outright control. Carmarthen was the scene of many violent election riots and vicious corruption. In the winter of 1755 a large crowd attacked the gaol and two rioters were killed. After a period of calm, severe rioting broke out in 1757 during which four people were killed, many injured and business premises attacked and looted. By the middle of the eighteenth century borough life had become completely dislocated and there were two corporations in existence. This situation was ended when a new charter was granted in 1764 which attempted to clarify who were entitled to vote. Voting was open and was recorded for all to see whenever there was an electoral contest. These however tended to be rare, expensive and violent affairs. Members were often returned unopposed in the eighteenth and early nineteenth centuries.

Of the two constituencies, representing the county was accorded the higher social status. A county member of parliament represented the powerful landed interest in parliament. There was a keen rivalry between the Dynevor and Golden Grove families to secure this honour. Yet no candidate during the eighteenth century could ignore the families and houses of Cwmgwili, Tre-gib, Edwinsford, Glansefin, Iscoed, Llanelli and Taliaris, to name but a few. Party labels and loyalties were much more flexible in 1750 than in the following century. Former Jacobite and Hanoverian sympathies survived as traditional family attachments to one or other of the two major political groups in the county. In Carmarthenshire the groups were known as the Reds, generally Tory, and the Blues, the Whigs. Marriage, inheritance and personal friendships or enmity could realign family connections. The rivalry was kept alive by membership of the Bluecoat Hunt or the Redcoat Hunt or by the support of a Blue or a Red candidate at a parliamentary election. Blue Street and Red Street in Carmarthen are a legacy of this rivalry.

In general the political history of the county in the late eighteenth and early nineteenth century is hardly noted for the ability of its members or the heat of its contests. There are, however, two exceptions. The first relates to an individual. In 1750 the sitting member for the county was John Vaughan who succeeded to the Golden Grove estates the following year. He was defeated in 1754 in a keenly fought contest by George Rice of Dynevor who retained the seat until his death in 1779. Rice's victory marked the end of the long domination of Golden Grove over the political history of the county. While the majority of Carmarthenshire's members of parliament during this period were fairly anonymous figures, Rice was a consummate political operator – a professional politician in a world of amateurs. He was a prominent supporter of the Duke of Newcastle and, as such, a Whig. His role was to manage elections for the government interest. This involved dispensing money from the secret service fund to buy support. In 1755 he spent £173 in the government cause in Radnorshire. The accession of George III in 1760 brought the Whig supremacy to an end as the new king was determined to take an active role in politics. While Newcastle went out of office Rice seamlessly transferred his loyalties to the new administration and continued his work, although now under the label of a Tory. Following Rice's death the seat was occupied by a member of the Williams family of Edwinsford in the Tory (Red) cause.

The second exception relates to the county's most famous election – the '*Lecsiwn Fawr*' (Great Election) of 1802. This contest pitched together not only the keen differences between the Blues and the Reds but a rivalry between old money – James Hamlyn Williams of Edwinsford – and new money in the guise of Sir William Paxton. Paxton was supported by J. G. Philipps of Cwmgwili, J. W. Hughes of Tre-gib and John Vaughan of Golden Grove. The election was fiercely contested. *The Times* noted that it 'is carried on with much party violence and proceeds slowly'.[9] Polling remained open for fifteen days at the end of which Williams was elected by 1,217 votes to Paxton's 1,110. The campaign is remarkable not only for the considerable sums of money spent by both sides in attempting to bribe the electorate, but because a record survives of how Paxton disbursed his funds. The total bill for his abortive campaign came to £15,690 4s 2d. This included 11,070 breakfasts, 36,901 dinners, 25,275 gallons of ale and 11,068 bottles of spirits. Williams was forced to sell timber from his estate to meet his bills. There were no other contests in the county until 1832. In 1820 the Dynevors resumed their representation of the county when the Hon. George Rice Trevor was returned unopposed for the seat.

Carmarthen borough was for most of the period occupied by the 'Blue' interest and its members were loyal Whigs. The 'Reds' however were always alert to any opportunities that might enable them to seize the initiative. Its political history during this period contains an undercurrent of violence, corruption and manipulation. The rival groups sought to interpret the borough charter for their own ends by creating electors (freemen) for their interest or disenfranchising rival supporters. Periods of opposition by either faction led them to use unscrupulous tactics. One family stands out in the politics of the borough during the second half of the eighteenth century: Philipps of Cwmgwili. Following the defeat of Griffith Philipps in 1741 the Whigs used the support of the mob to stage a return. When the Tories elected a mayor their rivals refused to accept the choice and produced an alternative through a common council. There were in effect two corporations.

Griffith Philipps won the seat in 1751 and the Tories in their turn wooed the town mob. In the autumn of 1755 there were severe riots in the town. Many of the rioters were armed and some were members of the suspected Jacobite Society of Sea Serjeants, a Tory dining club. A number of rioters were killed. In 1764 a new borough charter was obtained to try and resolve the corporate disputes. Griffith Philipps's son, J. G. Philipps, became the borough member in 1784. The Reds had to wait until 1796 before they were able to mount a serious challenge to him. Lord Dynevor's brother-in-law took up the Red cause and, amid scenes of violence and accusations of corporate irregularities, he was returned. The result was immediately challenged and was overturned on appeal, to the jubilation of John Vaughan of Golden Grove who identified himself closely with Blue-Whig cause. Vaughan's death and the bequest of his estate to the Campbells saw their entry into borough politics. They represented the seat at a number of elections until 1821 when J. F. Campbell succeeded his father as Lord Cawdor. The Tories seized the opportunity to turn the tables on their opponents. The ensuing contest pitched the ageing Sir William Paxton against a young, colourful Tory barrister – John Jones of Ystrad who had contested the seat on a number of previous occasions. The substance of his previous campaigns had been to prevent the Cawdors turning the borough into a family seat. After a ten-day contest Jones triumphed by 312 votes to 281. Jones's victory ended seventy five years of Whig control of the borough seat. He was an immensely popular figure – born in Carmarthen, Welsh-speaking and cultured. His library contained over four thousand books. Jones's popularity lasted through to the Reform Act crisis. All his election expenses were met by his supporters.

The second period in the examination of the political history of the county spans the era from the first Reform Act to the outbreak of the war. Between 1820 and 1830 there had been many calls for extending the vote and ending the obscenities of rotten and pocket boroughs. The Tories turned a deaf ear to all these calls. One of the first meetings in the county to demand reform was held in Carmarthen in January 1823. At the general election of August 1830 the issue of reform raised barely a flicker of interest in either county or borough contest. The two Tories George Rice Trevor and John Jones were both returned unopposed. When the Tory government resigned in November 1830 the incoming Whigs were committed to reforming parliament. Their Reform Bill was introduced in the Commons on 1 March 1831. It proposed widening the franchise in counties and boroughs and redistributing seats from small boroughs to large towns and populous counties. The most significant concern for Carmarthenshire was the proposal to enfranchise Llanelli as a contributory borough to Carmarthen. Both Jones and Trevor opposed the second reading of the Bill. The defeat of the Bill led to another general election. Trevor announced that he would not seek re-election for the county and Sir James Hamlyn Williams of Edwinsford was returned unopposed. Williams promised to support all the government's reform plans.

The contest in the borough was much more dramatic. Polling was abandoned amid scenes of violence and the sheriff was unable to secure the return of a member – one of the first occasions this had ever happened in Wales. A second election in August resulted in Jones defeating his Whig opponent Capt. John George Philipps of Cwmgwili by 274 votes to 203. The government was returned with an increased majority and introduced a second Reform Bill. It proposed adding a second county member to Carmarthenshire on the grounds of its increased population. Both Jones and Williams voted for this Bill which was rejected by the Lords. A third Bill was introduced in December 1831 which became law the following June.

What impact did the 1832 Act have on Carmarthenshire? Three new classes of voters were created in the counties: the £10 copyholder, £50 leaseholders and, at the instigation of the Tories, tenants paying £50 rent a year. Estimating the pre-reform electorate in the county is difficult but it was about three thousand. Following the Reform Act 3,887 voters were registered to vote, an increase of around 29 per cent. This was well below the average increase of 45 per cent for Welsh counties. Superficially very little appeared to have altered in the county. At the first post-reform election in 1832 George Rice Trevor and Edward Hamlyn Adams of Middleton Hall were returned. The changes for the borough were in comparison very significant. Llanelli became a contributory borough – an acknowledgement of its rapidly expanding size and economic power. Even with the addition of Llanelli, Carmarthen was the only Welsh borough where the electorate fell as a result of an act whose aim was to extend the franchise. The reason for this was that the enfranchisement of householders paying £10 rates was more than countered by the dis-enfranchisement of non-resident burgesses. While there were 723 eligible to vote in 1831 only 684 were registered in 1832. In the 1832 election John Jones was defeated by the Whig candidate W. H. Yelverton.

The period 1832–1914 witnessed a dramatic shift in the balance of political power. Age-old barriers and structures were being eroded while new interests and organizations were established. There were a number of important developments. Firstly, old rivalries between the Blues and the Reds were recast in favour of class-based loyalties to either the Tory/ Conservative cause or that of the Whig/Liberals. Landowners were drawing together not only in defence of their economic interests and lifestyle, but also in support of the Anglican Church. Lord Cawdor ended many generations of Golden Grove rivalry with Dynevor when he joined the Tories and helped secure in 1837 the county seat for John Jones. That county election was infamous because it brought into national focus the naked power of landlordism. The Tory amendment which was incorporated in the 1832 Act gave the vote to £50 per annum tenant-farmers. Clearly the aim was to strengthen the political position of the landlords. In 1837 Cawdor's agent R. B. Williams was writing to his master's tenants in Carmarthenshire with instructions of how to vote – 'Mr David Hopkins. I shall rely upon your giving a plumper for Col. Trevor at the approaching election who is the only candidate supported by your landlord. R. B. W'. Pressure was also exerted on Evan Evans of Llandybïe Mill for the prompt payment of his rent.[10] Eviction was a very real consequence if the 'request' was disobeyed. The events in Carmarthenshire were debated in the House of Commons. Tenant-farmers, many of whom had become politicized for the first time during the Rebecca

Riots and were inspired by Nonconformist attitudes to challenge and question injustices, were supporting the Whigs and later the Liberals.

There were further extensions to the franchise during Queen Victoria's reign. The second Reform Act of 1867 gave the vote to every male householder in borough constituencies and to every male householder occupying premises rated at £12 or more in the counties. As a result of the Act the borough electorate increased from 816 in 1866 to 3,190 in 1868. The county electorate showed a less dramatic increase, from 4,833 in 1866 to 8,026 in 1868. A further development occurred in 1884 when a third Reform Act extended household suffrage to the counties. Large numbers of colliers, steel and tinplate workers were enfranchised for the first time. A redistribution Act in 1885 divided the county into two distinct constituencies – East and West Carmarthenshire. The total registered county electorate in 1883 was 8,648. In 1885 the electorate for the West division was 9,969 and for the East 8,669.

A second feature was the gradual emergence of members from the industrial and business community to represent the constituencies. This development marked the slow decline of the landed interest as the natural political leaders of the county. While the lists of both county and borough members would continue to be peppered with the names of patrician Tory landowners (e.g. G. R. Trevor, Viscount Emlyn) and the occasional Liberal, such as W. R. H. Powell of Maesgwynne, they were becoming an endangered species. In 1837 the prominent local banker David Morris won the borough seat, which he retained until his death in 1864. The owner of the Black Ox Bank, David Jones of Pant-glas was elected the county member in 1852 and retained the seat until 1868. On his retirement he was succeeded by his brother John Jones of Blaen-nos who represented Carmarthenshire until 1880. The Llanelli industrialist C. W. Nevill was elected the member of parliament for the borough in 1872. While they owned landed estates these were the baubles of their wealth not its substance. In terms of faith they were firmly Anglican, at a time when most of their constituents were Nonconformist.

The emergence of Nonconformist Liberal members was a third important development. Following the 1868 election a number of Nonconformist tenant-farmers were evicted for defying the wishes of their Tory landlords and supporting the Liberals. Eighteen eviction notices were issued on the Cawdor estates in Carmarthenshire. These 'martyrs' of 1868 prompted the Liberal government to introduce a Ballot Act in 1872. The election of J. Lloyd Morgan as the Liberal member for West Carmarthen in 1889 marked a clear change. He was a barrister and the son of William Morgan, Professor of Theology at the Presbyterian College in Carmarthen. The following year another Nonconformist barrister Abel Thomas was elected for East Carmarthenshire. Most spectacular of all was the victory of one of the giants of the Welsh pulpit the Independent minister the Revd. Towyn Jones at the Carmarthen East by-election of August 1912. He succeeded in gaining the Liberal nomination ahead of Sir Stafford Howard and Sir Courtney Mansel. Possibly the most prominent of this group was the journalist and historian W. Llewellyn Williams who represented Carmarthen between 1906 and 1918. Williams was an ardent nationalist who had been active in the *Cymru Fydd* movement of the 1880s. He was a passionate advocate of the disestablishment of the Anglican Church in Wales, and in the years up to 1914 was a close ally of Lloyd George.

The final development was the slow, faltering emergence of organized labour onto the political stage. Rapid industrialization in the south-east of the county saw a great increase in the urban working class. Trade unionism followed in the wake of industrial expansion. After the extension of the vote in 1885, newly enfranchised workers mainly supported the Liberal Party. The formation of the Independent Labour Party in 1893 had no impact on Carmarthenshire. Even the formation of the Labour Representation Committee in 1900 did not prise away the loyalties of the working class to the Liberal cause. But there was a measure of disillusionment with a party that had been obsessed with Ireland and securing civil rights for Nonconformists. Workers wanted measures to alleviate their harsh living and working conditions. For an increasing minority of the proletariat the Liberal agenda was considerably at odds with their own. Within Carmarthenshire the two centres most clearly linked to socialism were Llanelli and Ammanford.

Before the early 1870s there was little sign of active trade-unionism in the Llanelli area. When six workers at R. J. Nevill's Wern foundry joined the Amalgamated Society of Engineers they were sacked. However, growing discontent over wages among tinplate workers provided the opportunity for the emergence of virile trade-unionism. In 1873 the Independent Association of Tinplate Makers recruited hundreds of members in Llanelli. The new unionism of the late 1890s, with its greater militancy, reached Llanelli when branches of the dockers' and gasworkers' unions were formed. The county's colliers helped form a union in 1882 – the Anthracite Miners. By the time of the great coal strike of 1898 it had over six thousand members and later became affiliated to the South Wales Miners' Federation. Industrial and social tensions were clearly evident in the 1893 colliers' strike in Tumble. A combustible mixture of proposed wage reductions, a less than solid strike – broken in part by English and Scottish 'blacklegs', and an influx of non-Welsh outsiders into a tight-knit community, spilled over into violence. The Llanelli area was certainly not immune to the impact of socialism. A touring speaker from the Marxist, Social Democratic Federation addressed a meeting at the Atheneum in 1892. Other meetings were held at Felin-foel and Ammanford. In the wake of all this activity and the lukewarm attitude of the Liberals to the growing demands of trade unionists, the Llanelli Trades' and Labour Council was formed on 4 January 1900. It was not until 1906 however that a branch of the ILP was formed in the town.

The drift towards the Labour Party was very slow. In the years before the First World War a variety of free thinkers, Christian evangelists and socialist speakers were drawn to Ammanford and the Aman Valley. This corner of Carmarthenshire was booming, primarily in response to the growing market for anthracite coal which its collieries produced in abundance. They were hoping to recruit from among its largely working class population. The first ILP branch was set up in Ammanford in May 1908. Among the more politically conscious and ambitious workers, opportunities for self education were sought out. Organizations supported by unions such as the SWMF offered tutorials and lectures, and even scholarships to Ruskin College Oxford. Out of this rather diffuse educational environment there emerged in Ammanford a remarkable group of worker intellectuals who met in an old vicarage which became known as the 'White House' (1913–22). The building was purchased by George Davidson, a wealthy socialist philanthropist more widely known for his pioneering educational work with adults in Coleg Harlech. Davidson's support enabled the group of about a dozen to hold regular lectures and tutorials in agreeable surroundings. A well-stocked library encouraged private reading and reflection, which these avid autodidacts embraced with relish. There were ambitious hopes – though never realised – that the White House would become a workers' forum. One of the most committed members of this group was the young Jim Griffiths.

Jim Griffiths, who became a significant figure in post-war British politics, described how as a young coal miner from Betws he first became involved with socialism:

> Harry Arthur – the socialist, pressed me to come to a meeting he had organized at what was then known as the Rechabites Hall (near the station in Ammanford). I went to the meeting and heard one of the ILP organizers, Herbert Eastwood, speaking on Socialism, and at the close of his address inviting us to join the ILP and form a branch. The address, which was idealistic and spoken with real religious fervour, appealed to me and my pal Tommy Thomas, and we both joined the ILP that evening.[11]

The first occasion the ILP contested a parliamentary seat in Carmarthenshire was in 1910. Dr J. H. Williams, a prominent local politician, was the candidate. He came a distant third and bottom of the poll, receiving just 12.6 per cent of the vote. The defeated Conservative candidate, a local squire, Mervin Peel, won twice the support given to Williams. At the by-election in 1912 he fared even worse and his vote fell to 10.3 per cent of the poll.[12] The party received very little backing from the colliers, but was aided by a group of militant suffragettes, a fact that Jim Griffiths argued partly contributed to the disappointing outcome. These were very inauspicious beginnings at parliamentary level for a party that would dominate the industrial area of the county for most of the twentieth century. At local level however, progress was being made in council elections. In 1913, five of the nine Labour candidates who contested the first election for Llanelli borough council were returned, and one Labour councillor was elected in Carmarthen.

A possible explanation for the reluctance of most workers to wean themselves away from supporting the Liberals was that the Liberal government of 1906–14 had embarked upon a substantive programme of social legislation. Also the period 1910–14 witnessed an eruption of union militancy in south Wales. In Carmarthenshire this culminated in severe riots in Llanelli during the national rail strike of 1911. Two strikers were shot and killed by the army. As news of the deaths spread an enraged crowd attacked the railway yard and four rioters were killed when explosive wagons ignited.[13] The ferocity of the events – looting and destruction by the mob, bayonet charges by the military, shocked the community. Respectable elements among the population may well have resisted the temptation to switch their political allegiances to a party affiliated to the union movement. Old loyalties would not be realigned until after the First World War.

Education

Education in Carmarthenshire for most of the period was a privilege and not a right. The provision that did exist was fairly closely tied to organized religion. In 1750 there was no state involvement in education. Elementary or primary education was mostly provided by charitable organizations. The origin and impact of the Circulating Schools has already been noted. During 1756–7 approximately fifty-three Circulating Schools were held in Carmarthenshire. The movement's leading patron was Madam Bridget Bevan of Laugharne, who continued Griffith Jones's work following his death in 1761. On her death in 1779 she left her estate of £10,000 to endow the schools. The bequest was challenged by her trustees and the funds were effectively frozen until 1804. The Madam Bevan Trust eventually came into existence in 1807 with a capital sum that had grown to £30,000. It continued to support the educational needs of the disadvantaged until 1854.

The effective end of the Circulating Schools in 1779 created a huge void in the provision of education. This was partly filled in the years after 1785 with the emergence of the Sunday School movement. Thomas Charles, who had been born in the parish of Llanfihangel Abercywyn in 1755 was the driving force behind this movement in Wales. These schools, which were immensely popular with pupils of all ages, were initially the preserve of Nonconformists, but were later adopted by the Anglican Church. Competition for members between the Anglican Church and the Nonconformists added a clear stimulus to the need to provide schools. People's desire for self-betterment through education drew them to schools irrespective of who was organizing them. The forays of both church and chapel into the educational field were regularized with the establishment of two voluntary societies – the Anglican National Society for the Education of the Poor (founded in 1811) and the Nonconformist British and Foreign Schools Society (founded in 1814). In the following half century they established a number of schools across the county. National schools were opened at Llanelli (1827), Abergwili (1834), and Marros (1840). Despite the strength of Nonconformity in the county the British Society was much less active than its church counterpart. To counter the shortage of teachers both societies used the monitorial system, where a teacher instructed the oldest pupils who would then teach the same lesson to the younger ones. The curriculum of each society was heavily weighted in favour of studying the Bible.

In addition to the initiatives of organized religion there were a number of other providers of elementary education in Carmarthenshire in the early part of the nineteenth century. First there were the 'dame schools'. These were privately run 'schools' which in most instances 'minded' children for a small fee while the parents worked. No formal training was required of the teachers – frequently elderly women – and any instruction which might be given was a bonus. The second group were 'works schools' set up by industrialists to educate the children of their workforce. Workers paid for the privilege through deductions from their pay. Industrialists benefited through having a more educated labour force. The outstanding example in Carmarthenshire was the Heol-fawr Copper-works school in Llanelli which was set up by R. J. Nevill in 1847. This developed from an older institution, the Llanelli Free School, also promoted by the Nevills. In 1818 the school had fifty-nine pupils although the average attendance at any one time was twenty-eight. It catered for the children of copper-workers and colliers. A copper-works school for the Mason and Elkington company was opened at Pen-bre in 1855. Older children paid 2d a week, infants 1d. Where a workman earned less than a £1 a week his children were educated free of charge. Other industrial schools were attached to tinworks at Carmarthen (fl.1844), Dafen (1850), New Dock

(1866) and Hendy (1885), and a chemical works at Pontamman near Ammanford. The final group were schools attached to the workhouses set up following the 1834 Act. These were opened at Carmarthen (1839), Llanelli (1840), Llandeilo (1840), Newcastle Emlyn (1842) and Llandovery (1844).

The provision of elementary education was very patchy. Government involvement in education started in 1833 when the Whigs granted £20,000 to be divided equally between the National and British Societies. Concern over illiteracy in Wales led to the production of the most notorious government report on Wales ever published. The infamy of the Education Report of 1847 is enshrined in our national consciousness. It was popularly labelled *Brad y Llyfrau Gleision* (the 'Treason of the Blue Books').

Its origins stemmed from a genuine concern about the lack of access to education among ordinary people, and the social impact this was having. The catalyst for the report was pressure from the member of parliament for Coventry, William Williams, who was born in the parish of Llanpumsaint. With recent events (the Rebecca Riots) in his native county clearly in mind, Williams told the House of Commons in 1846 that: 'An ill-educated and undisciplined population is one that may be found dangerous to the neighbourhood in which it dwells and that a band of efficient schoolmasters is kept up at much less expense than a body of police.' He urged the government to investigate the true state of educational provision in Wales.

The inquiry was undertaken by three Anglican barristers from England, with no knowledge of the Welsh language. Their report was a watershed in the history of nineteenth-century Wales. Its damning indictments on the morality of the Welsh ('savage in manner') and the status of its language ('distorts truth and favours fraud') were devastating and nothing short of libelous. The storm of controversy aroused by the report masked the very real issue that educational provision for ordinary people was at best erratic, and at worst deficient on a vast scale. It succeeded in uniting church and chapel in condemning its observations and galvanized them into renewed efforts through their voluntary societies to expand school provision.

The report on Carmarthenshire recorded a total of 179 day schools and 309 Sunday schools active within the county. The number of pupils attending day schools was 7,191 – 6.7 per cent of the population. Figures for those attending Sunday schools were however much higher, at 27,148 pupils. Significantly the breakdown of these figures showed that 24,371 pupils attended Nonconformist Sunday schools while only 2,777 went to those provided by the church. The overwhelming majority of the schools listed in the report had been founded in the thirty years before the inquiry. Only eleven of the schools were eighteenth-century creations. The oldest listed day-school was Vaughan's Charity school in Llangynog, founded in 1705. There were fifteen parishes in Carmarthenshire with no day-school provision at all in 1847. Those who visited the schools not only reported on the buildings and numbers but also conducted impromptu tests on the children. While frequently recording levels of crushing poverty, their observations were occasionally less than impartial. Enoch James vicar of Llandysul who examined Llanfihangel-ar-arth had this to report on the parish:

> Mrs Bevan's school left the parish in September 1846. Not a quarter of the children are attending any day-school at present. The attendance upon Mrs Bevan's school amounted to 80 or 90. The Dissenters availed themselves of it without scruple. The labourers are very ill off, and utterly unable to maintain a school for themselves. Even 2*s.* or 2*s.*6*d.* per quarter would exceed their means. Wages are not more than 10*d.* per day. Their misery is extreme. As far as they can manage it they are anxious to send their children to school. But for the Sunday Schools there would have been no education of the poor at all.[14]

Although the number of voluntary schools increased after 1847 there remained many areas of the country which had no access to education. In 1870 the government sought to rectify this situation by passing the School Boards Act. Locally constituted school-boards could raise rates to build and maintain undenominational schools. The schools were managed by boards elected by men and women. Among the new schools opened under the terms of the act were those in Llan-non (1873) and Kidwelly Hillfield Girls School (1887).

If opportunities for elementary education were limited then this was even more true for intermediate or secondary education. Only the very privileged received a secondary school education. In the main this was reserved for the sons of the gentry. Richer families sent their sons away to established public schools in England. Daughters of the gentry would be educated at home by governesses. Three loose categories of intermediate schools can be identified. First, schools based on the 'public school' model – fee paying and delivering a classical education based on Latin and Greek. In 1750 there was only one school in the county in this category, Queen Elizabeth Grammar School for boys in Carmarthen. The school was founded during the reign of Queen Elizabeth I in 1576 and was supported by church patronage. In 1847 the financial support of Thomas Phillips helped establish Llandovery College. The second category were dissenting academies. State discrimination against Nonconformists led them to establish on an *ad hoc* basis their own secondary schools. These were frequently much more enlightened than the grammar schools and focused on the sciences and mathematics in addition to the arts. Among the best known in the county was the Ffrwd-fâl Academy near Llansawel which was run by Dr William Davies. It catered for a small number of pupils who boarded in local farms. Although there were only thirty-four students on the register in 1846, demand for places in the school according to the 1847 Report was considerable. It prepared some students for Glasgow or London universities and others for careers requiring advanced knowledge of mathematics. The final category was the private venture schools, whose quality was rather variable. Some of these catered exclusively for girls such as the school at Laugharne which had sixteen pupils in 1880, nine of whom were boarders. The school catered for farmers' daughters and charged fees of £21 for boarders and £4 4s for day-scholars.

Concern over the lack of provision of secondary education in Wales during the late Victorian era led to the setting up of another educational commission, under the chairmanship of Lord Aberdare. Viscount Emlyn was one of the commissioners. Fears that it would replicate the injustice visited upon Wales by the 1847 report proved unfounded. The report noted a total of sixteen schools providing some form of secondary education within the county. A recent foundation was the Emlyn Grammar School, opened in Newcastle Emlyn in 1867. One of its alumni was Evan Roberts, the inspirational force behind the 1904–5 revival. With the exception of Llandovery College, none of the schools was in very robust health. Carmarthen Grammar School was described in 1880 as 'not very flourishing'.

The published recommendations urged the setting up of a system of intermediate schools. There was a delay before the recommendations were enacted, by the Welsh Intermediate Schools Act of 1889. A network of county schools emerged over the next decade or so. In Carmarthen the existing Queen Elizabeth Grammar School became a boys' school under the county scheme in 1895 along with the creation of a separate school for girls. The debate in Llanelli led to the establishment of a higher grade school in addition to a county school for boys and one for girls (1895). Llandeilo County School (1894) was originally for boys while the one in Llandovery (1896) was for girls. The largely rural nature of the catchment areas meant that they became dual schools very soon after their opening. Whitland and Llandysul county schools were shared with Pembrokeshire and Cardiganshire respectively. In 1914 in recognition of its rapid development a county school was opened in the Amman valley at Ammanford. The last of these admired and much loved schools to be established was in the Gwendraeth Valley in 1925. Initially these were fee-paying schools which offered a classical curriculum modelled on that of the English public school system. Gradually they offered scholarships to children whose parents were unable to afford the fees. The children who did not gain a coveted place in these new schools either remained in their elementary schools or they could transfer to a higher grade school such as the one opened in Llanelli in 1891. These higher grade schools provided an education with a vocational orientation – commerce, crafts and technical studies. While they were viewed by many as the poorer brethren in the state education system they provided many children with opportunities denied to their parents and they did help launch many a distinguished career.

The cause of higher education was rather better served than that of the elementary and intermediate sectors. Although there was no university provision in Wales until the opening of the college at Aberystwyth in 1872 there were developments in the higher sector. These developments were very closely linked to religion. Two distinct colleges were established in the town of Carmarthen. The oldest by far was the Presbyterian College which moved to the town in 1704. It can lay claim to being the oldest higher education institution in Wales. Over the course of the next century it taught a rather ambitious curriculum which included in addition to classics and theology, logic, mathematics, astronomy, natural sciences and conics. Although it was unable to grant degrees its work was at that level. The academy took students from a variety of denominations including the established Church. Many of its ideas challenged conventional orthodoxy. Thomas Perrott one of its masters was an Arminian, while Samuel Thomas was accused of Pelagianism. This was almost inevitable given the undenominational and progressive character of the college.

Increasing activity by the National Society was the spur for the creation of Carmarthen's second seat of higher learning. The National Society had from the outset been acutely aware of the need for a properly trained teaching profession to work in its schools. Initially its trainee teachers were sent to a training centre in Westminster. As the number of national schools in Wales increased, there were sustained calls to set up a locally based training college. Plans were laid for a college in Carmarthen and over £5,000 was collected. The Revd William Reed was appointed the first principal and the foundation stone for Trinity College was laid in 1847. Sixty students were admitted in 1848 when the college opened. Demand soon exceeded supply and student numbers were increased to a hundred and sixty.

A more disparate area of education was that of technical instruction. This sector was essential in facilitating and maintaining the economic and commercial progress made during the period. A mechanics' institute was opened in Llanelli in 1840 to provide evening classes in a range of scientific, technical and commercial subjects. The School of Art which had been opened in Carmarthen in 1854 provided instruction in technical drawing and building construction in addition to ceramic painting and design. Demand for places at the art school increased and exceeded the space available. New premises were opened in 1892 at Church lane, following a successful public subscription. A Technical Instruction Act was passed in 1889 and the county set up a committee to coordinate its response. A wide variety of courses was provided. Peripatetic lecturers visited local communities. The courses were specifically targeted to their perceived needs. Dairy schools were held in Llanybydder and Newcastle Emlyn in 1893–4. A lecturer in dyeing held classes in Carmarthen, Llanegwad, Llandybïe, Betws, Pencader and Pen-boyr. One of the more unusual initiatives was the acquisition of a mobile shoeing van in 1895 to tour around rural areas providing instruction for blacksmiths and farmers. In addition to the peripatetic classes the higher grade school at Coleshill in Llanelli which was opened in 1891, had been equipped with laboratories and provided evening classes in practical science and hygiene.

Religion

(a) The established Church

The condition of the Anglican Church in Carmarthenshire in 1750 was of an eminent and powerful institution in the throes of crisis. This was a protracted crisis shared with other counties making up the diocese of St Davids. The problems stemmed from the top down to parish level. St Davids was a poor diocese which by the middle of the eighteenth century was considered little more than a stepping-stone for ambitious bishops on their way to more lucrative and prestigious sees in England. Seventeen Englishmen were appointed bishops of St Davids during the eighteenth century. Many spent very little time at the bishop's palace at Abergwili and made no effort to understand their clergy or the needs of their flocks. Added to their absenteeism was a distinct lack of sympathy for the Welsh language, which in the more rural parts of the county was the only language spoken.

At parish level church buildings were falling into disrepair and the income from livings was pitifully small. Many parishes were combined with one vicar ministering to large scattered congregations. Not surprisingly the quality of ordinands was frequently low. Among the universal gloom there were a few beacons. Griffith Jones in Llanddowror was an inspirational preacher, organizer and enthusiast who made many new converts. The appointment of Anthony Ellis as bishop of St Davids in

1753 marked the slow recovery of the fortunes of the Church. Thomas Eynon, vicar of Llangynnwr was his commissioner. He was active in helping to improve the quality of ordinands. Many Oxford-educated men entered the church during this period. Two of the most eminent national figures in the revival of religion during the second half of the eighteenth century were born in Carmarthenshire. William Williams of Pantycelyn near Llandovery was ordained as a curate but was not given his own parish because he was considered to be too close to the Methodists. Thomas Charles was similarly overlooked within the church because of his suspect connections. Both would play central roles in the Methodist revival.

One of the outstanding bishops of this period who more than any other revived the fortunes of the church was Thomas Burgess (1803–25). Burgess was passionately committed to educational causes. After only a year in the diocese he set up a Christian Knowledge and Church Union Society (1804) and raised funds to provide scholarships to local grammar schools for candidates to the ministry. Among his other innovations was the provision of books and encouraging the creation of parish libraries. His greatest and most enduring legacy was to help found St David's College Lampeter, to train young men for the Anglican ministry.

Connop Thirwall, who was appointed Bishop of St Davids in 1840 continued further the work undertaken by Burgess. Thirwall was keen to dispel the notion that the Anglican Church was an alien institution foisted on Wales by the English state. The long tradition of Anglicization was clearly abandoned. Thirwall encouraged the use of the Welsh language in sermons and during services. He himself learnt Welsh and both preached and confirmed in his adopted language.

An accusation frequently made against the Church during the first half of the nineteenth century was that it was slow to respond to people's needs as society was changing. The dramatic increase in population and its redistribution within the county required a clear response from the church authorities. Moreover the dynamic growth of Nonconformity and its sustained chapel-building programme during the first half of the nineteenth century was in sharp contrast to the relative torpor of the Church, many of whose buildings were in disrepair. Thirwall started the process of creating new parishes in the industrial areas of the county. By 1900 there were new parishes in Llanelli (St Paul's and Christ Church), Carmarthen (St David's), Felin-foel, Dafen, Brynaman, Ammanford, Gorslas and Pontiets. A massive building and renovation programme covering all the churches in the county was launched. Much of the work up to 1870 was undertaken by the architect R. K Penson. Many crumbling medieval interiors were gutted and made over in the gothic style fashionable at the time. A more sensitive approach might, with hindsight, have preserved many fine features for posterity. Fifteen new churches were consecrated, while over thirty were rebuilt entirely. National Schools were built in many parishes. Despite the best efforts of such enlightened clerics as Burgess and Thirwall it is difficult to avoid the conclusion that the church was reacting to change rather than orchestrating it.

(b) Nonconformity and the Methodist Revival.

The rather moribund state of the Anglican Church in the middle of the eighteenth century was a cause of real concern to some of its more committed and enthusiastic members. Building on the evangelical tradition of Griffith Jones their concern was often translated into action. Carmarthenshire occupies an important place in the great religious awakening that took place during the eighteenth century. The Welsh revival started in 1735 at Trevecca with the conversion of Howell Harris. One of the oldest Methodist meeting-houses in Wales was Soar, in Cil-y-cwm, founded in 1740. William Williams, Pantycelyn (1717–91) soon joined Harris in preaching renewal and rekindling the embers of religion. They established close links with the leaders of English Methodism. John Wesley visited Carmarthenshire for the first time in August 1763 and returned to the county periodically until 1790. Some of the associations closely identified with his views (Wesleyan Methodists) while the majority of associations were Calvinistic Methodists. The early Methodists wished to remain part of the Anglican Church and to revive it from within. Many vicars were deeply suspicious of these committed and enthusiastic young men, and made life within the Anglican Church increasingly difficult for them. Peter Williams (1723–96) the celebrated author and biblical commentator from Llansadyrnin was refused holy orders because of his Methodism. William Williams was also refused ordination. 'Pantycelyn' as he became universally known blossomed into the chief hymn-writer of the movement.

The organizational heart of the Methodist movement was the *seiat* which was created by Harris. *Seiadau* aimed to bind the followers closer together by providing mutual spiritual support. There were seventy-one of these groups in existence in Carmarthenshire in 1750. Anglican clergy who were committed Methodists were much in demand and visited the various associations, preaching and conducting services. In the early nineteenth century Thomas Charles (then living in Y Bala) had emerged as the leading figure in the Methodist movement. He was reluctant to secede from the Anglican Church but the need to ordain ministers who were Methodists led to the long-deferred decision to leave. Thirteen candidates were ordained at Llandeilo in 1811. A new Nonconformist denomination had been born. Despite Methodism's undoubted contribution to renewing Christian values it was never as numerous as the older Nonconformist denominations in Carmarthenshire.

Methodism and its revival of interest in religion added a spur to the expansion of the older Nonconformist denominations, such as the Baptists and the Independents. Estimates of the numbers of adherents during the late eighteenth century are fraught with difficulties owing to the lack of precise figures. The *Baptist Register* in 1794 records 1,907 members in the county. Evan Griffiths, an Independent minister, estimated that there were 9,000 members in 1774. Prospective Independent and Presbyterian candidates for the ministry were able from the mid-eighteenth century to study at the Presbyterian Academy in Carmarthen. In the early nineteenth century the older dissenting churches were much more socially conscious and politically radical than the more conservative Methodists. David Rees (1801–69) from Tre-lech, a Congregational minister at Capel Als, Llanelli was the owner editor of the radical periodical *Y Diwygiwr* (The Reformer). With the economic development of south-east Carmarthenshire gaining pace during the first half of the nineteenth century, the Nonconformists, particularly the Independents, were quick to capitalize on the opportunities for ministering to the spiritual needs of the new communities. During this period in Wales a chapel was being opened on average every eight days. Nonconformity was fast outstripping the Church in providing new places of worship in locations best placed to serve the emerging communities.

Evidence of the religious profile of Carmarthenshire during the middle of the nineteenth century can be gained from the religious census of 1851. All places of worship were required to file returns indicating the number of people who could be accommodated and the numbers worshipping (morning, afternoon and evening) on 30 March, census Sunday. Its report clearly maps out the dominant position which the Nonconformists had established over the Anglican Church in Carmarthenshire. Within the registration county the total number of sittings provided by the 298 churches and chapels enumerated indicated that 88 per cent of the total population could be accommodated if they so wished. The seventy-nine Anglican churches in the registration county were dwarfed by the 215 Nonconformist chapels (there were in addition one Catholic and three Mormon churches). More revealing are the attendance figures for morning worship. These showed that 8,685 (23 per cent) people worshipped at an Anglican church while 28,357 (77 per cent) attended a chapel. While the ascendancy of Nonconformity was clearly shown, of equal significance is the fact that only 39 per cent of the total population of Carmarthenshire attended a church or chapel on census Sunday 1851. While Nonconformity was establishing a commanding presence over people's spiritual needs, society bore the clear imprint of secularization. Some denominations by the 1890s were reflecting carefully on whether their earlier successes had bred a sense of complacency. Their emphasis on respectability, temperance and Liberalism was possibly out of step with many of the inhabitants of the expanding urban communities.

Statistics for Carmarthenshire compiled by the *Nonconformist*, for submission to the *Royal Commission on the Church of England in Wales and Monmouthshire* (1910) showed further continuous growth in Nonconformity. The figures list a total of 414 Chapels which between them could offer sittings for 130,419 worshippers. While the capacity of the chapels had increased markedly, the estimated number of members as opposed to communicants was given as 27,173. Chapels had almost doubled while numbers of worshippers had declined. It is difficult not to conclude that Nonconformity in Carmarthenshire was at best stagnant, at worst on the brink of crisis. These figures were compiled in 1905, a year after the start of the last significant religious revival in west Wales. Enthused with an infusion of spirituality the number of converts increased. Some local rugby teams such as those at Ammanford and Llandybïe disbanded for the duration of the revival. The Apostolic Church with its headquarters at Pen-y-groes developed from this revival.

Culture

Many of the published works produced in Carmarthenshire were in Welsh. This in many ways reflected the status of Welsh as the vernacular language in the county. A sense of its ascendancy can be gained from data collected by E. G. Ravenstein for his *Celtic Languages of the British Isles: A statistical Survey* (1879). Out of a population of 115,710 in 1871 93.1 per cent (108,720) were able to speak Welsh. Remarkably a total of 37,800 could speak only Welsh. Welsh was the preferred language of leisure and learning, of play and prayer. It had survived tenaciously repressive penal laws and anti-Welsh educational initiatives such as the 'Welsh Not'. A leading pioneer in promoting the teaching of Welsh in schools and of bilingualism, was Llandovery-born Dan Isaac Davies (1839–87). He was one of the founders of the 'Society for the Utilisation of the Welsh Language' (1885), and used his position as a school inspector to encourage the teaching of Welsh.

Much of the literary output of this period is indebted in one way or another to the Church and Nonconformity. It is a tribute to the enduring legacy of William Williams Pantycelyn's genius that his hymns '*Iesu, Iesu rwyt ti'n ddigon*' and 'Guide me Oh thou great Jehovah' continue to stir audiences in the new millennium much as they did in the old. David

Charles (1762–1834) from Llanfihangel Abercywyn less well known than his elder brother Thomas, was the author of two much loved Welsh hymns – 'Rhagluniaeth fawr y nef' (Great providence of Heaven) and 'O fryniau Caersalem' (From the hills of Jerusalem). Increasing literacy combined with renewed interest in religion led to the publishing of Welsh-language religious periodicals. *Y Diwygiwr* (1835) was the Llanelli based radical campaigning periodical, edited by David Rees. Its motto was 'Agitate, Agitate, Agitate'. In the north of the county *Yr Haul* was published to serve the needs of the Anglican Church by the Llandovery printer and publisher William Rees owner of the Ton press. It was edited by David Owen (Brutus, 1795–1866) one of the most remarkable Welsh journalists and satirists of the century. His cutting invective won him praise and criticism in almost equal measure; in particular he lambasted his former Nonconformist associates mercilessly.

A further boost to the cultural life of the county was the revival of the eisteddfod. Bishop Burgess played a prominent part in supporting attempts to revive a national eisteddfod. The Carmarthen eisteddfod of 1819 was important because of the introduction by Iolo Morganwg (Edward Williams) of the *gorsedd* of the bards to the musical and literary festival. This fusion of tradition and culture became an integral part of the eisteddfod, and has remained largely intact down to the present day. Part of the first *gorsedd* ceremony, with the stone circle, took place in the garden of the Ivy Bush Hotel in Spilman Street. By the end of the nineteenth century it was common for towns, villages and even chapels to hold their own eisteddfodau. Competing in eisteddfodau provided an early opportunity for the young Brinley Richards (1817–85), from Carmarthen, to hone his considerable musical talents. He is perhaps best known for writing the music to the anthem 'God Bless the Prince of Wales' (1862). One of Carmarthenshire's most successful nineteenth-century *eisteddfodwyr* Watkin Hezekiah Williams (1844–1905) is more readily identified by his bardic name – Watcyn Wyn. Although his educational work at Ysgol y Gwynfryn tends to overshadow his poetry, during his lifetime he acquired a formidable reputation as a bard, winning both the crown (Merthyr, 1881) and chair (Aberdare, 1885) at national Eisteddfodau. An equally important figure from the neighbouring parish of Llandybïe was Thomas Matthews (1874–1916). Nowadays a largely forgotten and neglected figure, his contribution to the cultural life of Wales before the First World War was remarkable. An enthusiastic and visionary pan-Celtic nationalist, his main interests were the preservation and publication of early Welsh records, and with almost missionary zeal in the pages of *Cymru* he promoted the aesthetics of Welsh art particularly for use in schools.[15]

The visual arts are well represented in the county during this period. While its topography is not as spectacular as that of Snowdonia it attracted some of the most celebrated artists of the period. J. M.W. Turner visited Carmarthenshire twice, in 1795 and 1798. There were few professional artists resident within the county. John Lewis, a portrait and landscape painter, known to have worked throughout Wales but also based in Dublin and London, was resident in the county during the 1740s when he is known to have executed portraits of the Vaughans of Derllys, the Lloyds of Derwydd, and his well known portrait of Madame Bridget Bevan, supporter of the Circulating Schools. In 1785 the architect John Nash, a discharged bankrupt in the throes of an acrimonious divorce, arrived in Carmarthen. Over the next decade he reestablished his career and undertook several commissions in the county, most notably the redesign of Carmarthen Gaol and Llysnewydd Villa. The increasing affluence of Carmarthen provided opportunities for portrait painters and other craftsmen. David Brigstocke, father of Thomas, was a successful interior decorator based in the town. Stephen Poletti, a well known Italian ornamental plasterer, set up a business in Carmarthen. High quality furniture was made at the Carmarthen factory (*c*.1820–40) of David Morley. Hugh Hughes lived and worked in the town between 1822–27, and his portrait of the family of John Evans at breakfast has been described by Peter Lord as 'one of the highpoints of nineteenth-century Welsh painting'.[16] Thomas Brigstocke (1809–81) was born in King Street, Carmarthen, and after travelling widely on the continent and Egypt he established a successful career painting portraits of local worthies, military figures and Egyptian dignitaries. Gentry patronage helped sustain many artists. Some were extremely talented artists in their own right, such as Charles William Mansel Lewis (1845–1931) of Stradey Castle. He was a passionate and committed supporter of the arts in his local community, and in 1907 helped found Llanelli Art School. His close friendship with Hubert Herkomer helped support the career of this eminent Victorian artist.

Among the most important professional artists born in the county before 1914 were the portrait painter Carey Morris (1882–1968) from Llandeilo and J. D. Innes (1887–1914) who was born in Llanelli. Both trained at the Slade School of Art in London, although in Innes's case his initial training was undertaken at Carmarthen School of Art. Of the two, it is Innes's work which is now the most acclaimed. Many of his landscapes and later figurative work were clearly influenced and inspired by the Impressionists. His early death robbed Wales of a great talent.

In 1905 The Carmarthenshire Antiquarian and Field Club was formed to encourage the study of the history, archaeology, antiquities and folklore of the county. Among its founders was A. J. Stepney Gulston, a passionate antiquarian and gifted amateur painter.

VI

Industrial Change and Development *c.*1750–1914

Agriculture

For the greater part of its history the economic life of Carmarthenshire has been inextricably linked to farming. The nature of the agriculture practised within the county has in its turn, been linked to Carmarthenshire's topography. 52 per cent of the land in the county lies below 150m., with a further 38 per cent found between 150m. and 300m. The remainder – 10 per cent is above 300m. The fertility of much of the soil is by agricultural standards marginal, with that of the upland areas considered to be poor. Good quality farmland is at a premium and is confined to the larger river valleys and the coastal plain east of the Tywi.

Rural society was ordered very much in a hierarchical structure. The landed class ranged from peers of the realm to yeomen, some resident in the county others absentee. Their estates varied in size but in the main, apart from retaining a home farm for their own domestic purposes, the bulk of their land was rented out to tenants. The tenantry itself was divided between large tenants who employed labourers and small tenants who operated at or below subsistence level. Many of the smaller tenants often worked on an occasional basis for their larger neighbours. Below the tenants were the labourers who were employed by the larger farmers. During the middle of the eighteenth century the rural population was steadily increasing. Some young men, on the eve of marriage erected *tai unnos* (cottages built in one night) on the unenclosed commons surrounding villages and hamlets in the mistaken belief that freehold was acquired. Many communities tolerated these squatters while others reacted violently. Arthur Young noted in 1776 that the population of the countryside around Carmarthen had doubled in thirty years and that most of these people were living in poverty.

The traditional pattern of agriculture in the county was mixed farming – arable, pastoral and dairy. For much of the period under consideration two dominant features that stand out in the agricultural history of the county were its poverty and inherent backwardness. B. H. Malkin, writing in 1804, noted that the villages near the sea coast were frequently beautiful, but that in the north of the county their condition and that of the solitary cottages was the most miserable that could be conceived. He observed that 'the climate and fertility of this county are much celebrated though they are not found to be favourable to wheat. Barley and oats are the most profitable crops.' Regarding livestock he noted that 'the black cattle and horses bred on the hills, fill all the fairs of the neighbouring district and contribute in a great measure to the support of the farmers who depend much on the right of mountain'.[1]

Arable farming was mainly confined to the lower slopes of hills, and the valleys of the larger rivers where the soil was more fertile. The Revd T. Rees, writing in 1815, was effusive in his admiration of Carmarthenshire's farmers who 'may be allowed the merit, such as it is of ranking among the best in Wales'. Rees noted that good crops of barley and oats were produced but unlike Malkin he added that wheat was also grown with great success in several parishes. He singled out in particular Llangyndeyrn, St Clears, Llandybïe and the vale of the Tywi 'wherein it is grown to the most advantage …'.[2] During the French wars (1793–1815) considerable efforts were made to increase domestic cereal production in order to negate Napoleon's economic blockade of Britain.

Following a series of bad harvests during the closing years of the eighteenth century, and the scarcity of food due to the impact of the war, an anxious government sought information regarding the amounts and varieties of domestic crops available in 1801. Each vicar in the county was asked by the bishop to provide information regarding the acreage of various crops grown within his parish. The returns for Carmarthenshire are incomplete as only forty-eight of the seventy-seven parishes provided information. It is unlikely that the returns are very reliable as farmers suspected that the motive behind the survey might be to introduce new taxes for either the church or the state. Given these riders the acreage returns provide an illuminating snapshot of Carmarthenshire's arable farming in the middle of the longest war in modern British history. In line with other observations the dominant cereals produced were oats (19,817 acres) and barley (12,168 acres). Wheat production in the forty-eight parishes totalled 4,915 acres. Of the vegetable crops potatoes (1,111 acres), provided by far the largest acreage followed by peas, turnips and small quantities of beans.

Accompanying the acreage returns were various observations made by the surveyors. The notes inform us that

> The parish of Betws in general is a very poor corn land, and
> cannot at present produce half the bread for the support of the

inhabitants. But ... there are very good corn lands on the common, called Betws mountain. If it was inclosed and well manured
by a person capable of the business, I could venture to undertake there should be plenty for the consumption of the inhabitants and to spare likewise, as I find there was corn growing on
several parts of it some centuries ago.[3]

In Llandeilo Fawr it was noted that 734 acres of wheat produced 8,808
bushels, 1,262 acres of barley produced 25,240 bushels and 1,304 acres of
oats produced 32,600 bushels. The amount of land under cultivation in
Llandeilo Abercywyn was only 25 per cent of what it had been in the
recent past.

The year in which the French war broke out, 1793, also saw the
establishment of the Board of Agriculture. This was a voluntary
organization but it did receive a government grant. In an early report (1794)
it drew attention to the fact that Carmarthenshire's farmers by their practices,
'have impoverished the soil, and the soil, in its turn has impoverished
them'. The practice referred to was that of extracting one crop after another
from the same field until the yield was little more than the seed. The Board
of Agriculture produced an updated report in 1814, *The General View of
Agriculture and Domestic economy of South Wales*, drawn up by Walter
Davies. It noted that the climate was unfavourable for growing wheat with
the exception of the vales, the southern part of the county, and on Laugharne
Marsh. 'Carmarthenshire is perhaps the only county in South Wales that
imports wheat for its consumption.' Barley was more successful and
produced greater yields but it was 'generally ill-coloured'. One area was
singled out for comment: 'On the Newcastle Emlyn, or Teivy side of the
range of hills which divides the Vales of the Towy and Teivy, there is less
rain than in the vale of Towy and the soil is better calculated for barley and
turnips than any other part of Carmarthenshire.'[4]

The report proposed a number of ways of improving farming within
the county: enclosure of common land, the adoption of new farming
methods such as crop rotations and the introduction of new implements.
Enclosure of land in southern England involved parcelling out among
the farmers of a community the arable land in the open fields and the
common grazing land. In Carmarthenshire, enclosure almost exclusively
meant land which was termed 'waste' – uncultivated land. The 1814
report spelt out quite clearly the advantages of enclosure – a rise in the
value of the land (double its original value), the fences benefiting the
land by giving it shelter, 'the husbandman manures with a certainty of
reaping the fruit of his labour, and the produce of the stock are consequently
improved at least a twofold degree'. Yet there was also a downside to the
proposals. Enclosure could be achieved by two methods – common

consent or act of parliament. While the former method incurred few costs, the latter could be enormously expensive. The necessity of obtaining individual acts of parliament for each parish scheme was very costly. Smaller farmers who were unable to meet the cost frequently had to sell their land and become landless labourers. Cottagers and those with right to use the commons also lost out. In each scheme the lord of the manor obtained his share, usually between one-twentieth and one-fourteenth of the enclosed land.

During the French wars the pace of enclosure accelerated and many acts were passed, for example in St Clears 1807 (280 acres), Llanelli 1808 (400 acres), Llansadwrn 1809 (1,500 acres), Llandybïe and Llanarthne 1811 (4,700 acres). In 1795 it was estimated that the total amount of common and waste land which was unenclosed amounted to 170,666 acres. 33,813 acres of this total had been enclosed by 1885. Enclosure allowed enterprising farmers and landowners to introduce new methods. The most important of these were selective breeding to improve the livestock and crop rotation. While the standard method of crop rotation was a variant of the Norfolk four-course rotation, Walter Davies noted another method being trialled in Llangennech. A five-course system was used involving the rotation of barley, clover, peas, wheat and turnips. Rotating the clover and peas with the two cereals and turnips meant that the fertility of the soil could be maintained and sufficient winter fodder provided for the livestock. Unfortunately the practice does not appear to have been widely used. Few of the county's landlords were innovators who were prepared to experiment with new methods and actively encourage their tenant to embrace them. This is perhaps most clearly seen in the antiquated implements used and the inefficient practices perpetuated. Although carts were common many farmers preferred the less efficient sledge. Arable farmers in the county in the early nineteenth century used the heavy and cumbersome 'Welsh' plough despite the best counsels of their landlords. Occasionally when innovations were introduced estate-workers were reluctant to adopt them. Disputes frequently arose between landlord and servants. When, in 1815, H. Lewis of Gallt-y-Gog near Carmarthen introduced a short whip-rein plough onto his estate he was compelled to lock up his old ploughs so that the farm-servants did not have access to them.[5] Threshing of corn was still done by flail rather than by machine well into the nineteenth century. An exception to this trend was John Vaughan of Golden Grove the largest landowner in the county. Under his patronage a county agricultural society was founded in 1790. It distributed premiums to the value of £300 to innovative farmers.

One of the main reasons for the backwardness and poverty of agriculture in the county was the almost total reliance placed upon lime as a fertilizer. Given that much of the county consisted of hills subjected to heavy rainfall where the lime was needed to neutralize the acidic soil, its use as a fertilizer is perhaps understandable. The over-reliance for both arable and pasture was at the expense of other fertilizers such as manure. Between 1750 and 1850 along the northern rim of the coalfield where the carboniferous limestone outcrops occurred there developed a thriving industry to service the demand for lime. There were kilns dotted across the centre of the county from Llangadog and the slopes of the Black Mountain to St Clears. The heart of the industry was in the parish of Llandybïe. During the summer months long lines of horses and carts would gather along the turnpike roads at midnight for the journey to the kilns. They hoped to complete the round trip within twenty-four hours, or they would have to pay the toll again.

Carmarthenshire was well known for its livestock production – cattle, sheep and horses. In general sheep were reared in the upland areas in the north and north-east of the county, but some of the finest were reared around Kidwelly marshes. They produced the large quantities of wool necessary for an industry which could claim to span the rural/industrial divide, namely the production of woollen cloth. In the pre-industrial economy the production of meat and its dispatch to urban markets gave rise to the drovers. These tough independent minded men were regular visitors to the county where they bought cattle and pigs. Herds of animals were driven to marts in England along well-established routes which traversed the county. Villages such as Llansawel grew as centres to service the needs of drovers. Many of the cattle were the celebrated 'Welsh Blacks' ideally suited to the hilly terrain of the county. The sale of livestock to drovers was one of the main ways by which tenant-farmers were able to pay their rent. A ready market for butter and cheese was found in the industrial area around Merthyr. The opening of the south Wales coalfield and the creation of a railway network in the 1850s expanded this important source of farm income. Casks of salted butter and cheese were sent to these areas and also to Bristol. 'Sir Gâr' butter remains a well known local brand name.

Life for most tenant-farmers was very difficult and was accentuated by a number of factors. Between 1750 and 1851 it is estimated that the population of the county nearly doubled. As farming was the main source of employment enormous pressure was placed on the demand for farms. Competition for farms led landlords to reduce the length of leases to their tenants from those based on a number of lives, to a single life then a fixed term and finally an annual tenancy. This reduction caused insecurity for the tenant but greater flexibility for the landlord regarding rents. As life leases came to an end they were not renewed. By the 1840s there were no life leases on the Dynevor estate. Farm incomes were also being squeezed in the 1830s and 1840s by a range of taxes and charges of which tolls, rates and the tithe were the most despised.

Some smaller farmers, in order to make ends meet, worked the odd day here and there as agricultural workers on the larger farms of their neighbours. The role of the farmers' wives was central to maintaining the solvency of the farm. Besides their role in household management and child-rearing they frequently spun yarn and wove cloth to supplement the household budget. They also doubled up as dairy maids for producing butter and cheese. Some respite from this hardship appeared with the development of coal-mining and the metal industries in the southeast of the county. The accessibility of these areas even from the remotest parts of the county was made possible with the opening of the railways in the middle of the nineteenth century. Towards the end of the nineteenth century, some farmers and their sons became migrant workers, seeking work in the coal mines of the Aman and Gwendraeth valleys, lodging during the week, returning home at weekends. Such arrangements were only possible because of the support of the women in maintaining the farms.

The problems which continued to beset agriculture during the first half of the nineteenth century remained well into the second half. In 1843 the average rental for an acre of land was 12s 6d per annum. By the 1860s this had increased in many places by 50 per cent. With the general crisis in British farming in the last quarter of the nineteenth century rentals did decline as did wages and farm incomes. In Llangeler and Pen-boyr (which at one time was known as the garden of 'Sir Gâr') farm-servants who lived on the farm were paid between £10 and £20 per annum with maids receiving £6 to £14. Board and lodging was provided by the farmer. Farm labourers received a daily wage of 1s 6d with meals, 2*s* 6d without. The rates for craftsmen – stone masons, thatchers, etc. were between 3s and 4s per day and sometimes as high as 5s.[6] Compared with farm wages those paid to industrial workers and colliers were significantly higher. A Royal Commission on Land in Wales and Monmouthshire was set up by the Liberal government in 1893 to investigate problems in the countryside. During hearings in Carmarthenshire in 1894 evidence was taken from many tenant-farmers. Typical of these was Nathaniel Williams who farmed Talardd near Llandeilo. His detailed presentation crystallized the problems felt by this beleaguered group namely, insecurity of tenure, no compensation for improvements made to a property by a tenant, when he/she left, an inability to cull any game damaging crops, and illegal enclosures of common land. These economic problems were further accentuated by differences in religion, language and politics. Nathaniel Williams pointed out that one of the most visible symptoms of the agricultural crisis in his area was that 'labourers leave the land and crowd to the works and the towns.

In the hamlet of Gwynfe over fifty houses that were inhabited forty five years ago are now in ruins.'[7] Official figures support this view. According to census returns the number of men in the county engaged in agriculture fell between 1851 and 1891 by 38 per cent. The corresponding decline for women employed in farming was 68 per cent. Those who remained very often lived in considerable poverty in houses and buildings that were deteriorating through lack of repairs and neglect.

The Woollen Industry

Closely allied to agriculture is the woollen industry. Carmarthenshire had a number of advantages that facilitated the growth and development of this industry. Sheep farming was the main pastoral activity in the upland areas of the county. An abundance of good pasture at lower elevations ensured proper winter grazing, as animals were removed from their summer grazing (*yr hafod*) on the hills to the shelter of the valleys (*yr hendre*). With the exception of the areas flanking the coalfields where limestone outcrops occur, most of the water in the county is soft and ideal for the fulling and dyeing of wool. Fast flowing streams in the north of the county provided plenty of locations for water-powered mills.

Many references occur in local records before 1750 to textile workers operating in the county. There were weavers working in Llanelli (1745), Laugharne (1738), Llandybïe (1746) and Pen-bre (1705). In 1750 the industry was organized along domestic lines. Most textile workers worked part-time either to supply the needs of their own families or to supplement the income of their farms. The machinery they used were handlooms and domestic spinning wheels. Agricultural societies encouraged both spinning and weaving and offered premiums for the best yarn and cloth. Cloth was taken to fulling mills for finishing. Local records refer to the existence of *pandai* (fulling mills) in many areas of the county. In the middle of the seventeenth century there were fulling mills at Glyncothi, Abergorlech, Llangennech, Kidwelly and Carmarthen. Surplus cloth was taken to the local markets and the one at Meidrim became well known for its woollen products.

During the course of the nineteenth century the most important woollen producing area in Wales was established along the banks of the Teifi in the parishes of Llangeler and Pen-boyr. So dramatic was the growth in this area which centered around the communities of Dre-fach and Felindre that it was compared favourably with the West Riding of Yorkshire, and was nicknamed the 'Welsh Huddersfield'. The first weaver recorded in the area was Isaac Griffiths (1650). Over the course of the next century and a half the industry became firmly established and slowly expanded.

A *pandy* was established at Pentre-cwrt in the parish of Llangeler in 1698 and others followed at Felindre on Nant Brân, Cwm-pen-graig on Nant Esger and Dolwïon on Nant Bargoed. These fast flowing streams were ideal for powering the mills and cleaning and scouring the raw wool. During the first half of the nineteenth century the industry was still organized along domestic lines, both spinning and weaving were done by hand. Some innovations and changes were being slowly introduced. A water-driven scribbler carder was installed at the fulling mill at Cwm-pen-graig in the first decade of the nineteenth century. In 1820 a carding machine was introduced into the Dolwïon *pandy*. The gradual introduction of carding and spinning machines rendered hand-spinners superfluous. According to the 1841 census there were 328 weavers, 680 tailors and 106 woollen manufacturers in the county. Many of these were located in Llangeler and Pen-boyr.

This slow process of mechanization appears to have accelerated after 1850. Powerlooms were introduced and as J. Geraint Jenkins, historian of the industry notes, 'The region entered a period of unprecedented prosperity, but a prosperity that was to last no more than sixty years.'[8] Why this dramatic expansion? A number of factors explain this sudden growth. The area was close to the rapidly expanding industrial areas of the south Wales coalfield, where the traditional flannel shirts, socks and undergarments were very much in demand by colliers and industrial workers. The arrival of the railway at Pencader in 1864 and Newcastle Emlyn in 1895 opened up the area and provided a much-needed fillip for the industry. A final factor was ample local supplies of high quality wool.

Such was the pace of expansion in the area that by 1898 there were nineteen factories specializing in weaving in the parishes of Llangeler and Pen-boyr. It is estimated that 260 male weavers and the same number of women and children were employed in the two parishes. Three of these factories were operated by women. In 1899 it was remarked that there was hardly a location on the banks of the rivers in the two parishes where it was possible to build an additional mill or factory. As the industry expanded there was a notable improvement in the prosperity of the north Carmarthenshire communities. New houses replaced the insanitary and unhealthy thatch-roofed cottages. Similar developments took place elsewhere. The Cwmllwchwr mill near Ammanford was opened in 1871 as the coal industry in the area was starting to expand.

Labour relations within the industry were frequently less that harmonious. The first dispute occurred in 1872/3. In 1880 the workers remained out on strike for seventeen weeks. There were further strikes in 1891 and 1894. A Labourers' Union was formed in the Teifi valley in 1900, to represent the interests of all workers and it was later expanded to include the area around Pencader.

The arrival of the railways enabled larger mills powered by steam and supplied by coal to be built. This reduced the need to build mills alongside fast flowing streams. Following the opening of the Carmarthen–Lampeter railway in 1864 woollen mills were established at Pencader, Bronwydd and Llanpumsaint. In the years leading up to the Great War the industry was by and large prosperous and successful. An indication of the size of the industry in Carmarthenshire is given in the 1901 census which records 735 men and 162 women employed in the manufacture of wool and worsted. In addition to these 294 others were employed in dyeing and related textile production. This prosperity continued through the war years as government contracts for uniforms and blankets ensured a ready market. However in the harsh economic climate of the post-war period the slump in the industry was almost as spectacular as its growth had been before 1914. The inability of manufacturers to invest in new machines and fabrics contributed markedly to this decline. Welsh flannel products fell out of fashion even with its core market. During the 1920s twenty-one factories closed in the village of Drefach-Felindre.

An industry closely related to the manufacture of woollen cloth was the hat industry. In the first half of the nineteenth century Carmarthen was well known for the production of hats. The industry became established in the town because of the excellent felting quality of the wool produced in the county. By 1847 the vagaries of fashion and taste had moved against Carmarthen's hat-makers and a terminal decline set in.

The Iron and Steel Industry

The origins of the Carmarthenshire iron industry are to be found in the middle of the seventeenth century, at least a century before industrialization in Merthyr Tydfil transformed the Welsh economy. Carmarthenshire was well placed to meet the requirements of its small local market as it had large quantities of most of the essential raw materials needed for iron production – timber for producing charcoal, limestone, coal and seams of iron-ore. Navigable rivers and a coastal location frequently determined the siting of the works.[9]

Iron and later steel production in Carmarthenshire can be divided into two phases. The first phase relates to a small-scale industry which primarily served the needs of a rural economy. Some of the small works smelted iron while others imported iron bars and refined them in forges. This gave way to a second phase of rapid expansion and development when iron was replaced by steel and the bulk of the output was used to service a sister industry – tinplate.

One of the earliest furnaces for which there are records was at Pont-henri in the parish of Llangyndeyrn on the left bank of the Gwendraeth Fawr river. It was in operation in 1611 and was possibly established earlier. The furnace may well have used local supplies of iron-ore from Mynydd-y-garreg. Whitland forge was founded in 1636 by George Mynne and it is likely that it produced ammunition for Oliver Cromwell before his assault on Pembroke in 1648. The forge was located north of the town of Whitland in the parish of Llan-gain, where two tributaries of the Taf – the Gronw and Nant Colomendy – join. There were good supplies of timber for charcoal, and locally available limestone. Iron-ore was transported by ship to Carmarthen, then by mules to Whitland. In 1750 Whitland Iron Works was producing 100 tons of bar-iron. When it ceased production is unknown but it is not mentioned after 1800. A more important forge was opened just outside Kidwelly on the east bank of the Gwedraeth Fach. Its foundation was during the Commonwealth, sometime between 1648 and 1658. Unlike the other locations mentioned which remained essentially rural, Kidwelly later developed as one of Carmarthenshire's industrial centres.

There were three other small ironworks situated in isolated rural locations. The forge at Llandyfân near Llandybïe was located near a very small tributary of the Loughor – Nant Gwythwch. It produced 100 tons of bar-iron in 1750. A little to the west of Cynwyl Elfed at Cwmbrân was the smallest of these ironworks. Around 60 tons of bar-iron were produced annually in its forge. The isolated locations of both these ironworks meant that moving the bulky finished products was difficult and expensive. It is likely that pack-horses and mules were used. A plentiful supply of timber for charcoal was one of the main attractions of both sites along with a powerful water-supply for the forge wheels. The site at Llandyfân was in addition very close to limestone outcrops. Cwmdwyfran is the last of the three and in some ways the most significant because it was started by the man who became Carmarthenshire's leading ironmaster – Robert Morgan (1708–77) from Kidwelly. Morgan established Cwmdwyfran, in the parish of Newchurch, around 1740 and it was producing 120 tons of bar-iron in 1750. The location in the narrow steep-sided valley of the Gwili had considerable reserves of timber and water power, but none of the other raw materials needed for making iron. Iron-ore, limestone and later coal were all brought from the port of Carmarthen, some 4 miles away. A useful by-product of the charcoal making process was the oak bark which was removed from the wood and used for tanning leather.

In addition to Cwmdwyfran, Robert Morgan established two larger ironworks to meet the needs of Carmarthenshire's most important urban area and emerging industrial base. In 1748 he took over a forge in his home town of Kidwelly. He invested in the site which had a blast-furnace and a rolling mill, and increased production between 1750 and 1788 from

100 to 400 tons. More significantly for the subsequent industrial history of the county he also began upgrading the works, to manufacture tinplate. Around the same time as he was developing his operation at Kidwelly he was also planning a second works at Carmarthen. In 1747 he took out a lease from Lady Trevor for the old priory mill in the town. The main attraction of the site was the supply of fast flowing water. He set about building a furnace, two rolling mills and other works. Production started in 1748 and, by 1788, 400 tons of bar-iron was being produced, much of it exported from the wharf at Carmarthen. As at Kidwelly he built a tin-mill near the forge. In 1771, shortly before his death, Morgan bought the lease for the site from Lady Trevor for £3,000. The works remained in the family under the control of his son and his nephew. However, poor management by his successors led to a decline in the business.

If Robert Morgan was the county's industrial pioneer in the second half of the eighteenth century, then his equivalent in the early part of the next century was Alexander Raby (1747–1835).[10] He came to Llanelli in 1795 and started mining coal on land leased from the Stepney estate. A number of very small ironworks had been started in the area by Thomas Kymer and an English iron master named Yalden at Wern. In 1791 John Gevers and Thomas Ingman set up the short-lived Stradey Iron Works. In 1796, it was purchased by Raby. Iron ore and limestone for the works were supplied from Mynydd Mawr by means of a tram road. It produced 1,560 tons of pig-iron compared to only 290 tons produced at Carmarthen. During the French wars demand for iron increased and additional furnaces and forges were built. Raby lost money during a recession in the industry and concentrated his activities on coal-mining and copper-smelting. His energy, enterprise and business acumen all played a significant part in laying the foundations for Llanelli's future industrial expansion. Undaunted by the failure of an earlier venture a group of four partners set up the Pembrey Iron & Coal Company in 1816. Iron ore and limestone were brought to the ironworks via the Gwendraeth Valley Canal, while the coal was mined locally. The finished iron was exported through Pen-bre harbour which was built by the company and opened in 1819. Over the course of the period c.1750–c.1800 the iron industry had become well established within the county. The works in the Llanelli area clearly indicate the benefits that could accrue from an integrated transport system. Of greater long-term significance was the decision by Robert Morgan to expand his operations into the production of tinplate.

The nineteenth century witnessed a considerable expansion in the iron and steel industry in south-east Carmarthenshire, in and around the Llanelli coalfield. Why did this occur? There are a number of interrelated factors at work. The iron industry was to benefit from a number of important technical developments which assisted expansion, but more importantly opened up the possibility of mass-producing cheap steel. These discoveries included the hot blast method of smelting (1838) which allowed anthracite coal to be used, and the Bessemer (converter 1856) and Siemens (open hearth *c.*1875) methods of mass-producing high-quality low-cost steel. Steel, because of its greater strength and durability, rapidly replaced iron as the industry's main product. The coastal location of the area was a considerable advantage when local supplies of iron-ore became exhausted and the industry had to rely on imports of its primary raw material. Finally the pioneering work of Robert Morgan and others in developing the production of tinplate meant that the industry's output had a very strong local market.

The use of coke in the nineteenth century sounded the death knell of the small rural ironworks. In 1838 anthracite coal was used success-fully for the first time in smelting iron. A number of furnaces were opened in the Gwendraeth valley at Trimsaran and at Brynaman. In 1839 it is estimated that there were twenty-six furnaces in operation with a total production of 65,780 tons of anthracite pig-iron. The Llanelli coalfield with a coastal location and good supplies of coal assumed a primacy in the industry. As most of the output of the ironworks went into the production of tinplate most of the new works which were opened in the Llanelli area in the middle of the century also had their own tin mills attached. Dafen in 1846, was the first new ironworks to be opened which was specifically geared to producing tinplate. This was followed by others at Morfa (1851), Old Lodge (1852), Marshfield (1863) and Old Castle (1866).

The expansion in demand for tinplate after 1850 required further production capacity and additional steel works were opened. During this period, rationalization was taking place within the industry. Smaller companies amalgamated or became part of larger groups or consortia. Among the new works opened were the Llanelly Steel Company (1907), the South Wales Steelworks, Llanelli established by Richard Thomas & Company (1911) and the Bynea Steelworks (1912). A new powerful body was set up to represent the interests of the industry in 1906: the South Wales Siemens Steel Association.

The Coal Industry

The south Wales coalfield sweeps into the south-eastern corner of Carmarthenshire before disappearing under Carmarthen Bay near Kidwelly. The Gwendraeth Fawr river marks the western boundary of the coalfield. In Carmarthenshire two types of coal are mined – anthracite (*glo carreg*) and semi-anthracite. These two types contain the highest carbon contents of any coal mined. This factor proved to be both a blessing and a hindrance to the development of the industry. The high carbon content meant that the coal burned with intense heat while giving off very little smoke. It was ideal for domestic heating purposes, but was initially unsuitable for use in producing coke for smelting or for steam boilers.

There has been a long tradition of coal mining in the county of Carmarthenshire. Leland in his *Itinerary* wrote: 'Ther lieth a long on eche side of Wendreth Vaur Pittes, where menne digge Coles.'[11] The inhabitants of Llanelli also 'digge Coles'. He adds that two types of coal were produced – 'ring coles' for use in blacksmiths' forges (around Llanelli) and 'stone coles' (in the Gwendraeth Fawr valley). There is certainly evidence in the Welsh Port Books covering the Tudor period of coal being exported from Llanelli to the west of England and other locations. This sea coal trade as it came to be known would be a central feature of the industry.

The proximity of the coal seams to the coast was the reason for the early development of the Llanelli area. There were numerous coal outcrops in the mile and a half band that is bounded by Furnace, Felin-foel and Llangennech to the north, and by St Elli's church, Llanelli, Trostre. Llwynhendy and Bynea to the south. Much of the early coal-mining activity in Carmarthenshire was carried out by the landowners themselves. Many gentry families discovered that the income which could be generated from mining could provide a valuable supplement to their rental income. Some of the county's largest landowners – the Vaughans of Golden Grove, the Stepneys of Llanelli, the Mansels of Trimsaran and Stradey – all owned coal mines in and around the Llanelli area.

There were only two mining ventures of any importance in 1750. Robert Morgan leased land from Sir Thomas Stepney, at Llwyncyfarthwch and mined coal to supply his tinplate works at Carmarthen. Sir Edward Mansel of Stradey developed two small pits on his estate at Cwmddyche and Cae-main. After 1750 there was considerable activity on the Llanelli coalfield. Charles Gwyn operated coal pits at Llwynhendy and Cwmfelin during 1750–70; in 1754, John Allen was working coal at Wern, Caeau Gleision and Caecotton; and Daniel Shewen opened extensive mines at Penygaer and Bryngwyn during 1758–62. The most important of the early pioneers was Chauncy Townsend, a London merchant who in 1753 leased all the coal under the Stradey estates in Westfa and Borough hamlets. In 1762 he purchased all the unleased coal under the Mansell estates and in 1767 he sank the Genwen pit. He quickly established a dominant position in the locality. Other collieries opened at this time included Waunallt and St George's in 1766 and Pwll in 1768.

As the industry started to expand the easier and shallower seams were worked out and new and deeper shafts had to be sunk. This required capital investment as steam engines and pumps needed to be installed. Local landowners were either unable or unwilling to make this financial commitment. There was a gradual trend among the landowners from the middle of the century to lease out their collieries to industrialists rather than work the seams themselves. The attitude of Lady Elizabeth Stepney of Llanelli in 1787 was fairly typical: 'I don't like to work the coal myself anywhere.' Two years later she was instructing her agent to let the Betws collieries 'to the best bidder, on the best terms you can'.[12]

It was not until the 1790s that the next major phase of expansion took place. During this decade dominated by the war with France, there was a substantial increase in the price of coal from 47s to 67s a wey (equivalent to 4 tons). The firm of Roderick and Bowen opened three coalpits on land leased from Sir John Stepney and also re-opened the collieries started by John Allen some forty years earlier. In 1796 Alexander Raby arrived in the Llanelli area. He had at his disposal the colossal sum of £175,000 that he had received from the sale of his estate in Surrey. With a view to expanding his fortune he leased land from the Mansel estate and sank collieries at Cae-main, Cae-bâd, Cille, Caer-Elms and Cilfig. Raby's investments in the Llanelli coalfield can in part be explained by his need to supply coke for his blast furnaces in Furnace (1796) and Neath.

Local demand for the coal was fairly limited in the second half of the eighteenth century. In addition to coal for agricultural and domestic purposes, a small but increasing amount was used in the local iron and tin-works. The major markets lay further afield – other coastal towns in south Wales, the west of England and southern Ireland, and a very healthy market was established with the Cornish copper industry. Given the inadequate condition of the roads the only effective way to move large quantities of such a bulky commodity was by water – river, sea or canal. The creeks of the Burry inlet, especially that of the river Lliedi afforded a number of loading places for the small coastal vessels that plied their trade at this time. The significant expansion which took place in the early nineteenth century was due to two main factors. First the dramatic improvement in transport facilities – particularly the development of tramroads, railways and new port facilities – and second the emergence of a strong domestic market for Llanelli coal linked to the iron and copper-smelting industries. In 1820 up to 65,272 tons of coal was shipped from Llanelli.

In the early years of the nineteenth century a number of English entrepreneurs took a leading part in the development of the local coal industry. The three most important were General Warde, Ralph Pemberton and Alexander Raby. Warde owned nine collieries in the area, one of which, the Box colliery, he bought from Raby. Ralph Pemberton was a Middlesborough solicitor who in 1804 purchased the major proportion of the collieries owned by Roderick and Bowen. In 1808 he was responsible for sinking deep shafts, which for the first time enabled the major coal seams of the Llanelli coalfield to be accessed and fully exploited. Pemberton owned the Bres, Cefncaeau, Llandafen and St George's collieries.

The Llanelly Copperworks Company (fl. 1805) was content at first to rely for its coal supplies on the collieries owned by Raby, Warde and Pemberton. Why R. J. Nevill, its owner, decided to diversify into the production of coal is unclear. It is possible that the move was intended to secure coal supplies for his expanding works. In 1818 Nevill took over the management of Warde's collieries and by 1829 assumed the ownership. He acquired Raby's collieries in 1826. The copperworks opened the St David's colliery in 1841. This was the largest and deepest colliery west of the Loughor and employed 421 workmen.

Such was the pace of growth of the Llanelli coalfield that exports from Llanelli by the end of the 1830s were higher than those for all other south Wales ports, with the exception of Swansea. The export market was becoming truly international. Local producers were quick to take advantage of the demand for steam coal from the government and the East India Company. *The Cambrian* newspaper reported that in May 1836 5,000 tons of shipping was berthed in Llanelli harbour, loading coal for depots along the African coast and for Bombay.

Anthracite coal production before 1800 was on a much smaller scale than production of semi-anthracite. The coal was mainly worked from surface outcrops with no deep mining. Besides domestic use the main market appears to have been as fuel for the lime kilns. In 1609 Gerrard Bromley noted that 'there are coales founde wrought and digged in the say'd common called Mynith Mawre (in the parish of Llandybïe) ... for necessary ffyre and burning of lyme ...'.[13] Parish records refer fairly regularly during the eighteenth century to colliers. These pits were very small, employing perhaps two or three men. The key to unlocking the mineral wealth of this part of the south Wales coalfield was reliable and cheap transport. This in turn would enable owners to invest capital in steam winding and pumping machinery, in the knowledge that markets could be accessed. Although the Llanelly Dock and Railway Company line reached Pantyffynnon in 1835, Tir-y-dail in 1841 and Llandeilo in 1857 entrepreneurs were slow to take advantage of the opportunities that were available.

Collieries were opened in the Gwendraeth Fawr valley. By 1878 there were pits at Dynant, Pontyberem and Pontyberem south. The hazardous nature of the industry is evident in the numerous accidents and fatalities which routinely occurred. When colliers at Pontyberem in 1852 broke through old workings that were flooded, twenty-six men were drowned. Many of these mines tended to be small concerns run by individual owners. The Gors-las, Cross Hands and Pen-y-groes area for instance saw many small but profitable pits being sunk, with a daily output of perhaps no more than 100 tons. In the vicinity of the small community of Gors-las four pits were opened in the closing decades of the nineteenth century: Gilfach pit, Millers' pit, George pit and Pwllylledrim pit. Much of the output of these pits was also geared to lime-burning and the domestic market. The most significant venture in the area was the opening of the Great Mountain Colliery in Tumble in 1887. It provided the impetus for considerable development in the locality. By 1913 the colliery was employing 842 men.

The dramatic period of expansion in the anthracite coalfield was one of the most significant industrial features to affect the county in the second half of the nineteenth century. This was due in no small measure to a belated and long overdue appreciation of the superior heat-giving qualities of anthracite over other types of coal. Astute marketing, when agents gave away samples to tempt prospective importers, and the development of central heating requirements in large new buildings clearly played their part. Full advantage could now be taken of the integrated transport system of ports, harbours and railways developing from the coast. According to the Royal Commission on Coal (1919) the export of anthracite started in 1884. In 1886 Llanelli exported 80,000 tons and this increased to over 1.2 million between 1904 and 1911. The main destinations of the coal were France, Germany and Sweden. South Wales came to dominate the UK production of anthracite (producing 90 per cent of the total) and within south Wales almost half of its anthracite was mined in south-east Carmarthenshire.

Towards the end of the nineteenth century and the first decade of the twentieth the pace of expansion was such that collieries were opened annually, in an arc stretching from the Gwendraeth Fawr valley over to the Aman valley. The most spectacular growth occurred around Llandybïe and in the Aman valley. Development of anthracite collieries in the vicinity of Llandybïe appears in the initial phase to have been carried out by local men. D. Lloyd was a local man who opened Pwll-y-Lord and acquired coal rights in the Pantyffynnon, Saron and Capel Hendre area and opened the Parc colliery. These local coal pioneers had little knowledge of practical geology and tended to eschew scientific surveys. Location is all when opening a coal pit. When Lloyd was planning to sink Pwll-y-Lord he consulted with another local man Thomas Hughes of Cwmffaldau to advise him on the best location to tap the coal seams. Hughes was well known in the community and had an uncanny knack for knowing where the coal could most easily be found. The secret of his success apparently, was literally to taste the soil. Three other local men, John Davies, Llwyncoed, David Davies, Parc, and John Job, Llandybïe, between 1870 and 1875, opened a colliery in Caebryn called The Cottage Hall Colliery Company.

Colliers in this area called the limestone measures 'the farewell rock' as it marked the end of the coal-bearing seams. A small colliery was opened in Llandybïe within a few hundred metres of the 'farewell rock'. Work commenced on driving a level to open up the coal seams in 1890 at Pencae'r Eithin. The small company consisted of five local men. They had very little capital and the operation folded in 1903. In the twentieth century larger companies showed an interest, and the collieries at Tir-y-dail and Pencae'r Eithin came under the control of the Cleeves Western Valley Anthracite Ltd. The greater expertise and capital they had access to succeeded where the small partnerships had failed. In the space of thirty years the whole locality had been largely transformed. A cluster of collieries were opened, among them Ammanford Little vein (1891), Ammanford Red vein, Bettws Navigation, Bettws New Mine and Pantyffynnon (1902). As a result of this activity the hamlet of Cross Inn had metamorphosed into the busy urban community of Ammanford.

The Aman valley in turn experienced rapid expansion. Mines were opened in Cwmaman (Raven colliery 1907), Garnant and Brynaman. A rural valley of small isolated hamlets was transformed into an almost continuous urban ribbon settlement. By 1911 the population of the Aman valley (petty sessional district) was 23,034. The interlocking communities were close knit and overwhelmingly Welsh in language and culture. Welsh was the language at the coal face. The coal seams were also named in Welsh – *Y Wythïen Goch* (red seam), *Y Fawr* (the great), *Stanllyd, Bresen, Pumcwart, Trichwart* and *Y Wythïen Fach* (small seam). A strong sense of community, and identity with Welsh culture, was also noticeable in the Gwendraeth valleys. This helped support and sustain these areas through many difficult economic and social times.

This period of growth saw the number of collieries in the Carmarthenshire anthracite coalfield double from twenty-two in 1888 to forty-four in 1913. Between 1887 and 1902 the output of Welsh anthracite increased by 287 per cent. Half of this amount was exported. According to the 1901 census there were over 6,000 colliers working in the county (the largest industrial occupation by group). In the upper Aman valley the number of colliers employed doubled between 1896 and 1905 and almost doubled again by 1920.[14] By comparison there was very little increase in the numbers employed in the Llanelli coalfield.

The Tinplate Industry

There was a long tradition of producing tinplate in Carmarthenshire. Charles Gwynn of Kidwelly built a rolling mill at Bank Broadford a mile to the north of the town in 1737, the second earliest mill in Britain. In 1758

Robert Morgan of Carmarthen became a partner in the operation. Difficulties in production kept the output down to several hundred boxes per annum in the 1760s. Slowly the mill was expanded and production increased to what was claimed in a sale catalogue of 1799 as 3,000 boxes a year. If Kidwelly was the home of the industry in Carmarthenshire then its heartland and the town universally known as 'Tinopolis' was Llanelli. It was not, however, until the middle of the nineteenth century that sustained growth and expansion of the industry occurred. Following the example of Llanelli, satellite developments took place around Pontarddulais (including Hendy and Llangennech) and the Aman valley (Pantyffynnon, Ammanford, Glanaman and Brynaman).

The first of the new tinplate works to be opened was at Dafen (1847) and this was followed by the Morfa Works (1851–2, J. S. Tregoning), the Old Castle Works (1866) and the South Wales Works (1870–73). During the period 1846–70 the number of tinplate mills increased from nine to seventeen. Llanelli by 1873 was well on the way to becoming the most important production centre for tinplate in the UK. With the exception of the Dafen Works, the other three were situated on the flat coastal strip adjacent to the docks. The first stage in the production process required that plates of iron were heated, then passed through rollers to reduce their thickness. They were next dipped in sulphuric acid to remove any surface impurities before being coated with a thin layer of tin during the final stage. Trimmed sheets were gathered together in boxes. As the tinplate industry expanded other support industries were established to provide chemical and specialized engineering services. By 1852 the three mills of the Dafen Works employed 240 workers and the two mills of the Morfa Works employed 110 workers.

By 1874 the tinplate industry was firmly established in the Llanelli area. It then entered a period of considerable expansion. Three new works were built between 1874 and 1890 and existing works extended their capacity. The number of tinplate mills increased between these years from seventeen to fifty-four. This expansion was due mainly to the virtual monopoly of all foreign markets enjoyed by British producers. The lion's share of the export market was with the USA which bought 75 per cent of the output of the south Wales plants. Most of the tinplate was used for canning fruit, meat and fish. Between 1873 and 1878 the cost of a ton of tinplate fell from £133 5s to £61 7s 6d Such a dramatic fall was an added stimulus to the export market. The number of boxes of tinplate exported from the port of Llanelli increased from 15,041 in 1850 to 89,558 in 1870. This golden period was only halted as a result of the McKinley tariff (1891), which closed the American market to British tinplate.

Alongside this expansion there were significant changes in the nature of manufacturing. The most important of these was the replacement of iron with steel as the main constituent for tinplate. Plates made from steel produced fewer 'wasters', and the smoother surface of the steel meant that a lighter (and less expensive) coating of tin was required. Before 1875 the Dafen Works had attempted to produce steel (under licence) using the Bessemer method. Their early efforts were unsatisfactory because the quality of the steel produced was variable. The successful development of the Siemens open-hearth process at Landore, Swansea in the 1870s made cheap, reliable steel available to the tinplate industry. After this date steel gradually replaced iron in the manufacture of tinplate. As J. S. Tregoning said in 1886: 'For the best quality tinplate, nothing can compete with the Siemens open-hearth process.'

The changeover from iron to steel took place slowly because the supply of steel-bar was limited. In 1880 only Morewood's South Wales Works with two furnaces was producing steel in Llanelli. By 1885 a small steel plant had opened at the Morfa Works. This plant was built at a cost of £11,910 in 1885 and was capable of producing 350 tons of steel-bars and ingots a week. It was inevitable that iron forges would now close. Iron-making ceased at the South Wales Works in October 1884 and the Western management closed its forge in March 1885.

In the immediate aftermath of the McKinley Tariff Act 1891 the Llanelli firms do not appear to have been troubled by the loss of the American market as they were able to acquire new orders. What did harm them was the successful establishment of an American tinplate industry behind the tariff barrier. This resulted in severe depression between 1894 and 1898. By comparison with the 1890s, trading conditions during 1899–1913 were, on the whole, good despite some fluctuations (1903–6), and there was little difficulty in selling tinplate. From 1907 to 1913 the tinplate industry once again experienced boom conditions. High demand led to the expansion of plant. Twenty-seven new mills were built in Llanelli between 1907 and 1912. As the historian of the Llanelli tinplate industry, Harold Hancocks, concludes: 'Not since the boom of 1879–80 had such activity been known. Indeed, 1912–13 marks the zenith in the history of the tinplate pack-mills at Llanelli.'[15]

Relations between Llanelli producers in the years before the First World War were frequently divisive and acrimonious. An issue that divided the industry was the question of imported tinplate bar. These were cheaper than home-produced bars and were welcomed by the independent tinplate firms as a means of reducing manufacturing costs. The larger steel-tinplate firms protested at the dumping of cheap foreign steel. Their campaign to persuade the government to impose tariff protection failed in 1905. Following this failure the steel-tinplate works (with the exception of Richard Thomas and Company) formed the South Wales Siemens' Steel association in 1906 to try and ensure the control of prices and output. Fearing that this association 'would press out of the trade the tinplate maker who is not also a maker of his own steel' (*The Times* 19 September 1906), a number of independent producers decided to invest in their own steel-making capacity. A number of additional firms invested in the Llanelly Steel Company which resulted in the reorganization of the company in 1907. In 1912 a much larger operation, the Bynea Steel Company was opened.

Given the dominant position in the tinplate market of Llanelli it is sometimes easy to overlook the fact that works were also opening in other parts of the anthracite coalfield. Among the works opened elsewhere were those at Hendy (1866), Pontarddulais (1872 and 1875), Llangennech (1873), Pantyffynnon (1880), Glanaman (1881) and Ammanford (1889). These works, located away from the coast, tended to concentrate on blackplate which was used in roofing. With the concentration of the tinplate works on the coalfield the survival of one of the oldest works at Carmarthen would certainly appear anomalous. In 1820 the two mills consisted of two pairs of rollers, worked by five men. Weekly production amounted to 464 boxes. By 1850 the Carmarthen works specialized in blackplates. It succeeded in creating a small but viable market for its product. Although coal, iron-ore and limestone all had to be brought to Carmarthen the works survived in the shadow of its larger and more advanced neighbours until 1900 when it ceased production.

Other Industries

It is beyond the scope of this work to attempt to trace the development of all the other industries which were established within the county during this period. These were in the main dwarfed by the scale of those that have been covered. Three other industries have been selected in order to indicate the rich diversity that existed within Carmarthenshire.

Lead Mining

Lead mining was undertaken in many locations throughout the county. Thirteen sites have been identified across Carmarthenshire from the Casara mine in the parish of Myddfai to Pant-y-glein and Cystanog near Carmarthen and Tre-lech near the Pembrokeshire border. The majority of these were fairly small-scale undertakings with a limited lifespan. By far the most important and lucrative mines were in the very north of the county at Rhandir-mwyn. Gentry families were closely involved in the development. One of the largest mines in south Wales was owned by Lord Cawdor in the parish of Llanfair-ar-y-bryn. The mine at Nant-y-mwyn was

started around 1747 and by the 1780s, the 400 men employed were producing between 900 to 1,200 tons of ore a quarter. Lord Cawdor was
reputed to have cleared £300,000 in profit from the mine, an indication of
how lucrative this undertaking was. The very isolated location posed
serious difficulties regarding transport. Local farmers were sub-contracted
as hauliers to move the ore to Carmarthen and Llanelli. This helped supplement their incomes considerably. In 1823–5, 105 men were employed
by the Rhandir-mwyn mines.

Refining the ore produced lead and silver. The Cawdor family smelted
their own ores. A small works was built east of the town of Carmarthen
(c.1760). It was in operation until around 1800 when it closed. The equipment was dismantled and moved to Llanelli. During 1830 lead-smelting
became part of the business interests of the Nevill family. In 1849 the
Cambrian Lead and Silver Works started production. The most prosperous period for the lead-silver production at the Cambrian Works and the
Pembrey Lead Works was between the years 1850–70. The decline in
local supplies led to the works contracting. Lead-smelting ceased just
before the First World War.

Copper-Smelting

The establishment of copper-smelting in Llanelli was a central factor in
leading to the expansion of the Llanelli coalfield. Swansea was the centre
of the British copper-smelting industry towards the end of the eighteenth century. The introduction of copper-smelting to Llanelli was linked
to abundant supplies of good quality coal, and the presence of fire-clay
(used in lining the furnaces) at Llanelli, Llangennech and Pwll. A coastal
location ensured that copper ore from Cornwall could be imported easily.[16]
The Llanelly Copperworks Company was founded in 1805 and one of the
managers was Charles Nevill. Richard Janion Nevill, his son, joined the
board in 1817. This company was the most important single industrial
enterprise in Llanelli during the nineteenth century. The initial capital of
the company was £22,000 to which an additional £18,000 was subscribed
in 1807. In 1809 the works were enlarged and production was increased to
160 tons of refined copper per week. By 1856 production totalled 28,202
tons. Sales of refined copper produced by the company were valued at
£448,634 in 1862. The company was a major force in the industry. It
owned ships valued at £30,840 in 1846 and diversified into refining other
metals. The Cambrian Copperworks were taken over in 1849 and converted into lead and silver works. Collieries were acquired and railway
and dock developments promoted.

Llanelli Pottery

To those interested in ceramics, Llanelli is much more likely to be known for its pottery than for any trace of its industrial past. Many of its items are much sought after by collectors and command healthy prices at auctions. In 1840 William Chambers junior set up a small pottery in the town using local coal and imported Cornish clay. Thirty-four people are listed as working in the pottery in 1841. It was known as the South Wales Pottery (early items often bore the impressed mark SWP). The town and its hinterland were increasing in population and it was perceived that there would be a large local market for its functional and largely utilitarian ware. It posed a real challenge to the domination of the Cambrian Pottery (1764–1870) and indeed outlasted it by over half a century. Many of its products were decorated in transfers, some of the best known are Colandine, Whampoa, Amherst Japan and Swiss Sketches. They suggest a hint of the exotic, and the largely unattainable. Significant events were also commemorated such as the death of Prince Albert, the Crimean War or the visit of Garibaldi. Busts of John Wesley or plates celebrating Mari Jones were very popular with chapel-goers.

Chambers owned the pottery until 1855 when it was leased to Coombs and Holland.[17] W. T. Holland ran the business on his own between 1858 and 1868. He acquired some of the equipment and patterns from the small Ynysmeudwy Pottery (closed 1859) and the Cambrian Pottery (closed 1870) and produced fine quality earthenware. The pottery did experiment in the production of lithoplanes – thinly potted and made of porcelain which allowed the light to portray an image with almost photographic reality. If the history of the pottery in the closing years of the nineteenth century is fairly unremarkable then the opening years of the twentieth century is, by contrast, memorable. There was a real effort to decorate pieces by hand – sponge ware and the Persian rose pattern. This period saw the production of the most visible and nowadays among the most sought after items made by the pottery – the Cockerel Plate. Most of these colourful plates were painted by Sarah Jane Robert ('Auntie Sal'). More sophisticated in design and equally desired by collectors is the work of Samuel Shufflebotham who is best known for his flower and fruit painting. His work is almost always marked 'LLANELLY' or 'LLANELLY POTTERY'. A combination of increased costs resulting from producing hand-painted ware and the use of lower quality local clay from Mynydd-y-garreg which produced an inferior body, led to a decline in demand. Against mounting financial difficulties the pottery finally closed in 1921.

Transport and Communications

Roads

There had been little improvement in Carmarthenshire's roads since Roman times. In common with many areas of Britain their condition was considered to be very poor. Lord Ashburnham following a visit to his Carmarthenshire estates in Pen-bre and Llanddeusant noted in his diary the appalling state of the roads along which he had travelled. Since 1555 the responsibility for maintaining roads lay with the parish through which they ran. Over the next two centuries this provision was often flouted and frequently neglected with the result that the road system was in a very poor state.

In addition to the myriad of small trails and drovers' routes which criss-crossed the county, two important roads passed through Carmarthenshire. The road from London through to Ireland entered the county at Trecastle and descended via the Tywi valley to Llandeilo and Carmarthen before proceeding via St Clears to the Pembrokeshire border at Tavernspite. Many of the travellers who used the route were making for southern Ireland. The second road also emanating from Gloucester followed roughly the south Wales coast. Travellers on horseback could either enter Carmarthenshire by fording the river at Loughor, or via the bridge at Pontarddulais. The road followed the coast to Llanelli and then on to Kidwelly where it was possible to cross the Tywi estuary by ferry and thus avoid Carmarthen. It then merged with the upper road and entered Pembrokeshire at Tavernspite.

The increase in the volume of traffic using these roads during the middle of the eighteenth century led some parishes to transfer the cost of repair to private companies. These were called turnpike trusts and were established by individual acts of parliament. Users were charged tolls collected at gates and in return were theoretically assured of good roads. The system however evolved in a chaotic and haphazard way, and during the first half of the nineteenth century the companies were vilified by the majority of road users. They were the targets of sustained attack during the Rebecca Riots. Many of the trusts that came into existence were either inefficiently run or were too small to be viable. By the time of the Rebecca Riots there were eleven trusts operating roads in Carmarthenshire. Typical tolls were 3d for each horse pulling a cart or carriage, 10d per score of cattle and 5d per score of sheep. Journeys of even moderate distances could cover the roads of several trusts. Unless the return journey could be completed in twenty-four hours the tolls would be levied again. In 1844 an Act was passed to rationalize the turnpike system. Improvements in road surfaces and drainage did lead to better journeys along the main roads. Among these developments were those perfected by the civil engineer John Loudon Macadam. He favoured cambered surfaces and fine layers of stones laid on good foundations. Minor roads, however, continued to have poor surfaces until 1914.

Tram-roads

Roads with poor surfaces which were unable to take heavy load-bearing traffic were of little use to industrialists wanting to move large quantities of bulky commodities such as coal or iron ore. The solution they adopted was to construct tramways. Metal plates were laid on sleepers to spread the weight of wagons drawn by horses. Tramroads proliferated on the Llanelli coalfield from as early as 1750. One of the most ambitious schemes was for a 16 mile tramway from Llanelli into the upper parts of the coalfield. It aimed to access coal reserves at Mynydd Mawr and limestone at Castell-y-garreg, a mile and a half north of Gors-las. The Carmarthenshire Railway or Tramroad Company started to construct the line in 1802. Gors-las was reached in 1805. In 1834 an application was made to convert the tramway into a railway line. The line was rebuilt in the 1880s as the Llanelli and Mynydd Mawr Railway. Although most tram-roads were relatively short and tended to run from collieries to either canals or the coast, they played an important part before the coming of the railways in the industrial development of the county.

Canals

The location of Carmarthen, several miles inland but on a navigable river, provided as good an example as any of the advantages of moving large quantities of goods by water. The earliest canals to be built in Carmarthenshire were on the Llanelli coalfield. Two short canals were constructed by Chauncy Townsend in 1769–70. The first of these, the ¾ mile Dafen canal, ran from Llwynhendy to the sea at Dafen pill. The second was the Spitty canal (1766–70) which with its 1787 extension had a total length of 1¼ miles. It ran from Bynea to Spitty bank. Also in 1769 Thomas Kymer – who more than anyone saw the benefits of canal transport, started building a 3 mile canal from Kidwelly to Pwll-y-llygod.

Thomas Bowen, *c*.1770, probably built the first canal near Llanelli, the Trostre canal. It was only ½ mile long and connected his collieries with the Dafen river. Of similar length was the Llangennech canal (*c*.1775). Two canals were built around 1795. The ½ mile long Baccas canal was constructed by the Revd David Hughes to link his colliery with Pill-y-Cefen.

Roderick and Bowen connect their Wern colliery by canal with the small wharf they had erected known as 'Doc Canol' – a site later occupied by the Pemberton tinplate works. The construction of these canals was fairly simple – no locks, located in tidal areas, and not requiring parliamentary approval. Although these early canals did not form an interlocking system, they greatly improved the movement of coal in the pre-railway age.

By far the most ambitious canal building scheme in Carmarthenshire was the plan to improve the harbour at Kidwelly and construct a canal along the Gwendraeth valley to Cwm-mawr, with an extension eastwards across Pinged Marsh, through Pen-bre and on to Llanelli. An act of parliament was obtained in 1812 and the Kidwelly and Llanelly Canal and Tramroad Company was established. Construction work started in 1814 and the whole system was operational by 1837. When completed the canal was over 11 miles long, had five locks, three inclined planes, three aqueducts and cost £100,000. The Kymer and Pen-bre canals were linked to it. In many ways the scheme was out of date even on completion. Railways were the spirit of the age, as a cheaper, quicker and a more reliable means of transport. The decline of the canal was almost inevitable, as it was slower, less reliable and restricted by being unable to climb steep gradients. Its fate was ultimately sealed when the canal company amalgamated with the railway to form the Burry Port and Gwendraeth Valley Railway. The final indignity was that the new company's track was mainly laid between 1869 and 1886 on the bed of the old canal.

Railways

South Wales was the birthplace of steam railways, when the first journey was made by Richard Trevithick in Merthyr in 1804. His pioneering work however was adopted very slowly. In Britain the great period of railway building was in the 1830s and 1840s and Carmarthenshire was part of this process. The first significant project was proposed by the Llanelly Railway and Dock Company which received its first act of parliament in 1828. It was planned to transport coal, iron-ore and limestone from the anthracite areas to Llanelli. A further act of parliament in 1835 allowed the company to construct a line through Pontarddulais to Llandeilo with branch lines to Cwmaman and Brynaman. Tir-y-dail was reached by 1841 and Brynaman in 1842. The progress of the main line northward thereafter was rather slow. Publicity material issued by the company in 1839 to tempt investors noted that:

> The recently discovered advantage of the use of anthracite coal in reference to blasting furnaces, stoves, steam power purposes

and for malting, and which, to an immense extent of tonnage, may be brought down to Llanelly docks, is of itself, a most important circumstance as contributing to the revenue of the Company.

Linking Wales to the expanding English network was one of the main aims of the South Wales Railway which was formed in 1844. A line was constructed from Chepstow and reached Carmarthen in October 1852. The industrial area of the county was integrated into the national rail network. In 1863 the Great Western Railway (or 'God's Wonderful Railway' as the GWR was affectionately known) absorbed the South Wales Railway Company and from 1872 the broad gauge which it favoured was replaced by the standard gauge which predominated on the national network.

Just before it was absorbed by the GWR, the Llanelly Railway and Dock Company in 1861 secured approval for additional branch lines from Pontarddulais to Swansea and along the Tywi valley from Llandeilo to Carmarthen. The former would carry mainly raw materials for industry and the rapidly expanding export market, while the latter would open up a rich agricultural area. Llandovery was reached by 1858. Further expansion into central Wales to join the line south from Craven Arms in Shropshire was delayed by two civil engineering problems. Both of these were resolved in 1868 firstly by the construction of a 700 ft viaduct at Cynghordy and secondly the opening of a 1,000 yard tunnel under the Sugar Loaf mountain on the Carmarthen Brecknock border. A link was now established with the large industrial conurbations of the Midlands and Lancashire.

The expansion of the GWR across the southern part of the county in the early 1850s by-passed the Gwendraeth valley. Industrialists in Llanelli were very keen to exploit the mineral deposits in the Mynydd Mawr area around Tumble. With the Gwendraeth valley canal facing stiff competition from the railways it was decided in 1865 to discontinue the canal. In 1866 the Burry Port & Gwendraeth Valley Railway came into existence. The first coal train made the 11 mile journey from Pontyberem to Burry Port Docks in July 1869. Twenty collieries were joined to the line. Passenger traffic was introduced in 1909 and 57,000 people were carried during the first six months of operation. In 1921 the company became a subsidiary of the GWR.

Carmarthen was emerging as the hub of the county's railway network. To the lines going along the Tywi valley to Llandeilo and central Wales, westwards to Fishguard and along the south Wales coast to England, a new line to Lampeter was opened in 1864. It was not until 1895 that a branch from Pencader linked Newcastle Emlyn into the network. This was a considerable boost to the woollen industry in north Carmarthenshire.

Railways made a dramatic impact on the economic and social life of Carmarthenshire. The economic benefits are fairly obvious – cheap reliable transport of heavy goods on a large scale from points of production to markets or other works. Isolated areas were opened up for industrial development and many new job opportunities were created. Links to urban areas through the national rail network helped provide a boost for industries such as woollen production and dairy farming. It became easier for farmers to buy lime for their land. Railways themselves created a large number of new jobs, from 'gangers' on track maintenance to porters, drivers, station-masters, signalmen, etc. There was, however, a negative side. Canals were clearly a casualty of the coming of the railways. In Carmarthenshire railways virtually ended the need for drovers. The end was not immediate but by the close of the century long-term droving had virtually ceased.

There were also significant social benefits. Cheap passenger transport from the middle of the nineteenth century contributed to social mobility and in some areas speeded up the process of rural depopulation. With the almost incessant demand for labour from the south Wales coalfield many of the passenger journeys made by young men and women were all too frequently one way. Most small communities were now in fairly easy reach of the markets and shops in Llanelli, Carmarthen and Swansea. Railways were responsible for bringing many inhabitants of the rural hinterland into contact with urban life. The reverse was also true. *The Cambrian* in 1884 (August) published the revelatory account of a young reporter sent from Swansea to cover a political rally in Cwmaman:

> Following advice which was certainly not the best, one got landed at dusty Llanelly with more than an hour's wait. Then at snail's pace to Pantyffynnon and then slower still to Garnant in primitive railway carriages filled with the Welshest of Welsh people whose only anxiety, individual and collective, seemed to be to ascertain whether certain '*moch*' (pigs), were at the end of our train, or were left behind for another journey.

Harbours and Docks

A coastal location was undoubtedly a central factor in the development of industry during the industrial revolution. By a considerable margin, the most important harbour and dock complex in the county was at Llanelli.[18] Coal had been exported from the town since Tudor times. Large-scale development, however, occurred during the nineteenth century. New Dock and Llangennech Dock were opened in 1834. Exports included coal, tinplate and copper, while iron ore, copper ore and tin were imported. A small but flourishing ship-building industry emerged in Llanelli in the 1860s. The first iron ship to be built was the 220 ton *Premier* which was launched in 1863. Towards the end of the century the Llanelly Harbour Trust was formed under the terms of the Llanelly Harbour Act (1896), and plans were made to build a larger and more modern facility – the North Dock (1903).

Further along the coast at Burry Port a small harbour was built between 1830 and 1832. A floating dock – called the East Dock – was constructed and opened by 1840 to cope with a projected increase in anthracite exports. The dock had a rather chequered history and struggled to operate at full capacity. Management optimism did result in plans to upgrade the port and these came to fruition in 1888. An estuary location did present problems of silting and alterations in the channels approaching the docks. Kidwelly also emerged as a coal exporting port due to the enterprise of Thomas Kymer who built a dock as an outlet for his coal pits. These were linked by canal. Navigation problems linked to the movement of offshore sand effectively stymied plans for further development. By the 1840s Kidwelly's existence as an active port was effectively at an end.

VII

War, Depression, Recovery: 1914–2005

Society

During the period covered by this chapter Carmarthenshire has undergone a greater variety of changes at a more rapid pace than at any other time in its history. These changes and developments have largely been a consequence of external factors such as war and economic depression. The population of the county continued to grow in the period following the Great War, peaking in 1931. As the shadow of the hungry thirties fell over the county the population declined as people left to search for work in other, less blighted parts of Britain. It was not until the 1980s that this downward trend was reversed and the population of the county started once again to increase. This recovery was not, however, universal as the population of Llanelli continued to decline. Part of this recovery was due to inward migration as people were drawn to the county by the twin attractions of cheaper housing and a pleasant, largely rural environment with strong community values.

Table 3. Population Census Figures for Carmarthenshire 1901–2001

Year	Population
1901	135,328
1911	160,430
1921	175,073
1931	179,100
1951	172,034
1961	168,008
1971	162,562
1981	164,000
1991	166,834
2001	173,635

Of the external factors the most dramatic were the two world wars which in no small measure define the twentieth century. On the anvil of war nineteenth-century society was largely destroyed and a new one was forged in its place. Rapid technological advance blended with destruction, reconstruction and enormous social and political development were its characteristics.

The Great War, 1914–18

The outbreak of war in the summer of 1914 was hardly unexpected. What took people by surprise was the scale and ferocity of the campaigns, as initial hubris gave way to weary resignation and ultimately despair. Britain's declaration of war on Germany was greeted with enthusiasm and thousands of young men descended on recruiting stations to join the army, in the misguided belief that it would all be over by Christmas 1914! Many Carmarthenshire men found themselves in France within a month of the outbreak of hostilities as part of the British Expeditionary Force. These were reservists. Among them was a young farm-servant named Sam who noted his initial thoughts in an understated way on a postcard sent from France to his employer, Mr James of Hengrofft Farm, Trap: 'Dear Sir I hope you are quite well for I am quite safe so far. I have had a little hard time out here sir. I will be glad when I can come home again'.[1]

It is not possible to establish with any degree of accuracy the total number of men and women from the county who served with the various branches of the armed forces during the Great War. A government survey established that there were 20,506 men of military age (20 to 35) in the county in 1914–15, with an additional 5,706 men aged 36 to 40. As an agricultural county with a significant industrial base in mining and heavy industry, there were many reserved occupations vital to the war effort. A letter was published in the *Carmarthen Journal* in October 1914 complaining of the lack of response to volunteering from young men in the 'agricultural regions'. Whatever the initial reluctance Carmarthenshire men (and a small number of women) fought and served in most theatres of the war in significant numbers. The conditions they endured and the scenes they witnessed were unimaginable to the general public. Many kept war diaries to record their experiences. An extract from the diary of Lieutenant Robert Peel of Taliaris, serving with the Royal Field Artillery in Gallipoli during 1915, provides some indication of the horrors witnessed, and the extreme privations endured by men on active service:

> Nov 27/28/29 Thunderstorm, torrential rain, blizzard and frost –
> great suffering among infantry. During this period all ranks at
> Sulva bay went through the greatest hardship – Nov 27 at 5.30

pm a fierce thunderstorm set in with torrential rain, this continued on and off all night till 1 am when weather turned cold & the
blizzard period began. This period lasted till the evening of the
28th when a hard frost luckily dried up the ground and made
existence more bearable – The infantry in 1st line of trenches
were in a most luckless state many dying from exposure others
being drowned – men in reserve trenches and rest camps were in
little better conditions there being no overhead cover available.[2]

Lt Peel survived Gallipoli and was posted to the Western Front where he
won the Military Cross. He died from wounds received at Ypres in 1917,
the second member of his family to fall in the service of his country – his
brother predeceasing him while serving with the South Wales Borderers
in 1914.

The advent of new technology ensured that some aspects of the war
were unlike any previous major conflict. This was the first war when
aircraft were used in any significant numbers. One of Carmarthenshire's
most decorated servicemen from this war was a young flying officer from
St. Clears, Ira 'Taffy' Jones (1896–1960). The diminutive Jones in later life
wrote a number of books about aviation history. In one he recalls his
feelings about the enemy.

On May 27 1917 I remember seeing the burnt out bodies of a
pilot and an observer, their identities then unknown to me, being
taken out of the tender which was to take me to Choques.
Looking down on the blackened and unrecognisable remains, of
what had so recently been two high spirited youngsters like
myself, I felt a dreadful bitterness and anger against the whole
nation of conquest-hungry barbarians beyond the Rhine. I
prayed fervently: "Oh, God! Please let me kill at least one German
before I die."[3]

In a remarkable burst of activity, Jones greatly exceeded his expecta-
tions. Between May and November 1918 he shot down forty German
aircraft, making him the thirteenth highest scoring British fighter ace in
the First World War.

The impact of the war on the economy was considerable. There was
an increased demand for woollen cloth, coal and steel. Farming played a
key role in the war effort as the need to become as self-reliant as possible
was brought into sharp focus when merchant ships were sunk by German
U-boats. As losses mounted on the Western Front and conscription was
introduced in 1916, many farm-labourers were called up. Women assumed
the roles occupied by the men and frequently single-handedly managed

farms. Their enfranchisement in 1918 was in part a reflection of the heroic effort they had made during the four and a half years of conflict. The fatalities sustained by the county's military are given in Table 4. As a crude measure the ratio of recruits to fatalities is roughly 10 to 1.

Table 4. Carmarthen County War Memorial: Roll of Honour.
Those who died in The Great War 1914–1918

Nurses	Officers	N.C. Officers	Other Ranks
3	123	254	1533
		Total: 1913	

Apart from the human cost the social and political impact of the war was considerable. A shared sense of grief, which touched almost every family in the county, led some to demand greater equality and enhanced opportunities. The more politically aware became disillusioned with liberalism and turned instead to socialism. The fragile unity with which the Liberal party had entered the war broke down in 1916 over the issue of conscription. Llewellyn Williams, the MP for Carmarthen, was a prominent opponent of conscription which he considered betrayed the libertarian values that were the bedrock of the party. He voted against the first reading of the Conscription Bill and became an outspoken critic and enemy of his former friend Lloyd George. At the 1918 election he did not receive the endorsement of the coalition government – the so-called coupon, and did not sit in parliament again. For the squirearchy, according to H. M. Vaughan 'the crowning catastrophe of the Great War dealt the final and fatal blow'. High taxation, loss of income, social change and the deaths of many heirs contributed to this social group 'becoming a thing of the past'.[4]

The Second World War, 1939–45

The outbreak of war in September 1939, in contrast to events in 1914, was not greeted with any enthusiasm. For the second time in under a generation the future was marked by uncertainty. By the late 1930s, the failure of appeasement to assuage Hitler's demands made war much more likely than in the years following his assumption of power in 1933. Carmarthenshire would play a very significant role in the war effort. Britain was slow to rearm, and as part of the tentative process the RAF selected a coastal site at Pen-bre burrows to set up a depot and a bombing range. Royal Ordnance constructed a new munitions plant on the site of the former Great War armaments factory. During the war its output of munitions was crucial in supporting the military and the thousands of women who worked long shifts played an important if unsung role in the war effort.

The great expanse of flat land and relatively isolated location at Penbre made it ideal for military purposes and particularly the needs of the air force. Construction work started in 1938 and the following year the No. 2 Air Armaments school was set up there. During the spring of 1940 this hitherto isolated part of Carmarthenshire was awash with activity. As the Battle of Britain was fought out in the skies over southern England the airfield was taken over by fighter command. Sixteen Spitfires from 92 Squadron were based at Pen-bre. They played an important supporting role in the Battle of Britain by defending the western approaches. In the summer of 1940 the strength of the base was 633 officers and aircrew. Unlike the Great War where the direct impact of the conflict on the civilian population was limited to war work and various restrictions, the Second World War ensured, courtesy of the *Luftwaffe*, that everyone was in theory at risk. On 10 July 1940 Pen-bre was attacked by the German air force. Three high-explosive bombs were dropped on the Royal Ordnance Factory, killing twelve people and seriously injuring fourteen others. The following day the town of Kidwelly was bombed. The Spitfires of 92 Squadron flew out from Pen-bre on 8 September 1940 and were replaced on the same day by the Hurricanes of 79 Squadron. This was a much more cosmopolitan force which included Czechs, Poles and free French.

RAF Pen-bre continued to experience considerable activity. The following extract from the Operations Record Book of 79 Squadron for 25 September 1940 gives a brief insight into these turbulent times:

> At about 21.00 hrs E/A (enemy activity) appeared over the aerodrome and dropped 12 incendiary and three HE (high explosive) bombs. No damage was done but one private of 9th Gloucester Regiment defending the beach was seriously wounded. The wounds proved fatal.

In March 1941 a new all-Polish Squadron – 316 – was formed at Pen-bre. The contribution of the officers and men at the aerodrome resulted in twenty-eight enemy aircraft being shot down with a further twenty-eight being damaged. Following the departure of Fighter Command in June 1941, No. 1 Air Gunnery School assumed residency of the base and would remain there for the duration of the war. This was a period of rapid expansion for the base which by 1944 had a strength of 1,529 RAF personnel and 243 WAAFs. In the lead up to the invasion of Europe large numbers of allied forces, mainly American, were billeted temporarily in and around Pen-bre. In addition to Pen-bre there were other developments.

At Pendine 3,000 acres were purchased by the War Office from the Llanmiloe estate of Major G. Jones for the development of a weapons' testing establishment. Many of the county's mansions were used for the war effort. Soldiers were based at Stradey and Dynevor Castles, and evacuees were billeted at Edwinsford. Although it is difficult to provide an accurate figure for the number of casualties from the Second World War some indication can be gained from the Commonwealth War Graves' Commission which lists 593 dead on their register, whose details include Carmarthenshire. The actual figure is higher since not all the dead would have included a reference to the county.

Among the most important social developments of the twentieth century is the creation of the welfare state and ensuring equality of opportunity in education. The county made great strides in both these fields after 1914. At the time of the outbreak of the First World War, standards of health-care provision in the county were very poor. There were three hospitals in existence, two were in Carmarthen – the Infirmary which had been founded by voluntary contributions in 1847 and had opened in 1858, and the three-counties asylum at St David's opened in 1865. The third hospital was a small voluntary foundation at Llanelli. In 1920 the *First Report of the Welsh Consultative Council on Medical and Allied Services in Wales* highlighted just how inadequate the medical provisions in the county were. Catering for a population of over 170,000 there were 44 GPs, 67 trained midwives, 23 qualified nurses, a 45-bed hospital in Llanelli and a 35-bed hospital in Carmarthen. The Maternity and Child Welfare Act of 1918 and the Public Health Act of 1936 empowered but did not oblige local authorities to provide maternity hospitals. There was no such provision in Carmarthenshire. In order to try and establish a maternity hospital for the county Lady Dynevor made a radio appeal in 1935. The Local Government Act of 1929 ended the operation of the Poor Law and lifted the spectre of the workhouse which had haunted many of the elderly in their last years. Some former workhouses were used for providing healthcare. In Llanelli the workhouse in Bryntirion became a small hospital.

The creation of the National Health Service (NHS) in 1948 would, over the course of the next half century, radically improve the standards of healthcare provision in the county. Carmarthenshire became in 1948 part of the Welsh Regional Hospital Board. This took over Llanelli District hospital and the County Infirmary in Carmarthen, both of which were voluntary institutions with more than a hundred beds, and also the small public assistance institution at Bryntirion. The first significant hospital to be built in the county by the NHS was the West Wales General Hospital at Carmarthen. Work on this project commenced in 1954 and new departments and facilities have been added over the intervening years. In 2002 it had 376 beds available. A new 230-bed general hospital named after Prince Philip was opened in Llanelli in 1990. In addition to these large hospitals there are smaller hospitals at Llandovery, Mynydd Mawr (Y Tymbl), Aman Valley (Glanaman) and Bryntirion. Some of these cater exclusively for geriatric patients. Since its inception the NHS has significantly improved the quality of life for the inhabitants of Carmarthenshire. The average size of its GP practices – 1,637 in 2000 – is slightly lower than the average for Wales of 1,695. One area of concern however is the percentage of the population registered with an NHS dentist which, at 42.4 per cent in 2000, is among the bottom three health groups in Wales. During the financial year ending in March 2000, the total expenditure on health services by the NHS providers in the county was £88.7 million. The service had become a substantial employer providing jobs for 2,627 people.

In the field of education a number of developments have occurred. During the Second World War the passing of the 1944 Education Act finally realized the goal of free secondary education for all, albeit with the crucial caveat that it should be according to age, aptitude and ability. This introduced selection for secondary school through the eleven plus examination. The tripartite system of grammar, technical and modern schools which the 1944 Act envisaged was not well suited to a largely rural county such as Carmarthenshire where scattered communities could not sustain the three different schools proposed by the new law. Harold Wilson's Labour government removed the element of selection at eleven by requiring local education authorities in 1965 to submit plans to establish non-selective comprehensive schools. The progress of this reorganization in Carmarthenshire was rather piecemeal. The first scheme was in Llandeilo when Llandeilo Grammar School and Llandybïe Secondary Modern School merged in 1969 to create Tre-gib County Secondary School, located in a new purpose-built school at a site in the grounds of a former mansion in Ffair-fach. Other reorganizations occurred in Ammanford, Llanelli, Gwendraeth, Carmarthen and Whitland.

Possibly the most interesting development has been the emergence of the Welsh-medium schools. There has been a sustained revival of interest in Welsh culture and the Welsh language during the last quarter of the twentieth century. This has been reflected in the emergence of an active and committed Welsh schools movement. Initially this was very much a grass-roots organization aimed at securing nursery and playgroup provision through the medium of Welsh. Mudiad Ysgolion Meithrin became a very effective and well-organized pressure group. Reorganizations along comprehensive lines offered opportunities for Welsh-medium secondary schools to be established. As a county with a large number of Welsh speakers it should perhaps come as no surprise that there was such a demand for Welsh-medium education. Welsh-medium secondary schools were opened in Llanelli (Ysgol Gyfun y Strade, 1977), Carmarthen

(Ysgol Gyfun Bro Myrddin, 1978) and Cefneithin (Ysgol Gyfun Maes-yr-yrfa).

In addition to the main developments a number of other educational changes occurred. During the early part of the twentieth century, when the county's industrial base was much greater, technical education expanded. From rather inauspicious beginnings, as a series of summer schools for men involved in the local mining industry, a mining and technical institute was opened in Ammanford in 1927. It expanded and in 1942 incorporated a secondary technical school. Subsequent developments have seen further expansion and amalgamation with other technical colleges in the county, located at Llanelli and Carmarthen to form the multi-campus further education college – Coleg Sir Gâr. In Llanelli, Coleg Sir Gâr offers a tertiary provision since local English-medium schools lost their sixth forms following comprehensive reorganization.

Perhaps the most emotive of the changes taken by the local education authority affects small rural schools and decisions to close them. Of the 114 community primary schools in the county at the start of the academic year 2005–2006, seven have twenty or fewer pupils. These schools are at the very heart of their communities and closure notices inevitably lead to protracted campaigns by anguished parents. One of the first campaigns of the new millennium was waged by the parents of Henllan Amgoed school. While very often stays of execution are won, the long-term trend is towards consolidation.

Economic Change and Development

Enormous changes to the economic structure of the county have taken place since 1914. These are best illustrated by the selective consideration of the fortunes of three of the most important of Carmarthenshire's industries – coal, tinplate and agriculture.

The Coal Industry

During the First World War production of anthracite remained fairly steady at around 2.4m tons per annum. Although jingoism was prevalent throughout the country some militant miners sought to use the crisis of war to press their case for improved conditions. In some ways their increased militancy was a reaction to attempts by coal-owners to dismantle pre-war agreements regarding working hours and wages. Matters came to a head in July 1915 when there was a major strike in south Wales. The editorial of the *Carmarthen Journal* could barely contain its anger at the action of the miners: 'We can only stand looking on aghast, at what seems to us an outrage upon the very soul of patriotism' (16 July 1915). Following the intervention of Lloyd George and other members of the wartime coalition government, the ten-day stoppage was brought to an end. The miners secured a wage of 3s 4d a day plus 50 per cent for underground workers. While the miners had made significant advances in their wages many in the nation at large felt that they were holding the country to ransom. In order to avert future damaging disputes the government took over control of the south Wales coalfield in 1916, and the rest of the British coal industry a year later. To determine the future organisation of the coal industry after the war, a royal commission was set up which, much to the surprise of the coal-owners, recommended nationalization when its report was published in 1919. However the wartime coalition government led by Lloyd George rejected the proposals, a decision which contributed to the deteriorating industrial relations of the 1920s, and also to the decline in support for Liberalism in the coal-field constituencies.

The end of the war did not result in a crisis for the anthracite coalfield immediately. As Jim Griffiths recalled in *Glo-carreg: Memories of the Anthracite Coalfield*: 'For a few years in the nineteen-twenties, the anthracite coalfield enjoyed an Indian summer. The movement for clean air brought an increased demand for smokeless fuel and *glo-carreg* is the best smokeless fuel of all. The real boost to the anthracite trade came from the opening up of a new market in Canada.'[5] Anthracite production in Carmarthenshire, which had fallen to 1.7m tons in 1921 recovered to 2.5m tons by 1922. Alongside the new markets the anthracite coalfield underwent a rationalization of ownership. The driving force in this process was Sir Alfred Moritz Mond who first became involved in the south Wales coal trade in 1910. He observed the chaotic state of affairs in the anthracite coalfield where production before the war was in the hands of over one hundred independent companies. Mond set about forming his own combine and the Amalgamated Anthracite Collieries Company (AAC) came into existence in 1924. In the same year it took over the Cleeve's Western Valleys Anthracite Collieries Ltd. Following Mond's lead the United Anthracite Collieries Ltd (UAC) was formed in 1924. It grouped together among others: Great Mountain Collieries, Ammanford Colliery Company Ltd, and Pontyberem Anthracite Colliery Company. UAC had a combined output of 600,000 tons per year.

Tensions between labour and capital were, however, never far below the surface. These emerged with great ferocity in the anthracite coalfield in 1925, in what Hywel Francis called the forgotten strike: 'Events that for a short while, in that long hot summer gripped the imagination of the British Labour Movement and must have struck fear and horror in the hearts of those bold shareholders who had sunk their capital in the new coal combines of West Wales.'[6] The focal point of the strike was Ammanford and its cause in essence was the desire by management to amend employment practices which the colliers with equal tenacity sought to defend. Before the emergence of the combines the colliery owners and the workers operated a 'seniority rule'. When demand for anthracite fell away in the summer months, miners were allowed to seek temporary employment in the adjacent steam-coal collieries and they could later claim back their previous job when anthracite production once again expanded in the winter months. In addition a miner could not be laid off at the discretion of the manager; he was protected by the date of his employment and those most recently employed would be the first to be made redundant. When the UAC took over Ammanford No. 1 Colliery a new manager was appointed and there began a series of incremental changes to rearrange working practices. The chairman of UAC, F. A. Szarvasy, considered these to be essential if 'satisfactory profits could be earned'. There were attempts to eliminate the New Year and Good Friday holidays and the short Saturday shift. As a result of a change in working methods in the Boxer district of the colliery, men were placed on minimum wage rates as piece rates were considered inadequate. The colliery agent gave 116 miners notice to end their contracts and refused to recognize the matter as a dispute. The lodge offered a seniority list which was ignored by management. It appeared that the UAC was attempting to by-pass the seniority rule. The dismissal of Will Wilson, a collier, in April 1925 in a further breach of custom and practice led to a strike.

Five local pits struck in sympathy with the victimized miners. In sympathy it spread to the Dulais and Neath valleys. When pickets in Ammanford confronted miners who wished to work there was an outbreak of violence. There was serious violence in late July. The town of Ammanford and some of the surrounding villages were very much under the control of the strike committees. At Saron colliery shots were fired and a man was wounded. During the so-called 'battle of Ammanford' (5 August) there was serious rioting between police and strikers. Against this deteriorating situation the owners reflected on their position. An agreement was reached whereby the conditions existing prior to the strike would continue. The seniority rule had been preserved in what was seen as a momentous victory. However, 198 miners were prosecuted for their part in the disturbances and 58 were imprisoned for periods varying from one to eighteen months.

Industrial relations continued to remain the most intractable of problems during this period. In 1926 the AAC merged with its main rival the UAC. The new group controlled 2 million tons of anthracite production (40 per cent of the Welsh total). In 1928 the Llewellyn and Buckland group was bought by Mond who now controlled 80 per cent of south Wales production. Proposals to extend the working day while at the same time reducing wages were the immediate cause of the general strike of 1926. It still remains the greatest display of union solidarity in British labour history. It paralysed the country for nine days before the TUC called off the action. The miners remained out for a further nine months. The *Amman Valley Chronicle* noted that: 'If the present crisis continues it is proposed to establish soup kitchens locally and to open a distress fund' (20 May 1926). Enormous suffering was borne by the families of the miners and the shopkeepers who depended on their custom. When the miners were finally forced to accept defeat in December 1926 it left a bitter sense of animus against the owners and the government.

While the rest of the coalfield slipped into depression in the early 1930s, the demand for anthracite proved to be remarkably buoyant. Production peaked in 1934 at 6,133,934 tons. South-east Carmarthenshire offered a haven for some of the army of unemployed miners in the rest of south Wales. As Table 5 shows there were more men employed in the Gwendraeth and Aman valleys in 1935 than in 1913, albeit in fewer pits.

Table 5. Colliery Manpower by Valley, selected years: 1913–81[7]

Valley/Area	1913		1935		1947		1961		1981	
	Men	Pits	Men	Pits	Men	Pits	Men	Pits	Men	Pits
Llanelli/Burry Port	1642	18	368	6	634	2	415	1	–	–
Gwendraeth Valley	4214	14	7224	16	2946	8	1478	3	1121	1
Amman Valley	7900	35	7112	20	4422	13	2555	5	693	1

The outbreak of war in 1939 provided a much needed fillip to the fortunes of the coal industry. In order to increase production the so-called 'Bevin boys' were drafted into the industry. The old tensions involving wages and working conditions were never far below the surface. The failure of the Porter tribunal to meet the full claim put in by miners for a wage of £6 a week underground and £5 10s for surface workers led to mass stoppages in many British coalfields. By early March 1944 the strike was almost complete in south Wales. The *Carmarthen Journal* described the events as 'An outrage – It is a stab in the back ...' (10 March 1944). A letter from a man in Saron, H. G. Tidmarsh, to his nephew Glan Rees on active service in Italy (20 March 1944), offers an interesting insight into local opinion, and some salutary advice on the perils of overseas service:

> As perhaps you have heard we have been having a little trouble of late in the local collieries. I have been talking to some of

them. They either cant or do not wish to take their own jobs or lives seriously. As you know it is important that we keep all our factories going at full speed, and to do that as much coal as possible is needed. Well now Glan, just a word of advice which I know you will take in the right spirit. In your travelling about from place to place, 'Keep away from the Drink', it will do you no good.[8]

The strikes were quickly resolved and hastened the introduction of a new national agreement. This wartime dispute led miners to aim for continued nationalization after the war, as the only way to avoid the highly divisive conflicts within the industry. Jim Griffiths was one of the Labour Government ministers who accepted the proposals that the state, in the guise of the National Coal Board should take over the coal industry. This duly occurred on 1 January 1947. The history of the coal industry in the county in the post-war period is one of decline punctuated by the opening of new super-pits – Cynheidre (1960), Betws (1975), then further decline.

Table 6: Selected Colliery Closures in Carmarthenshire: 1949–92[9]

Colliery	Closure	Colliery	Closure
Pontyberem	1949	Ammanford No. 2	1976
Trimsaran	1954	Cwmgwili	1980
Llandybïe	1958	Morlais	1981
Saron	1956	Cynheidre	1989
Carwe	1960	Betws	1992
Great Mountain	1962		
New Cross Hands	1962		
Wernos	1965		
Pantyffynnon	1969		

In 1981 2,800 were employed in the county's coal industry. This represented 5.6 per cent of all county employment. By 1997 the figure had fallen to 500 (1 per cent of county employment). Betws colliery is the last deep mine in the anthracite coal field. Following its closure in 1992 it reopened after a management buy-out in April 1994 and remained in operation until 2003. There remains a demand for high quality anthracite coal and there are large reserves remaining in the county, but as an industry the once mighty King Coal has almost passed into history.

The Tinplate Industry

During the period immediately following the end of the Great War the loss of tinplate production was more than offset by the phenomenal rise in profit per box which reached a peak of 7s 6d in the first half of 1918. However the return to peacetime conditions created difficulties, particularly in obtaining raw materials (notably coal) and skilled labour. When the immediate difficulties were overcome the industry started to prosper. Tinplate prices rose from the controlled wartime price of 30s 3d a box to 55s a box in May 1920. This position did not last long.

The collapse of the post-war boom and the intensification of competition resulted in a frantic search for orders. By the beginning of 1921 all the Llanelli works with the exception of the Morfa and Old Lodge Works were idle. Although there was a slight recovery towards the end of 1921 it was effectively a temporary respite and the trend was very much downwards. In May 1925 there were 5,000 Llanelli tinplate workers unemployed. As F. J. Rees, manager of Llanelli steelworks, remarked: 'We are passing through a period of gloom and despondency unequalled during the last 25 to 30 years.' The onset of the Great Depression in the wake of the Wall Street Crash compounded the gloom. In 1930 the industry was operating at 69.9 per cent of its capacity. This fell to 50 per cent capacity in 1931–2. By January 1931, 7,000 Llanelli tinplate workers were either wholly or partly unemployed. The crisis was accentuated by Britain's decision to leave the Gold Standard which led to the breakdown of the Anglo-American tinplate agreement which controlled the export trade. Half the mills in the industry were idle by the end of 1931. J. S. Tregoning & Company was particularly badly hit with the Morfa Works closed throughout the second half of that year.

Towards the end of 1932 demand for tinplate started to improve. In August 1933 W. J. Frith, chairman of Richard Thomas, confidently declared that 'the worst is over'. The industry enjoyed a measure of prosperity – although with reduced capacity until 1938. The price per box improved from 14s 4d in 1931 to 23s 5d per box in 1937. Two factors helped the recovery of the industry. First, an international tinplate cartel was set up in 1934 to regulate competition. Second, there was a prodigious increase in the domestic demand for canned foods. Production soared, reaching 251,200 tons in 1935 – an increase of 186 per cent over 1930. This upsurge peaked in 1937 when it became clear that there was overproduction in the industry.

In the interwar period there were significant moves towards amalgamation in the Llanelli area. With the exception of Richard Thomas, which amalgamated with the Grovesend Company in 1923, none of the firms owning tinplate works in Llanelli amalgamated in the 1920s. The turning point came in 1932 when a tariff was placed on imported steel-bar. Between 1933 and 1936 Richard Thomas bought two Llanelli tinplate works – the Pen-coed Works of Folland and Company (October 1935) and the Morfa Works of J. S. Tregoning (March 1936). The Old Castle and Western Works effectively operated as a single concern. In April 1939 five tinplate firms – Old Castle, Western (Llanelli), Kidwelly, Ashburnham (Burry Port) and Teilo (Pontarddulais) – combined to form the Llanelly Associated Tinplate Company Ltd.

The Second World War proved to be a mixed blessing for the tinplate industry. Early in 1939 the government's efforts to put Britain on a wartime footing brought a boom in production. Tinplate was required in increasing quantities for gas mask canisters and food reserves for the military. All the Llanelli works made a full recovery from the disastrous conditions of 1938. The Old Castle Works produced 622,471 boxes in 1940, its highest output since 1937. However these conditions were fated not to last. Export licences were withdrawn in 1941 and under the lease-lend arrangements, the USA was allowed to supply tinplate to British markets in the Middle and Far East. Exports declined sharply. Closures were inevitable. In 1941 the Llanelly Association closed its Ashburnham, Kidwelly, Old Lodge and Western Works. In the same year Richard Thomas closed its South Wales Works and the Morfa Works were closed in 1942. From 1942 until the end of the war tinplate production in Llanelli was confined to the Old Castle Works, Llanelly Association (Teilo and Burry Works) and R. T. Mills (of Richard Thomas). Despite this contraction and supporting the view that every recession has a silver lining, handsome profits were being made: Llanelly Association's profits totalled £316,805 during the years 1940–43.

It was clear that the continued overcapacity in the industry and the need to invest in modern plant, necessitated drastic solutions. There was little argument against the closure of out-of-date plants such as the Old Lodge and Kidwelly Works. The overall capacity of the Llanelly Association was reduced from forty-three to twenty-six mills. In August 1945 the tinplate manufacturers established the Tinplate Scheme Ltd to supervise the financing of redundancy proposals. Eventually £509,204 was set aside for this purpose. If Llanelli was to have any post-war future as a centre of tinplate production then investment in new plant was essential. The new Labour Government pledged its support to back the restructuring of the industry. It was planned that three new cold reduction plants be sited in south Wales in close proximity to the new hot strip-mill planned for Port Talbot. The Llanelly Association was adamant that one of the cold reduction plants should be built at Llanelli – the heart of the tinplate industry, and where there was a large reservoir of highly skilled labour available.

Even with government support no one company could provide the necessary funds for such a massive restructuring scheme to secure the industry's future. A further round of amalgamation took place. The merger of Richard Thomas & Company with Baldwin's Ltd to form Richard Thomas and Baldwin (RTB) was the first stage in the programme. Of greater significance was the formation of the Steel Company of Wales in 1947 of which RTB was the major subscriber but to which the Llanelly Association also contributed. With the site of the new strip-mill agreed for Port Talbot, it was anticipated that Llanelli would be the front runner to acquire the first of the new cold reduction plants. However, this was far from being a done deal. The local member of parliament, Jim Griffiths, entered the fray. He lobbied determinedly both publicly and in private the case in favour of Llanelli. Jim Griffiths believed that the government had a responsibility to provide alternative sources of employment. Although the industrialists favoured a site at Felindre (north of Swansea), Trostre, despite its marshy location and greater distance from Port Talbot, won the day. Why was Trostre successful? The *South Wales Evening Post* expressing the Swansea view, was explicit in its assessment: 'There is no doubt whatever that the decision was largely influenced by Mr Jim Griffiths, the Minister of National Insurance on behalf of Llanelly.'

Work on the Trostre site started on 27 August 1947. The five-stand cold-reduction mill came into operation in November 1951. Originally designed to produce 135,000 boxes per week, by 1962 its output had risen to 250,000 boxes per week. Trostre's opening marked the passing of the era of the Llanelli pack mills which had begun with the opening of Dafen Works in 1846. The surviving works gradually closed. In 2005 Trostre was part of the Anglo-Dutch steel company Corus and was the largest single employer in the Llanelli area, providing work for around 900 men and women.

Agriculture

Since 1914 farming in the county has witnessed sustained changes. The most important relates to the pattern of landownership and employment, and the nature of farming within Carmarthenshire. In 1914 there were 8,700 agricultural holdings in Carmarthenshire but only around 12 per cent of these were owned by the occupier (1909 – 11.57 per cent owner occupier). While the number of holdings declined over the next sixty years to 5,440, by 1973 the percentage owned by occupiers had surged to 68.2 per cent (1970). Over roughly the same period the number of workers, both seasonal and regular, employed on these holdings had fallen sharply from 7,929 in 1921 to 2,956 in 1970. Increased mechanization and the move towards family farms have contributed to this trend.

Important changes have occurred to the nature of the farming within the county. There has been a substantial fall in the area of land under tillage, from c. 70,000 acres in 1914 to 15,000 acres in 1972. This decline is greatest in the growing of cereal crops such as wheat and barley. An adverse knock-on effect of this has been the virtual elimination of corn-milling, one of the most rural of industries. As arable farming has declined it has been paralleled by a rise in pastoral farming. The number of cows and heifers more than doubled after 1914 and there have been significant increases in the numbers of sheep reared in the county. Wool, dairy products and meat are now the staples of the county's agricultural economy. Between the wars the county became an important producer of dairy products. The creation of the Milk Marketing Board in 1933 was of benefit to farms in Carmarthenshire as it allowed them to gain the security of a steady income. Local cooperatives such as the ones at Ffair-fach and Carmarthen processed the milk into a range of dairy products. New cream-eries were opened at Llangadog (1957/8) and Newcastle Emlyn, with the latter specializing in producing mozzarella cheese. In the last quarter of the twentieth century the farming industry has appeared to lurch from one crisis to another – first BSE and more recently foot and mouth (2001). Farm incomes during this period were failing to keep pace with those in other sectors of the economy and heaped further misery on an already beleaguered industry. Enterprising farmers tapped into the potential of tourism by offering quality rural accommodation, pony trekking and fish-ing. The potential for eco-tourism and organic farming may ultimately pro-vide a life-line. Many family-run farms can only survive if there is an additional income to that generated by the farm.

The break up of the landed estates was underway before the First World War, but the momentum increased rapidly afterwards. Since the Second World War both the Dynevor and the Golden Grove estates have been broken up and sold. The fate of many of the larger and smaller country houses in the county has been depressing. Many have been abandoned and have slowly fallen into terminal neglect rendering demolition as the only safe option. Of the larger houses, Glanbran, Dolaucothi, Tre-gib, Middleton Hall and Pant-glas have all been demolished. Edwinsford is in total ruin.[10] The picture is not entirely gloomy. Some sites and houses have been secured. Remarkably, after the architectural strippers had removed many of its features, Aberglasney was saved from demolition by a trust, and is now an important tourist attraction. Newton House and grounds have been acquired by the National Trust. The grounds and remaining outbuilding at Middleton Hall have, with lottery funding, become the site of the National Botanic Gardens of Wales.

Regeneration and Recovery

Central and local government have adopted a proactive approach to mitigate the effects of economic change. During the Second World War light industry was encouraged to locate within the county. The motor component company Llanelly Radiators opened in 1942 and later, Fisher and Ludlow, part of BMC, followed suit. Hopes that south-west Carmarthenshire would become a significant force in the automotive industry did not materialize. The closure of the Duport steelworks in 1981 with the loss of 1,100 jobs was a severe blow to the economy of the county. Since then there has been a change in employment patterns. More people now work in the public and service sector than in manufacturing and agriculture. In 2000, of the 50,000 employee jobs located in Carmarthenshire 49 per cent were occupied by men and 51 per cent by women. While male full-time jobs accounted for 41.6 per cent of the total, female full-time jobs only made up 23 per cent of the total. The average gross annual earnings for the United Kingdom in 2003 was £24,600 compared with £19,700 for Carmarthenshire. Carmarthenshire's average weekly wage at only 80 per cent of the UK average is among the lowest in Wales. In order to alleviate the effects of these structural changes the government through the Welsh Development Agency and in partnership with the county council has encouraged the establishment of new businesses in the county. By 2002 no fewer than twenty-eight industrial estates, business parks and workshops had been set up to mitigate the effects of unemployment. Tourism has become an important seasonal employer and has benefited from recent developments in Middleton Hall, Aberglasney and Dynevor Park. In May 2000 the first National Botanic Garden to be built in Britain for nearly two hundred years was opened at a 568 acre site at Middleton Hall near Llanarthne. The project was supported by a £21.7 million grant from the Millennium Commission and matched by £20 million from other sources. Its centrepiece is the critically acclaimed Great Glasshouse designed by Lord (Norman) Foster. This is the largest single-span glasshouse in the world and its gently curved profile fits in smoothly with the surrounding contours of the countryside. The first years of its existance were beset by financial problems and lower than anticipated visitor numbers. Financial restructuring and growing support from the general public will hopefully secure its future.

To support these developments there have been improvements to the county's road network. The extension of the M4 motorway into Carmarthenshire led to improved links being established with Llanelli, and the construction of a dual carriageway between Pont Abraham and St Clears. There has been significant progress towards eliminating congestion bottle-necks at Carmarthen, Whitland, Llandeilo, St Clears and Kidwelly with the opening of bypasses. While the county's road system has improved this has been paralleled by a decline in its rail network. After the Beeching report (1963) a number of branch lines were closed: Carmarthen to Llandeilo, Carmarthen to Lampeter, and passenger services ended along the Aman and Gwendraeth valleys. The main line from London to Fishguard still traverses the county, but the only other passenger route in operation is the Central or Heart of Wales Line from Llanelli via Llandovery to Shrewsbury. Despite many fears regarding its future it has managed tenaciously to survive through astutely marketing its tourist potential.

As areas of Carmarthenshire have suffered the effects of de-industrialization, urban reclamation schemes have commenced. The scars and dereliction of former collieries, tinplate works and steel mills have been removed. The WDA and the county council were behind the largest and most ambitious of these regeneration schemes in Llanelli. Since 1990, £60 million has been invested in transforming 2,000 acres of industrial dereliction into quality residential, industrial, commercial and leisure facilities. The star attraction, which was officially opened in 2002, is the 22 km. Millennium Coastal Park which has cost £30 million. A derelict coastal plain has been reborn as a sustainable leisure and tourist attraction incorporating many water features. On the former site of the Duport Steelworks is the Sandy Water Park. Within the park there are woodlands, marinas, cycle paths, coastal walks and the new National Wetlands Centre of Wales. The town centre of Llanelli has also been transformed with the opening of the St Elli covered shopping area. There are plans to restore Llanelly House, one of the finest surviving eighteenth century town houses in Wales, to its former glory. It is hoped that it will become a key component in the cultural life of the town. A less ambitious development has been made in Carmarthen around the old market which with its eclectic variety of stalls has once again become an important trading centre.

Politics

The political history of the county since 1914 has been varied and at times dramatic. Carmarthenshire has not lost its ability or capacity to surprise. There was no general election during the course of the war and the parliament of 1910 was extended until hostilities were over. The Representation of the People's Act (1918) allowed women over 30 to vote in national elections for the first time. Accompanying the Act, parliamentary constituencies were revised to take into account demographic changes. This measure redrew the political landscape in Carmarthenshire. The county which had previously had three seats, was now reduced to two. A constituency of Carmarthen was formed by uniting the former East and West divisions. The old Carmarthen Boroughs constituency disappeared. Llanelli was given its own member and became a separate borough division of Carmarthen. The impact of these changes on the county was profound. Whereas the total electorate of the three former constituencies in 1910 was around 28,500, following the extension of the franchise the Llanelli constituency alone was 49,000 and that of the new western constituency 36,000. The changes almost mirrored the socio/economic division of the county into agricultural/rural and industrial/urban. Now that the industrial areas of Burry Port, the Aman and Gwendraeth valleys had been joined to Llanelli it afforded the Labour party a better opportunity to concentrate its political resources in order to make a political breakthrough. At the 1918 'Coupon' Election both constituencies returned National Liberal supporters of Lloyd George's coalition. While John Hinds was returned unopposed for Carmarthen, the Revd Towyn Jones faced a stern challenge in Llanelli from Dr J. H. Williams who won 49.9 per cent of the vote for Labour and placed the party well and truly on the political map as a credible alternative to the Liberals.

At the 1922 general election Dr J. H. Williams finally won the seat for the Labour party. His triumph was due to a number of factors. The party's organization in the Llanelli area had been transformed and the trade unions were far more supportive of Labour than they had been before the war. The Labour Association appointed a new young organizer, Jim Griffiths, who proved to be an inspirational and effective choice in galvanizing support for the party. Perhaps of greater significance was the change in attitude towards socialism in general and towards the Labour party in particular, which many working-class people considered to be a better reflection of their own hopes and aspirations than Liberalism. Labour's victory in the 1922 parliamentary election in Llanelli marked the start of the longest period of unbroken political domination by one party in Carmarthenshire's history. In 1936 Jim Griffiths succeeded Dr J. H. Williams as the member of parliament. His political career was in sharp contrast to that of his predecessor. Whereas Williams adopted rather a low profile in the House of Commons, the parliamentary career of Jim Griffiths (member of parliament for Llanelli 1936–70) is the most distinguished of all the members who have represented one of the county's constituencies.

Carmarthenshire is linked with two important political figures in the twentieth century. The first of these, Jim Griffiths (1890–1975) was born into a mining family in y Betws and at the age of 13 he followed the path of most of his contemporaries to work in the local colliery. He became involved in local politics and attended Ysgol y Gwynfryn/White House in Ammanford, a sort of informal political finishing school for those of a left-wing persuasion. Griffiths became a committed socialist and opposed the 1914–18 war. During the war he was appointed the first secretary of the Ammanford Trades and Labour Council. His early talent as an organizer and motivator led to his selection as the Labour party agent for Llanelli. In 1925 he became miners' agent to the Anthracite Association and from 1934 to 1936 he was president of the South Wales Miners' Federation. Once in parliament Jim Griffiths transcended the rather insular world of mid-twentieth century Welsh political life, winning a reputation for himself as a skilled operator in the much larger bear pit of British politics. When Labour's years in the political wilderness ended with their landslide victory in the 1945 election Jim Griffiths was appointed Minister for National Insurance (1945–50), a key role in consolidating and expanding the welfare state. He was responsible for two major pieces of legislation – the National Insurance (Industrial Injuries) Act 1945 and the National Insurance Act of 1948. Much to his surprise he was appointed Colonial Secretary in 1950 a role he threw himself into with his customary energy. Jim Griffiths never forgot his roots and he devoted a great deal of time to Welsh issues and concerns during the party's years in opposition – particularly that of Welsh separatism. He himself favoured a measure of devolution while maintaining the economic unity of the United Kingdom. When Labour returned to office in 1964 Jim Griffiths was appointed the first Secretary of State for Wales. During his time as MP for Llanelli he fought eight elections and never once secured less than a 65 per cent share of the vote. He retired from political life in 1970.

Denzil Davies replaced Jim Griffiths as MP for Llanelli and successfully defended the seat in the nine general elections between 1970 and 2001. The new member was an able and personable politician who during his early years in parliament ascended the ministerial ladder when Harold Wilson appointed him Minister of State for the Treasury in 1975. During the Thatcher years (1979–90) he occupied a number of prominent and high-profile shadow cabinet positions, notably Welsh affairs and defence. However over a period of years he became disenchanted with certain aspects of the party's defence policies and returned to the back benches. The days when Labour's vote in Llanelli could be weighed rather than counted were also passing gradually into history. Denzil Davies saw off a spirited challenge from Plaid Cymru in 1970, although their candidate was the immensely popular rugby coach of Llanelli RFC, Carwyn James, who could only secure a 16.8 per cent share of the vote. At the 2001 general election Davies's majority over Plaid Cymru in a reduced turnout almost halved to 6,385 votes compared with 12,110 in 1997. At the elections to the newly created Welsh Assembly in May 1999 Labour failed to win Llanelli which returned Plaid Cymru's Helen Mary Jones. If it is premature to write Labour's political obituary for the Llanelli constituency then at the very least it is facing the prospect of more challenging times in the new millennium.

In the newly created constituency of Carmarthen the representation between 1918 and 2002 has been shared rather unequally between three political parties. The most successful political party in British political history – the Conservative Party – was not one of them. Although the county has been unable to provide the Conservative Party with any MPs since 1918, it has nevertheless contributed to its fortunes. At the 2005 General Election the party was led by Michael Howard, who was raised and educated in Llanelli. For almost fifty years the Liberal party retained its grip on Carmarthen, the rural farming interest narrowly keeping at bay for most of the time the Labour vote, which was concentrated on Carmarthen and some of the smaller towns. Labour won the seat for the first time in 1929 when Daniel Hopkin was returned, only to lose it again at the 1931 election, the nadir of the party's fortunes as a serious political force. Daniel Hopkin regained the seat for Labour in 1935 but was unable to retain it during one of Labour's greatest triumphs in 1945. The seat was establishing a tradition of independence and of bucking against national trends. Hopkin Morris held the seat for the Liberals from 1945 until his death in 1957 when Lady Megan Lloyd George, a convert from the Liberals recaptured the seat for Labour at a by-election. Lady Megan was the first woman to be returned to parliament for either of the seats in the county. She was active in presiding over the Parliament for Wales campaign. No Liberal member has been returned since Morris's death. In 1955 Plaid Cymru contested the seat for the first time and their candidate Jennie Eirian Davies, although polling a respectable 3,835 (7.8 per cent) votes, was a distant third behind the Liberals and Labour.

The most dramatic election during this period was the by-election in July 1966 following the death of Lady Megan. Plaid Cymru had been making slow if unspectacular progress in the constituency. Their candidate in the 1966 general election, Gwynfor Evans, recorded the highest ever share of the vote for the party when he came third with 16.1 per cent. This hardly suggested that the seat was within the party's grasp, and few were prepared for the dramatic events of four months later.

Plaid Cymru's roots in Carmarthenshire go back almost to 1926 when the party was founded. A branch was set up in Llanelli soon after the Pwllheli founding meeting. The second important political figure linked with the county is Gwynfor Evans (1912–2005). Gwynfor, as he was universally known, "embodied the soul of Welsh nationalism".[11] He was described in the *Western Mail* on the occasion of his ninetieth birthday, as one of the greatest and most influential Welshmen of the twentieth century. It is difficult to refute this assessment. By the time he moved to Llangadog in 1939 the number of Plaid members in the county had slumped to six. During the war the local party was opposed to the War Office's policy of sequestering land in the Epynt area. Many party members including Evans were pacifists. In 1946 he started a new branch in Gwynfe recruiting fifteen members and another branch in Llangadog. Plaid Cymru's early rural roots are clearly discernible. Its appeal was largely to those who were concerned about the erosion of what they perceived to be a unique way of life – essentially rural and linguistically and culturally Welsh, in the face of an overpowering homogeneous Anglo/Welsh society. In some ways the 1966 by-election was a protest vote and Plaid Cymru frequently posed the question to undecided voters: 'Why add one Labour vote to Wilson's majority of 96?' In other ways there were very real local issues which needed addressing such as proposals to amalgamate farms, the need for new roads and by-passes in the county, and the closure of rural railways. Critics labelled Plaid Cymru's candidate 'Gwynfor Dual Carriageways'. Permeating many of Plaid Cymru's policies was the view that 'London does not recognise how serious the situation is in Wales, and does not intend to act effectively'. (*Be Your Own Masters* – Gwynfor Evans campaign leaflet 1966.) At the poll Gwynfor Evans secured 16,179 votes and established a comfortable majority of 2,436 over the defeated Labour candidate. When asked to assess the significance of the 1966 by-election Gwynfor Evans observed:

> The impact on Wales has been permanent and has never ceased. The Party has grown constantly at all levels, in Carmarthenshire and in Wales. The by-election was like a kick-start. The effects went very deep in places for example – Gwynedd. We won Caernarfon and Meirionnydd in a General Election only eight years later. This was the first time we took seats in a General Election. All kinds of movements such as the Welsh Schools' movement seemed to leap forward after 1966.[12]

Gwynoro Jones recovered the seat for Labour in 1970 against the national trend, which saw Harold Wilson lose the general election. He retained the seat in the first of the two general elections in 1974, after several nail-biting re-counts by the slimmest of margins – three votes. If Plaid Cymru was disappointed with its performance in February 1974 they more than made up for it in the autumn election. Wilson had led a minority Labour administration since February and he considered the time propitious to make further inroads into Conservative support nationally in order to establish a majority in parliament. While Labour achieved this goal, the party lost the Carmarthen seat. Although Gwynoro Jones succeeded in increasing the Labour vote, the main beneficiary from the sharp fall in support for the Liberal and Conservative candidates was Plaid Cymru's Gwynfor Evans. Plaid Cymru was unable to establish any sort of tenure on the constituency which reverted to Labour at the 1979 election. The natural inclination and composition of the constituency did not fit the profile for a safe Labour seat. As a large rural and predominantly Welsh-speaking area it had more in common with Liberal and even some Conservative constituencies. Labour held the seat throughout the long period of Conservative governments (1979–97) and the first Tony Blair administration (1997–2001) first with Dr Roger Thomas, then Dr Alan Williams. Issues relating to the Welsh language, bilingualism and the countryside tended not to figure prominently on the party's national agenda but they mattered increasingly to many living in the constituency. In 1997 the parliamentary constituencies in the county were redrawn. The town of Carmarthen and the western part of the county were added to south Pembrokeshire to create the new constituency of Carmarthen West and South Pembrokeshire which Labour's Nick Anger won. A new constituency of Carmarthen East and Dinefwr was formed. Although predominantly rural the addition of Ammanford and Glanaman from the Llanelli constituency did counter the loss of the town of Carmarthen. At the 2001 general election the seat was taken by Adam Price for Plaid Cymru, and was Labour's only loss in Wales. Kidwelly was added to Llanelli where the net effect of the boundary changes was to reduce the Labour vote.

Political activity is by no means the monopoly of established parties. Individuals and groups occasionally drew together under the spur of some external threat, and galvanized themselves in the process into non-partisan community action. These David versus Goliath struggles are occasionally successful. Two post-war examples from Carmarthenshire are testimony to the will and tenacity of local people triumphing over state and commercial interests. The first concerned a plan by Swansea Corporation in 1960 to construct a reservoir in the valley of the Gwendraeth Fach near Llangyndeyrn. Local people were incensed by this proposal and waged a successful campaign which united the community to ensure their valley's survival. The campaign in this close knit and thoroughly Welsh locality contained cultural issues to which the authorities appeared crass and insensitive. This peaceful and quiet corner of Carmarthenshire captured the attention of local and national media in a way vaguely reminiscent of the Rebecca movement. An action committee was set up to coordinate the opposition campaign. There were numerous meetings, letters, marches and considerable lobbying of local and national politicians. One of the most successful tactics employed by the protestors in October 1963 was to blockade farm gates and deny surveyors access to the threatened land. After a protracted and increasingly acrimonious campaign Swansea corporation abandoned its plans in 1965 and sought instead an alternative location near Rhandir-mwyn. This proved less contentious and Llyn Brianne reservoir was opened in 1972.

The second successful example was the proposal by McAlpine in the early 1980s to extend its quarrying operations at Pentregwenlais into neighbouring Carmel Woods, an area of outstanding natural beauty. An alliance of community and environmental interests was successful in halting the scheme, which had it come into fruition would have destroyed Pant y Llyn, the only example in mainland Britain of a turlough, a seasonal lake whose level rises and falls in parallel with the water table. In March 1996 the new owner of the quarry, Tarmac, adopted a much more conciliatory approach to its relations with the community. This resulted in the opening in July 1999 by His Royal Highness the Prince of Wales, of the Carmel National Nature Reserve.

Over the period 1914–2002 the structure of local government within the county has changed in many ways. While the county council had responsibility for a wide range of functions following its creation in 1888, the rapid pace of population growth and urbanization led to the formation of urban districts, which assumed their own functions. A number of these have already been noted. Rural districts were also formed into councils and operated at a level below that of the county. These were based on such areas as Llandeilo Fawr, Whitland and Llanybydder. Below these the county was divided into parish councils. This rather chaotic system survived until local government in Wales was reformed in 1974. In what was the most significant change to the internal map of Wales since 1542, the old counties, county boroughs, rural and urban districts were swept away and replaced by new counties and districts. The three counties of west Wales were spectacular casualties in this reorganization. Carmarthenshire, Cardiganshire and Pembrokeshire were replaced by a new 'super' county named after the ancient Welsh kingdom of Dyfed. The former county of Carmarthenshire was divided into three districts – Carmarthen, Dinefwr and Llanelli. As in Roman and medieval times the administrative centre of the new county of Dyfed was Carmarthen. In universal terms the new structure did not prove to be an unqualified success. Many were still deeply attached to the unique characteristics and traditions of the former counties and were unable to identify closely with Dyfed. Almost from the outset there were calls to restore the *status quo*. The sheer size of the new county left many bewildered and wondering why a reform, whose aim was to bring local government closer to the people, appeared to have moved it further away. As it transpired, the shelf-life of the new structure was in historical terms very short. In 1997 a further round of local government reorganization took place with the creation of new unitary authorities. The former county of Carmarthenshire re-appeared out of the post-Dyfed experiment as a new unitary authority.

Only the parish councils, renamed community councils, were virtually unscathed by these reforms.

The issues of separatism and devolution were central to the politics of nationalism advocated by Plaid Cymru. Gwynfor Evans as president of Plaid Cymru was one of the architects of their programme. Labour's half-hearted commitment to devolution in 1979 was a factor in the overwhelming rejection of the proposal by the electorate in the 1 March referendum of that year. Devolution was well and truly off the political agenda under the Conservative governments led by Margaret Thatcher. They were even prepared to renege on their 1979 manifesto pledge to establish a separate Welsh television channel. This prompted Gwynfor Evans to announce his intention to fast unto death unless the commitment was honoured. Remarkably the government performed a U-turn and agreed to set up what became, in November 1982, S4C. When Labour returned to power in 1997 devolution was a central part of its constitutional reforms. Although the menu on offer to Wales was at very much a lower tariff compared to the one proposed for Scotland, Labour's determination to secure the proposals was much more apparent and real than it had been two decades earlier. Despite this there was still a reservoir of scepticism against the policy in Wales. Few who are interested in such matters will forget the tension as the referendum results were announced across Wales. With the outcome very much in doubt until the end, what appeared to sway it was appropriately enough the result from Carmarthen. Gwynfor's adopted county tipped the balance of the votes in favour, ahead of the 'No' vote. In the first elections for the new National Assembly, Plaid Cymru won both the Llanelli and the Carmarthen East and Dinefwr seats. Labour was returned in Carmarthen West and South Pembrokeshire. The Welsh Assembly is likely to assume a greater role over our lives in the future and it may well alter the relationships between the various parties in the county.

Culture

Much of the cultural life of the county has been rooted in the Welsh language. Since 1914 there has been a slow and steady decline in those speaking and using the language. In 1911, 84.9 per cent of the population was able to speak Welsh. This had fallen to 66.5 per cent by 1971. Over the last two decades of the twentieth century, this decline has been arrested as a result of a number of initiatives, two of which were the creation of S4C, and the decision to make Welsh a compulsory part of the National Curriculum. Much of this has been due to the influence of Plaid Cymru and the general national revival which has made it both fashionable and advantageous to be bilingual in the 'new' Wales. While the importance of the *gymanfa ganu* (hymn singing festival) and local eisteddfodau, although they are still arranged, has lessened in importance over the course of the century, there has been an upsurge in Welsh-medium broadcasting and publishing for recreational as well as educational purposes. One of the most admired Welsh singer-songwriters of the post-war era is Dafydd Iwan (1942–) who was born in the Aman valley and brought up in Brynaman. A fervent nationalist, his protest songs in particular struck a chord with many young Welsh speakers reaching political maturity during the 1960s and 1970s.

A number of literary figures from Carmarthenshire have made important contributions to Welsh culture beyond the confines of their native county. David Rees Griffiths (1882–1953) younger brother of Jim Griffiths, was better known by his bardic name of Amanwy. He was a prolific poet and *eisteddfodwr* who had won over fifty-two chairs by 1923 and later became an accomplished local journalist. Largely self-taught, Amanwy was one of a flourishing literary group that existed in Ammanford in the years before the Great War. He is possibly one of the finest collier poets ever to have written in the Welsh language. A good friend of Amanwy was D. J. Williams (1885–1970). D. J., as he was universally known, came from Llansawel but left to work in Betws colliery. He later became a teacher and established himself as a short-story writer and author of a much acclaimed biographical account of life on a farm in north Carmarthenshire – *Hen Dŷ Ffarm* (The Old Farmhouse).[13] In 1936 D. J., who was a leading figure in the fledgling nationalist party Plaid Cymru, gained national prominence for his role in the arson attack on the RAF bombing school at Penyberth in Lleyn. Another contemporary of Amanwy's was the well-known historian of Nonconformity, Gomer Roberts (1904–93) from Llandybïe. Howell Elvet Lewis (1860–1953) was an outstanding poet and hymn-writer. Elfed, as he was popularly called after his birthplace (Cynwyl Elfed), gained a great reputation in Welsh literary and religious circles although he spent much of his adult life as a minister in London.

The most celebrated Anglo-Welsh writer linked with the county in the twentieth century is Dylan Thomas (1914–53). His family came originally from Brechfa but Dylan's father was born in Johnstown on the outskirts of Carmarthen. Dylan's own connection with the county is through the boat house at Laugharne with its dramatic setting overlooking the Taf estuary. Dylan arrived at the Boat House in 1949, the property being rented to him by Mrs Margaret Taylor (wife of historian A. J. P. Taylor), his most consistent benefactor – and lived there for four and a half years until his death in 1953. During his time in Laugharne he only completed six poems in the famous blue garden shed at the end of the cliff walk. 'Over Sir John's hill' was one of the first poems he wrote in Laugharne.

Whether or not Laugharne provided the inspiration for his best known work *Under Milk Wood* is open to debate; what is certain is that most of the writing was undertaken there. Shortly before his death the last portrait of Dylan Thomas was completed by Gordon Stuart, a young Canadian who later became well known as a gifted landscape artist as well as a renowned portrait painter. Following his death in New York, Dylan's body was brought back to Laugharne and is buried in the local churchyard where it is marked by a simple wooden cross. The author Richard Hughes (1900–1976) once said that some people thought that writing was something to escape to, whereas in his case it was something to escape from. He settled in Laugharne in 1934 and while indulging in his passion for sailing, also managed to complete his second novel *In Hazard* (1938) in a gazebo located in the castle. From the north of the county, Earnest Lewis Thomas (Richard Vaughan, 1904–83) who was born in Llanddeusant wrote a trilogy of novels, starting with *Moulded in Earth* (1951) set in the farming communities lying in the shadow of the Black Mountains.

In the visual arts the one outstanding figure is Edward Morland Lewis (1903–43) from Ferryside. After training at Carmarthen School of Art he attended the Royal Academy schools in London before enrolling in Walter Sickert's private art school. His work was preoccupied with tone, and he used a relatively muted range of colours. Much of Lewis's work consists of landscapes from around his native Ferryside and the town of Carmarthen. He was killed during the war in North Africa in 1943 before his talent had fully matured. Another product of Carmarthen Art College who established a considerable reputation, and acquired a dedicated following, was John Elwyn (1916–97). His subject material reflected a rural life that was slowly passing – farms, animals and chapels. A much more contemporary approach to art is given by William Wilkins (1938–) who has lived in Llandeilo since the age of two. His figurative work using a range of bright colours is carefully constructed in a pointillist style. The wider public may well be more familiar with his inspirational efforts to restore the gardens at Aberglasney as chairman of the trust which secured the survival of 'the garden lost in time'. Tom Nash (1931–) from Ammanford has worked in Paris and Provence and has won international acclaim as an abstract artist. One of his biggest projects was to assemble a series of large reflective panels on the side of Dryslwyn castle, a rare example of the environment directly incorporated into a work of art. He was for many years a lecturer at Llanelli School of Art. Among the newer generation of artists working in Carmarthenshire, one of the most intriguing and significant is Peter Finnemore from Pont-iets. Trained as a photographer, much of his recent work is conceptual, encompassing both photography and video. His work emphasises cultural identity, community, landscape and relates to issues of space and being, drawing heavily on his own roots in the Gwendraeth Valley. Some of his short films and photographs are set or taken in his own garden and home, using the ordinary to explore wider issues. In 2005 he was one of the artists who represented Wales in the Venice Biennale, and he also won the Gold Medal for Art at the National Eisteddfod.

With an increase in leisure time many have embraced organized sport as a recreational pastime, either as participants or as spectators. From the viewpoint of team sports the popularity of rugby within the county is almost universal. Many of the village sides before the advent of the national leagues were involved in the West Wales League. The only first-class club in the county is Llanelli RFC, better known as the 'Scarlets' to their legions of devoted fans. Between 1972 and 2000 the 'Turks', the team's other nickname, won the WRU Challenge Cup a record eleven times. The greatest day in the club's history was 31 October 1972 when they defeated the mighty New Zealand All Blacks, by nine points to six. Carwyn James, Llanelli's coach was meticulous in his preparation for what was the second fixture of the tour. The previous year he had master-minded the British Lions to a famous series victory in New Zealand. When the All Blacks arrived in Britain they were determined to avenge their defeat by beating Carwyn's team. James was a great believer in the psychology of sport. Ray Gravell, one of the heroes of the victory re-called Carwyn taking the team to see the All Black's opening fixture in Gloucester, and insisting that the team sit as close to the touch line as possible. 'Seeing them close up took away any air of invincibility – they did not seem any bigger, fitter or leaner than us. Our victory has entered the folklore of the town – the day the pubs ran dry'.[14] Among the sporting heroes from the county were a group of extraordinarily talented rugby players. A quartet of famous outside-halves – Barry John, Phil Bennett, Gareth Davies and Jonathan Davies prompted some sporting journalists to speculate as to the existence of a 'fly-half' factory somewhere in the Llanelli hinterland.

One of Carmarthenshire's more unusual sporting links is with motor cycle-racing and world land speed record attempts. The magnificent 8 mile long stretch of wide golden sand at Pendine are aptly known as the 'sands of speed'. The beach had long been used for horse racing, but from 1905 motor-cycle speed trials were organized on the beach. Pendine's popularity as a venue grew in the 1920s. Large crowds of up to ten thousand motor-cycle enthusiasts would turn up for the Welsh TT races. Its ability to offer a measured mile with plenty of distance either side led to it becoming a favoured location for attempts on the land speed record. In 1924 Malcolm Campbell established a new record on the beach with a speed of 146 mph. In the following three years there was intense rivalry between Campbell and J. G. Parry Thomas to become the fastest man on four wheels. When Campbell broke Parry Thomas's record of 174 mph by reaching a speed of 180 mph in February 1927, the response was tragic. On 3 April 1927 Parry Thomas was killed when his powerful 27 litre engine car, Babs, somersaulted following a mechanical failure. The car was buried in the sand. In 1969 a decision was taken to exhume the wreck. After a lengthy restoration Babs is displayed for part of the year in the new Museum of Speed which was opened in the village in 1996.

In the future the county is likely to face a number of important challenges. Following the decline of its heavy industrial base – coal, steel and tinplate – Carmarthenshire has become a post-industrial society and economy. The vibrancy and self-esteem of its diverse communities is in many ways linked to the economic health and well being of the county. Ensuring that former industrial communities have a real future – particularly for their young people – will be a major priority for economic planners both locally and nationally. There are also challenges facing the rural heartland of the county. Issues relating to agriculture, transport, education, culture and demographic change are all very much alive and will need addressing. The county does have a number of advantages not least of which is a strong sense of community and local identity which will help it weather these challenges. Alongside these is the pleasant and varied environment which is so attractive to both visitors and locals. Enabling the marriage of these features to the revolution in information technology might well be one way forward. While the scars and relics of former industries have been expunged from the landscape, pride in the heritage and culture of the county as reflected in its museums and societies will enable future generations to understand the forces that helped shape and mould 'Sir Gâr'.

References

Chapter 1

1 F. C. Wardle, *Transactions of the Carmarthenshire Antiquarian Society*, vol. 13 (1918–19), p. 50.
2 Sir J. E. Lloyd (ed.), *A History of Carmarthenshire*, vol. I (Cardiff, 1935), p. 26.
3 Sir J. E. Lloyd (ed.), *A History of Carmarthenshire*, vol. I (Cardiff, 1935), p. 37.
4 G. J. Wainwright, *Coygan Camp. A Prehistoric, Romano-British and Dark Age Settlement in Carmarthenshire* (The Cambrian Archaeological Association, Cardiff, 1967), p. 12.
5 John Davies, *A History of Wales* (London, 1994), p. 7.
6 H. N. Savory, 'Prehistoric Carmarthenshire (since 1935)' in *The Carmarthenshire Antiquary*, vol. III, pt. 2 (Carmarthen, 1960), p. 52.
7 Royal Commission on Ancient and Historical Monuments, *V County of Carmarthen* (London, 1917), p. 102.
8 Richard Fenton, *Tours in Wales (1804–1813)*, edited by John Fisher (London, 1917), p. 336.
9 Sir J. E. Lloyd (ed.), *A History of Carmarthenshire*, vol. I (Cardiff, 1935), p. 51.
10 Anthony H. Ward, 'The Cairns on Mynydd Llangyndeyrn' in *The Carmarthenshire Antiquary*, vol. XII (Carmarthen, 1976), p. 12.
11 Anthony H. Ward, 'Field Survey of the Carmel Cairn group near Llandeilo' in *The Carmarthenshire Antiquary*, vol. XXIII (Carmarthen, 1987), pp. 3–10.
12 Sir Cyril Fox, 'Burial place of dwellers in the upper Taf Valley; Carmarthenshire in the Bronze Age' in *Archaeologia Cambrensis* (1925), p. 288.
13 *Archaeologia Cambrensis* (1860), p. 101.
14 Williams (et al), 'Recent archaeological work on Merlin's Hill, Abergwili' in *The Carmarthenshire Antiquary*, vol. XXIV (Carmarthen, 1988), p. 11.

Chapter 2

1 Dr. G. D. B. Jones, 'Excavations at Carmarthen 1968' in *The Carmarthenshire Antiquary*, vol. V (Carmarthen, 1969), pp. 2–3.
2 Heather James, *Excavations in Roman Carmarthen 1978–1990* (Carmarthen, 1993), p. 32.
3 Royal Commission on Ancient and Historical Monuments, *V County of Carmarthen* (London, 1917), p. 93.

4 Michael G. Jarrett, 'Excavations at Llys Brychan, Llangadog, 1961' in *The Carmarthenshire Antiquary*, vol. IV (Carmarthen, 1961), pp. 2–7.
5 W. N. Yates, 'The Age of the Saints in Carmarthenshire' in *The Carmarthenshire Antiquary*, vol. IX (Carmarthen, 1973), pp. 68–9.
6 A. O. H. Jarman, *The Legend of Merlin* (Cardiff, 1960), p. 26.
7 Sir J. E. Lloyd (ed.), *A History of Carmarthenshire*, vol. I (Cardiff, 1935), p. 122.
8 Joan Thirsk (ed.), *The Agrarian History of England and Wales*, vol. 1 (Cambridge, 1967), pp. 308–20.

Chapter 3

1 R. R. Davies, *The Age of Conquest Wales 1063–1415* (Oxford, 1987), p. 223.
2 Roger Turvey, *The Lord Rhys Prince of Deheubarth* (Llandysul, 1997), p. 9.
3 R. R. Davies, *The Age of Conquest Wales 1063–1415* (Oxford, 1987), p. 306.
4 R. A. Griffiths (ed.), *Boroughs of Medieval Wales* (Cardiff, 1978), p. 149.
5 R. R. Davies, *The Age of Conquest Wales 1063–1415* (Oxford, 1987), p. 391.
6 Roger Turvey, 'Twelve days that shook south-west Wales: The Royal Letters, Owain Glyndŵr and the Campaign of July 1403' in *The Carmarthenshire Antiquary*, vol. XXXVII (Carmarthen, 2001), p. 15.
7 The Dwnn family of Kidwelly were one of the few Welsh families to emerge into prominence during the middle of the fifteenth century. Sir John Dwnn served Edward IV and became an outstanding patron of the arts. See Peter Lord, *The Visual Culture of Wales: Medieval Vision* (Cardiff, 2003) pp. 252–257.

Chapter 4

1 Howell A. Lloyd, *The Gentry of South-West Wales 1540–1640* (Cardiff, 1968), p. 35.
2 *The Itinerary of John Leland. The Antiquary*, vol. V, 3rd edn. (Oxford, 1769), p. 23. Leland's tours were conducted between 1536–39.
3 E. A. Lewis, *Welsh Port Books 1550–1603* (London, 1927), pp. 61–7.
4 John Davies, *The Carmarthen Book of Ordinances 1569–1606* (Llandybie, 1995), p. 2.
5 John Rowland Phillips, *The Civil War in Wales and the Marches*, vol. I (London, 1874), p. 251. A Royalist account of events in Newcastle Emlyn, 7 May 1645, p. 251.
6 John Rowland Phillips *The Civil War in Wales and the Marches*, vol. II (London, 1874), p. 273. Rowland Laugharne, 12 October 1645.
7 Ibid., p. 353; unsigned letter, 8 May 1648.
8 Ibid., p. 358; T. Sands, 3 May 1648.
9 Glanmor Williams, 'Stephen Hughes (1622–1688): Apostol Sir Gâr: The Apostle of Carmarthenshire' in *The Carmarthenshire Antiquary*, vol. XXXVII (Carmarthen, 2001), p. 29.
10 Sir J. E. Lloyd (ed.), *A History of Carmarthenshire*, vol. II (Cardiff, 1939), p. 109–11.
11 Erasmus Saunders, *A View of the State of religion in the Diocese of St David's About the beginning of the 18th Century* (London, 1721), p. 4–5.
12 Peter D. G. Thomas, 'Jacobitism in Wales' in *The Welsh History Review*, vol. 1, no. 3 (1962), p. 292.

Chapter 5

1 *Journals of the House of Lords* (1792), pp. 511–512.
2 B. H. Malkin, *The Scenery, Antiquities and Biography of South Wales* (London, 1804), II, p. 469.
3 Russell Davies, *Secret Sins: Sex Violence and Society in Carmarthenshire 1870–1920* (Cardiff, 1996), p. 233–4.
4 Thomas Campbell Foster, *The Times*, 7 October 1843.
5 Evidence of Mary Thomas, Llanelli, 6 December 1843. *Report of the Commissioners of Inquiry for South Wales* (London, 1844), p. 359.
6 David Williams, *The Rebecca Riots* (Cardiff, 1971), p. 116.
7 H.O.45/454 letter dated 19 June 1843 and enclosed in a letter sent by Lord Dynevor to the Home Office, 20 June 1843.
8 *Royal Commission on Land in Wales and Monmouthshire, Report* (London, 1896), p. 702.
9 *The Times*, 31 July 1802.
10 Hansard's *Parliamentary Debates*, 3rd Series, vol. XLIII, 671–2.
11 *James Griffiths and his Times* (Ferndale), p. 17.
12 See Deian Hopkin, 'The Rise of Labour in Llanelli 1890–1922' in Geraint H. Jenkins and J. Beverley Smith (eds), *Politics and Society in Wales 1840–1922* (Cardiff, 1988), pp. 169–170.
13 See Deian Hopkin, 'The Llanelli Riots of 1911' in *The Welsh History Review*, vol. 11, no. 4 (1988), pp. 497–500.
14 *Reports of the Commissioners of Inquiry into the State of Education in Wales* (London 1847), p. 220.
15 Dylan Rees, 'Thomas Matthews M. A. (1874–1916), Llandybïe: historian, writer and art critic' in *The Carmarthenshire Antiquary*, vol. XL (Carmarthen, 2004), pp. 129–138.
16 Peter Lord, 'Artisan Painters in Carmarthen' in *The Carmarthenshire Antiquary*, vol. XXVII (Carmarthen, 1992), p. 53.

Chapter 6

1 B. H. Malkin, *The Scenery, Antiquities and Biography of South Wales* (London, 1804), II, p. 538.
2 Revd T. Rees, *A Topographical and Historical Description of South Wales* (1815), p. 273.
3 Board of Agriculture Acreage returns for Wales: Carmarthenshire, *Bulletin of the Board of Celtic Studies*, 1951, part 2, p. 63–4.
4 Walter Davies, *General View of the Agriculture and Domestic Economy of South Wales*, 1814, vol. I, p. 482–3.
5 Walter Davies, *General View of the Agriculture and Domestic Economy of South Wales*, 1814, vol. II, p. 194.
6 Daniel E. Jones, *Hanes Plwyfi Llangeler a Phenboyr* (Llandysul, 1899), pp. 336–7.
7 *Royal Commission on Land in Wales and Monmouthshire*, vol. III (London, 1895), p. 108.
8 J. Geraint Jenkins, *The Welsh Woollen Industry* (Cardiff, 1969), p. 256.
9 See Michael C. S. Evans, 'The Pioneers of the Carmarthenshire Iron Industry' in *The Carmarthenshire Historian*, vol. IV (1967).

10 M. V. Symons, *Coal Mining in the Llanelli Area*, vol. I (Llanelli, 1979), p. 95–100.

11 *The Itinerary of John Leland. The Antiquary*, vol. V, 3rd edn. (Oxford, 1769), p. 23.

12 David W. Howell, *Patriarchs and Parasites. The Gentry of South-West Wales in the Eighteenth Century* (Cardiff, 1986), p. 94.

13 Gomer M. Roberts, *Hanes Plwyf Llandybïe* (Cardiff, 1939), p. 213.

14 Russell Davies, *Secret Sins. Sex, Violence and Society in Carmarthenshire 1870–1920* (Cardiff, 1996), p. 30.

15 Harold Hancocks, 'History of the Tinplate manufacture in Llanelli' (unpublished MA thesis, University of Wales Swansea, 1965), p. 250.

16 R. S. Craig, R. Protheroe Jones, M. V. Symons, *The Industrial and Maritime History of Llanelli and Burry Port 1750 to 2000* (Carmarthen, 2002); for the copper industry, see pp. 108–135.

17 Gareth Hughes and Robert Pugh, *Llanelly Pottery* (Llanelli, 1990), p. 15.

18 R. S. Craig, R. Protheroe Jones, M. V. Symons, *The Industrial and Maritime History of Llanelli and Burry Port 1750 to 2000* (Carmarthen, 2002); chapter 8, pp. 374–426.

Chapter 7

1 Postcard sent from France to Mr James, Trap, 25 September 1914 (author's family papers).

2 CRO Carmarthen, Peel Diary, 27–29 November 1915.

3 Ira Jones, *Tiger Squadron* (London, 1954), p. 51.

4 Herbert M. Vaughan, *The South Wales Squires* (London, 1926), p. 4.

5 James Griffiths, 'Glo-Carreg. Memoirs of the Anthracite Coalfield' in *The Carmarthenshire Historian*, vol. V, 1968, p. 13.

6 Hywel Francis, 'The Anthracite Strike and Disturbances of 1925' in *Llafur*, vol. 1, no. 2, May 1973, p. 53.

7 Ray Lawrence, *South Wales Coalfield Directory*, vol. 1 (South Wales Miners Library, 1998), pp. 116–117.

8 H. G. Tidmarsh to Glan Rees, 20 March 1944 (author's family papers).

9 Ray Lawrence, *South Wales Coalfield Directory*, vol. 1 (South Wales Miners Library, 1998), p. 384.

10 For a comprehensive list of houses in Carmarthenshire, which have been demolished or are in a perilous state, see Thomas Lloyd, *The Lost Houses of Wales* (Elmswell, 1986), pp. 54–67.

11 *The Times*, 22 April 2005.

12 Interview with Gwynfor Evans, 19 August 2002.

13 D. J. Williams, *Hen Dŷ Ffarm* (Llandysul, 1953).

14 Interview with Ray Gravell, 28 May 2002.

Select Bibliography

Official Papers

County Of Carmarthen, Royal Commission on The Ancient and Historical Monuments and Constructions in Wales and Monmouthshire, (London, 1917).

Evidence, Report and Appendices, Royal Commission on Land in Wales and Monmouthshire, (London, 1895, 1896).

Report, Evidence and Indexes of the Royal Commission appointed to inquire into the Church and other Religious Bodies in Wales (1910).

Return of Owners of Land, 1873. England and Wales.

Report of the Commissioners of Inquiry for South Wales (1844).

Reports Of the Commissioners of Inquiry into the State of Education in Wales, three volumes (1847).

Report of the Committee appointed to inquire into the condition of Higher Education in Wales (1881).

Printed Works

Annals, A. E., and Burnham, B. C., *The Dolaucothi Gold Mines: Geology and Mining History* (Cardiff, 1983).

Archaeologia Cambrensis.

Archaeology in Wales.

Arber-Cooke, A. T., *Pages from the History of Llandovery*, vol. 2 (Llandovery, 1976).

Baker-Jones, L., (ed.) *The Glaspant Diary 1896: A Chronicle of Carmarthenshire Country Life* (Carmarthen, 2001).

Barnes, T. and Yates, N., (ed.) *Carmarthenshire Studies* (Carmarthen, 1974).

Cragoe, Matthew, *An Anglican Aristocracy The Moral Economy of the Landed Estate in Carmarthenshire 1832–1895* (Oxford, 1996).

Craig, R. S., Jones, R. P., Symonds, M. V., *The Industrial and Maritime History of Llanelli and Burry Port 1750 to 2000* (Carmarthen, 2002).

Daniel-Tyssen, J. R., *Carmarthen Charters* (Carmarthen, 1878).

Davies, J., *The Carmarthen Book of Ordinances 1569–1606* (Llandybïe, 1996).
Davies, R., *Secret Sins: Sex, Violence and Society in Carmarthenshire 1870–1920* (Cardiff, 1996).
Davies, R. R., *The Age of Conquest: Wales 1063–1415* (Oxford, 1991).
Edwards, H. T., *Cwm Aman* (Llandysul, 1972).
Edwards, J., *Llanelli: Story of a Town* (Derby, 2001).
Edwards, J. (ed.), *Tinopolis: Aspects of Llanelli's Tinplate Trade* (Llanelli, 1995).
Evans, J. T., *The Church Plate of Carmarthenshire* (London, 1907).
Grigg, R., *History of Trinity College Carmarthen 1848–1998* (Cardiff, 1998).
Griffiths, R. A. (ed.), *Boroughs of Medieval Wales* (Cardiff, 1978).
Howell, D., *Land and People in Nineteenth Century Wales* (London, 1978).
Howell, D., *Patriarchs and Parasites: The gentry of south-west Wales in the Eighteenth Century* (Cardiff, 1986).
Hughes, L., *A Carmarthenshire Anthology* (Llandysyl, 2002).
Hughes, G., *A Llanelli Chronicle* (Llanelli, 1984).
Hughes, G., and Pugh, R., *Llanelly Pottery* (Llanelli, 1990).
Hughes, G., *The Scarlets: A History of Llanelli Rugby Club* (Llanelli, 1983).
James, H. (ed.), *Sir Gâr: Studies in Carmarthenshire History* (Carmarthen, 1991).
James, H., *Excavations in Roman Carmarthen 1978–1990* (Carmarthen, 1992).
James, T., *Carmarthen: An Archaeological and Topographical Survey* (Carmarthen, 1980).
Jenkins, D., *Llanelly Pottery* (Swansea, 1968).
Jenkins, G., *The Welsh Woollen Industry* (Cardiff, 1969).
Jones, D. J. V., *Rebecca's Children: A Study of Rural Society, Crime and Protest* (Oxford, 1989).
Jones, F., *Historic Carmarthenshire Houses* (Llandybïe, 1987).
Jones, Ira, *Tiger Squadron* (London, 1954).
Labour Party Wales, *James Griffiths and his Times* (Ferndale).
Lawrence, R. (ed.), *The South Wales Coalfield Directory*, vols 1 and 2 (1998).
Lewis, E. A., *The Welsh Port Books 1550–1603* (London, 1927).
Lloyd, J. E. (ed.), *A History of Carmarthenshire*, two volumes (Cardiff, 1938 and 1939).
Lloyd, T., *The Lost Houses of Wales* (London, 1986).
Lodwick, V and J., *The Story of Carmarthen* (Carmarthen, 1994).
Molloy, P., *A Shilling for Carmarthen* (Llandysul, 1980).
Morgan, D., *The Story of Carmarthenshire* (Cardiff, 1909).
Morris, W. H., *Kidwelly Tinplate Works*.
Parry-Jones, D., *Welsh Country Upbringing* (London, 1948).
Phillips, J. R., *Memoirs of the Civil War in Wales and the Marches 1642–9*, two volumes (London, 1874).
Prys-Jones, A. G., *The Story of Carmarthenshire*, two volumes (Llandybïe, 1959, 1972).
Jones, Daniel E., *Hanes Plwyfi Llangeler a Phenboyr* (Llandysul, 1899).
Rees, E. (ed.), *Carmarthenshire Memories of the Twentieth Century* (Llandybïe, 2002).
Rees, W., *An Historical Atlas of Wales From Early to Modern Times* (London, 1951).

Rhys, R., *Cloi'r Clwydi* (Llandybïe, 1983).

Roberts, G. M., *Hanes Plwyf Llandybïe* (Cardiff, 1939).

Saunders, E., *A View of the State of religion in the Diocese of St. David's about the beginning of the 18th century* (Cardiff, 1949).

Symonds, M. V., *Coal Mining in the Llanelli Area*, vol. 1 (Llanelli, 1979).

Tarmac Papers

Turvey, R., *The Lord Rhys: Prince of Deheubarth* (Llandysul, 1997).

Vaughan, H. M., *The South Wales Squires: A Welsh Picture of Social Life* (London, 1924).

Wainwright, G. J., *Coygan Camp: A Prehistoric, Romano-British and Dark Age Settlement in Carmarthenshire* (Cardiff, 1967).

West Wales Historical Records

Williams, D., *The Rebecca Riots: A Study in Agrarian Discontent* (Cardiff, 1971).

Williams, D. J., *Hen Dŷ Ffarm* (Llandysul, 1953).

Williams, L. J., *Digest of Welsh Historical Statistics*, vol. 1 (Cardiff, 1986).

Local periodicals

Aman Valley Historical Society Transactions.
The Carmarthenshire Historian.
The Carmarthen Antiquary, The Carmarthenshire Antiquary, 1941–2005.
Transactions of the Carmarthenshire Antiquarian and Field Club, 1905–1939.

Unpublished theses

Bainbridge, A., 'Agriculture in Carmarthenshire' (University of Wales, MA 1976).

Cragoe, M., 'The Golden Grove Interest in Carmarthenshire Politics', 1804–21' (University of Wales, MA 1986).

Davies, D. Russell, 'A Social History of Carmarthenshire 1870–1920' (University of Wales, Aberystwyth, Ph.D. 1989).

Hancocks, H., 'History of the Tinplate manufacture in Llanelli' (University of Wales Swansea, MA 1965).

Rees, R. D., 'The Parliamentary Representation of South Wales 1790–1830' (University of Reading, Ph.D 1962).

Index